JOURNAL FOR THE STUDY OF THE OLD TESTAMENT
SUPPLEMENT SERIES
210

Sheffield Academic Press

The Vow and the 'Popular Religious Groups' of Ancient Israel

A Philological and Sociological Inquiry

Jacques Berlinerblau

Journal for the Study of the Old Testament
Supplement Series 210

For my parents, Laurette and Rubin,
with great love and admiration
for their love and their tolerance

Copyright © 1996 Sheffield Academic Press

Published by Sheffield Academic Press Ltd
Mansion House
19 Kingfield Road
Sheffield S11 9AS
England

Printed on acid-free paper in Great Britain
by Bookcraft Ltd
Midsomer Norton, Bath

British Library Cataloguing in Publication Data

A catalogue record for this book is available
from the British Library

ISBN 1-85075-578-7

CONTENTS

Part I
THE MECHANISMS OF THE ISRAELITE VOW

ACKNOWLEDGMENTS

The present text is an exhaustive revision of my original doctoral thesis, which was completed in the Spring of 1991 at New York University. My three doctoral advisors, to whom I am always grateful, were Dr Baruch Levine, Dr David Sperling and Dr Hamid Dabashi. Throughout my sojourn at N.Y.U. I was greatly influenced by Dr. Moss Roberts and Dr. Juan Corradi. The lectures of the latter convinced me to become a scholar, those of the former a sociologist.

In the intervening years I have had the pleasure of studying and teaching sociology at the New School for Social Research. I would like to thank Dr Sondra Farganis for years of intellectual and moral support. Dr Mustafa Emirbayer kindly read and critiqued the introduction to the present work. Dr. Rayna Rapp performed the same service for my seventh chapter.

I acknowledge appreciatively Dr David J.A. Clines and Philip R. Davies of Sheffield Academic Press. Both were instrumental in bringing this project, and others, to fruition. Ms. Carol Smith, also of Sheffield, is to be thanked for her meticulous editing of the current work.

I owe a debt of gratitude to Julius Sperling and Henry Resnick, librarians at Hebrew Union College–Jewish Institute of Religion in New York. For years both have generously given of their time to assist me with German translations and countless bibliographical queries.

Jimmy Eisenberg, Jason Freitag, Beth Godley, Natalie Indrimi, Camala Projansky and Claudia Schaler are true and devoted friends who directly and indirectly made this work possible. Also to be thanked are my students and colleagues at the City University of New York. May this great and noble institution persevere. For reasons which I am not quite able to put into words, the cities of Brooklyn, Paris, Jerusalem and Rome must also be thanked; they are all inextricably bound to the writing and researching of this book. The shortcomings of the present text are, of course, attributable only to myself (and the aforementioned cities).

I dedicate this work to my parents, Laurette and Rubin. If I were to treat my children with half as much wisdom, generosity and kindness as they treated me, I will surely have accomplished much.

Jacques Berlinerblau
Brooklyn, New York
February 1996

ABBREVIATIONS

AB	Anchor Bible
AfO	*Archiv für Orientforschung*
AnOr	Analecta orientalia
AS	K. Jackson, *The Ammonite Language of the Iron Age*
BA	*Biblical Archaeologist*
BASOR	*Bulletin of the American Schools of Oriental Research*
BASORSup	*Bulletin of the American Schools of Oriental Research, Supplements*
BBB	Bonner biblische Beiträge
BDB	F. Brown, S.R. Driver and C.A. Briggs, *Hebrew and English Lexicon of the Old Testament*
Bib	*Biblica*
BibOr	Biblica et orientalia
BKAT	Biblischer Kommentar: Altes Testament
BZ	*Biblische Zeitschrift*
BZAW	Beihefte zur *ZAW*
CBQ	*Catholic Biblical Quarterly*
EBib	Etudes Biblique
EH	A. Berthier and R. Charlier, *Le sanctuaire Purique d'El-Hofra à Constantine*
GKC	*Gesenius' Hebrew Grammar*, ed. E. Kautzsch, trans. A.E. Cowley
HAR	*Hebrew Annual Review*
HAT	Handbuch zum Alten Testament
HKAT	Handkommentar zum Alten Testament
HSM	Harvard Semitic Monographs
HUCA	*Hebrew Union College Annual*
ICC	International Critical Commentary
IDB	G.A. Buttrick (ed.), *Interpreter's Dictionary of the Bible*
IDBSup	*IDB*, Supplementary Volume
ISBE	G.W. Bromiley (ed.), *International Standard Bible Encyclopedia*, rev. edn
JAAR	*Journal of the American Academy of Religion*
JANES	*Journal of Ancient Near Eastern Studies*
JAOS	*Journal of the American Oriental Society*
JBL	*Journal of Biblical Literature*

JCS	*Journal of Cuneiform Studies*
JEH	*Journal of Ecclesiastical History*
JJS	*Journal of Jewish Studies*
JPS	*Tanakh: A New Translation of the Holy Scriptures According to the Traditional Hebrew Text*
JNSL	*Journal of Northwest Semitic Languages*
JSOT	*Journal for the Study of the Old Testament*
JSOTSup	*Journal for the Study of the Old Testament* Supplement Series
KAI	H. Donner and W. Röllig (eds.), *Kaanäische und Aramäische Inschriften*
KAT	Kommentar zum Alten Testament
NCB	New Century Bible
Or	*Orientalia* (Rome)
OTL	Old Testament Library
PEFQS	*Palestine Exploration Fund, Quarterly Statement*
RA	*Revue d'assyriologie et d'archéologie orientale*
RB	*Revue biblique*
RevExp	*Review and Expositor*
SB	Sources bibliques
SBLDS	SBL Dissertation Series
SBLRBS	SBL Resources for Biblical Study
SC	Sources chrétiennes
SJLA	Studies in Judaism in Late Antiquity
TWOT	R.L. Harris, G.L. Archer and B. Waltke (eds.), *Theological Wordbook of the Old Testament*
TZ	*Theologische Zeitschrift*
UF	*Ugarit-Forschungen*
VT	*Vetus Testamentum*
WBC	Word Biblical Commentary
ZAW	*Zeitschrift für die alttestamentliche Wissenschaft*
ZDMG	*Zeitschrift der deutschen morganländischen Gesellschaft*

INTRODUCTION

I am seeking to rescue the poor stockinger, the Luddite cropper, the 'obsolete' hand-loom weaver, the 'utopian' artisan, and even the deluded follower of Joanna Southcott, from the enormous condescension of posterity. (E.P. Thompson, *The Making of the English Working Class*.)

In most cases the grassroots historian finds only what he is looking for, not what is already waiting for him. Most sources for grassroots history have only been recognized as sources because someone has asked a question and then prospected desperately around for some way—any way—of answering it. (E.J. Hobsbawm, 'History From Below: Some Reflections'.)

Basic Questions and Goals

The Israelite Vow: A 'Popular Religious Practice'

Old Testament scholars have often maintained that the making of vows was a component of ancient Israel's 'popular religion'. H.L. Ginsberg, in an article devoted to the study of Psalms and inscriptions of thanksgiving, refers to vows in the northwest Semitic world as 'a popular religious practice' (1945: 161 n. 8). In a discussion of the perplexing votive regulations of Lev. 27.1-8, Jacob Milgrom observes: 'That such vows were popular in early Israel is evidenced by King Jehoash's reference to monetary contributions to the Temple of Jerusalem that stem exclusively from "the money equivalent of persons" (2 Kings 12.5)' (1990: 489).

A similar view may be identified in the most recent—and certainly the most comprehensive—discussion of the Israelite votive system. In his monograph, *Vows in the Hebrew Bible and the Ancient Near East*, Tony Cartledge opines:

> the very presence of so many vow-like prayers within Israel's 'hymnbook' is an indication of the popularity and meaningfulness of the practice. In my view, the prayers of the psalmists are not just those of a religious expert or professional hymn-writer. The laments in particular may express the needs and hopes of ordinary people, and utilize motivational tactics (such as vows) that are common to more popular forms of religion... The

presence of vows (always personal) in virtually every other society of the ancient Near East, and in form very similar to vows practiced in Israel, shows that vow-making was an important element of popular or 'folk' religion throughout the ancient Near Eastern world of the first millennium (1992: 27-28).[1]

From the outset it must be stated that I do not have any substantive disagreement with the basic opinion expressed by each of these scholars. By the final chapter of this study it will be maintained, albeit with certain qualifications, that the Israelite vow was indeed a 'popular religious' practice. In this respect, the present contribution differs only superficially from previous discussions of this issue.

Yet those who have posited the existence of a connection between the vow and 'popular religion' have yet to demonstrate precisely *how* they arrived at this conclusion. The quotations cited above essentially exhaust all of the scrutiny which each of these exegetes has devoted to this question. As such, no substantive analysis of those texts which might confirm this view has been forwarded. Further, these researchers—as well as many other students of the Old Testament world (see Berlinerblau 1993)—have refrained from defining or discussing the crucial and irritatingly multivalent term, 'popular religion'. Insofar as many distinct conceptualizations of the latter abound in the relevant scholarly literature, these unadorned references to the alleged 'popularity' of the vow are susceptible to varied and contradictory interpretations.[2]

In this study, by contrast, a detailed argument will be advanced as a means of assessing the plausibility of this claim. In so doing, a variety of sociological and text-critical methods will be developed and applied to those northwest Semitic and biblical texts in which the vow is mentioned. These initiatives have been formulated in response to three essential sets

1.   See also Cartledge 1988: 998; Wendel 1931a: 17; Brekelmans 1963: 2553 and Oesterley and Rowley 1963: 1025. For a discussion of the popularity of vows and oaths in Hellenistic Judaism, see Lieberman 1942: 115-41.

2.   As will be seen, the term 'popular religion' can be interpreted in a number of different ways. For example, some view it as the religion practiced by the *majority* of the population (e.g. Dever 1987: 220). Others interpret this construct as a type of religiosity associated with certain social groups (e.g. non-privileged economic strata; see below). Elsewhere, when scholars refer to a religious act as 'popular' they are calling attention to the fact that it is *frequently* practiced by the members of a particular society. The exegetes mentioned above have not specified which definition they are employing. Consequently, it is almost impossible to understand what they have in mind when they refer to the vow in the context of 'popular religion'.

of questions, none of which have been addressed by students of the Israelite vow.

To begin with, I ask: what does 'popular religion' actually mean? As will become clear, this question is inextricably tied to another: what is 'official religion'. Thus, before labeling vow-making as an aspect of Israelite 'popular religion' it will be necessary to clarify what is signified by this term and its analytical opposite. By drawing upon sociological, anthropological and historical research, I shall put forward working definitions of these constructs which are applicable to the pre- and early post-exilic periods targeted in this study.

My second congeries of questions concerns the textual sources which we use to study the vow and Israelite 'popular religion'. In a discussion of historiography in the pre-Hellenistic Near East, the historian R.J. Collingwood observes:

> History of this kind I propose to call *theocratic history*; in which phrase 'history' means not history proper, that is scientific history, but a statement of known facts for the information of persons to whom they are not known, but who, as worshippers of the god in question, ought to know the deeds whereby he has made himself manifest (1956: 14; see also Diakonoff *et al.* 1991: 16; Ginzburg 1979: 87).

Theocratic historians are not beholden to the virtues of 'objective assessment', 'questioning authority', 'seeing things from both sides' and a variety of other values which modern academicians, in theory, strive for in their scholarship. Cool detachment, the disciplined assassination of one's prejudices, the sober and disinterested investigation of 'the facts', are not ideals shared by members of this guild. Theocratic historians are passionate and partial. Success in their calling is measured not in the 'critical distance' (Walzer 1988: 12-16) they maintain from their most cherished beliefs, but precisely in their capacity to effectively persuade their readers that these beliefs constitute truth itself.

The authors of the Old Testament are by no means immune from the charge of being 'theocratic historians'. Nahum Sarna observes:

> It is obvious, however, that the biblical writers were not concerned with the objective recording of details and processes of historical change, as a modern historian would be. The biblical writers were not consciously engaged in what we call historiography. Rather, their concern was with the didactic use of selected historical traditions (1988: 37).

Rather than offering disinterested accounts, the biblical literati adhere to a 'party line' (see Smith 1987: 22; Lang 1983: 19) and aggressively endorse and chronicle the truths of the 'Yahweh-alone' ideology as they understood them. William Dever notes that these writers 'were more concerned with viewing history as the *magnalia dei*, the "mighty acts of God"' (1990: 83). Such a state of affairs has a profound impact upon the historical accuracy of the Old Testament. As Keith Whitelam remarks:

> The text is not a witness to historical reality, only to itself. It is a witness to a particular perception of reality (1986: 52).[3]

Insofar as the Hebrew Bible 'is a religious book and not a history book' (Garbini 1988: 14) it becomes necessary to ask the following questions: To what degree may valid historical information be extracted from a text whose authors were clearly beholden to a Yahwist 'party line'? What hazards confront the researcher who wishes to plumb the Old Testament for details regarding 'popular religiosity'? How may biblical verses which discuss the Israelite vow—or any practice for that matter— be analysed for accurate reports regarding 'popular religious groups'? What exegetical techniques may be employed as a means of bypassing distortions of accuracy inherent to works of 'theocratic history'?

My final set of questions seeks to explain *why* the vow might have been a component of ancient Israel's 'popular religion'. While biblical researchers may refer to an aspect of Israelite worship as 'popular', they typically refrain from offering any sort of theory which might account for this state of affairs. In this study I shall attempt to explain the 'fit' or congeniality which existed between the vow and certain types of Israelites. What was it about this practice that made it so appealing to those social groups usually categorized (see below) under the rubric of popular religion? Conversely, I shall ask: what sociological attributes of certain Israelites may account for their attraction to the vow?

In the forthcoming study the reader will be introduced to a variety of methods and theoretical approaches that will permit us to evaluate the plausibility of the association between the vow and 'popular religion'. A few students of this practice have displayed extraordinary intuition in labeling this practice as 'popular'. My goal is to demonstrate that their hypothesis is essentially correct. In order to do so, however, it will be necessary to articulate the core assumptions, the methods, and the

---

3. For variations on these themes see Day 1989: 5; Sperling 1986: 7; Smith 1987: 7; McCarter 1987: 137; Dever 1990: 123 and 1991: 196; Holladay, Jr. 1987: 249 and Ackerman 1989:109. For a discussion of these problems as they relate to Antiquity in general, see Diakonoff *et al.* 1991: 14-21.

theories which lead to this conclusion. If the sub-discipline of Israelite 'popular religion' studies is to advance beyond its current state then these must be made explicit. Thus, a sociological understanding of certain basic concepts (namely 'popular religion' and 'official religion') is needed. Further, an attempt must be made to develop an exegetical methodology which is cognizant of the snares of 'theocratic history'.

It is hoped that the experimental strategies developed here will shed light not only on the particular question of the vow's 'popularity', but on the more general issue of how those studying ancient Israel should engage with the 'popular religion' construct. In so doing, the first small steps toward recovering a seemingly lost component of ancient Israel's religious heritage will be taken.

'Popular Religious Groups': Sociological Questions

In order to understand what 'popular religion' or a 'popular religious group' (to use the term employed here) actually is, a considerable amount of theoretical groundwork will be necessary. Consequently, this section will be devoted to an extensive exposition of key issues explored by social scientists and historians who have studied this construct. Developments in Old Testament scholarship will be compared to this non-biblical research. By this means I shall generate the working definitions of Israelite 'popular religious groups' and Israelite 'official religion' which will be used in this study.

The Study of 'Popular Religion' in Non-biblical and Biblical Research
It is only in recent years that the subject of 'popular religion' has become the object of widespread, intensive and unbiased scholarly scrutiny. As Peter Williams notes, professors of religion in the United States traditionally viewed this sort of research as 'at best irrelevant and at worst reprehensible' (1989: 6).[4] Accordingly, what little attention 'popular religion' did receive was generally not adulatory. As many contemporary students of this issue have observed, earlier generations of scholars frequently stressed the 'vulgar' (Brown 1982: 16), 'hopelessly irrational' (Brandes 1990: 186), 'naive', 'primitive', 'prelogical', 'infantile' (Gurevich 1990:

---

4.   As such, the study of 'official religion' was often posited as the sole legitimate area of inquiry among academicians who studied religion (Vrijhof, 1979b: 694; see also Towler 1974: 149).

xiv), 'socially retrograde' (Kselman 1986: 31) and idiotic (Schneider 1990: 24) disposition of 'popular religion'.

In the last quarter of a century or so, this situation has begun to change. An international and interdisciplinary core of scholars (with pivotal loci in Northern and Western Europe, Latin America and the United States) has devoted serious and sustained attention to the study of this issue. With each passing year more new titles on 'popular religion' come trickling forth from university presses. It is now not unusual to find sessions at academic conferences or issues of journals devoted exclusively to this theme.[5]

The trajectory of 'popular religion' research in biblical scholarship runs more or less parallel with the one found in non-biblical fields. As with the study of religion in general, most scholarly works on Israelite religion written prior to the seventies were exclusively concerned with its 'official' dimension (see Berlinerblau 1993). A deprecatory stance toward 'popular religion' can also be detected in Old Testament studies. C.J. Labuschagne's remark, 'Popular theology is the result of a process of corruption and perversion of true Yahwism, imperceptibly moving with the prevailing spirit of the times, like a putrefaction transmuting one living cell after the other', stands as an emblematic statement of this approach (1964–65: 123). At roughly the same time that researchers working in other disciplines began to take an interest in 'popular religion', a similar movement was developing—though somewhat less intensely—in biblical studies. The increased concern with this issue is evidenced in J.L. Crenshaw's comment that 'In the past, far too little attention has been given to the actual religion of the "man in the streets" in ancient Israel, the spotlight of scholarly scrutiny being turned on the officially sanctioned religion of Israel' (1970: 392).[6]

In an article written fifteen years later, P.D. Miller could point to heightened attention given to a subject which formerly garnered very little interest:

5.   See, for example, *Social Compass* 19 (1972); *Social Compass* 29 (1982) and *Concilium* 186 (1986). Further, a sort of elective affinity can be observed between 'popular religion' studies and various innovative theoretical approaches such as the French *Annales* school (Schneider 1990: 25); see also Ginzburg 1991: 1-2; Badone 1990a: 7; the Italian *microstoria* school (see Muir and Ruggiero 1991); gender studies; peasant studies; 'grassroots history'; subaltern studies and so on.

6.   There were, however, a few studies of Israelite 'popular religion' prior to Crenshaw's 1970 remark (see Berlinerblau 1993).

Is the proper subject of investigation the Yahwism described in the biblical sources as normative, or is it the popular religion which may have been very different from or even opposed to Yahwism ?...The recrudescence of interest in the history of Israel's religion has brought with it a renewed attention to this question but hardly a consensus about either the nature of popular piety or the sources for its reconstruction (1985: 215; see also Vorländer 1986: 63).

Local Definitions

One of the dividends of the increased—and less disdainful—scrutiny accorded this issue (in non-biblical research), has been the emerging realization that 'popular religion' is an extremely difficult term to define. Ellen Badone notes: 'As a scholarly category, "popular religion" is problematic' (1990a: 4). François-André Isambert, in one of his characteristically perceptive examinations of this issue, writes: 'The very concept of *popular religion* has been the object of numerous attempts at definition and frequently renewed debates, giving the impression of the infinite repetition of the same errors' (1982: 13). A similar sense of frustration may be detected in Michael Carroll's observation that 'popular religion' is a term 'whose meaning has become increasingly less clear over the past two decades' (1992: 6).[7] It is for these reasons that I consistently surround the term 'popular religion' with menacing quotation marks. These grammatical bodyguards serve as a warning to those who would view this construct as unproblematic and conceptually unambiguous.

It should come as no surprise then that there presently does not exist any consensus as to what 'popular religion' actually means. While there may be some theoretical similarities among the approaches of researchers who engage with this issue, there has not surfaced any recognized dominant paradigm or school to which the majority of scholars pledge their allegiance. Consequently, numerous definitions of 'popular religion' abound, but none has yet achieved hegemonic status.

This (not necessarily unfortunate) circumstance is due to a variety of factors. To begin with, the international and interdisciplinary composition of this field's practitioners has resulted in a somewhat atomized discourse, in which no theoretical center can easily be forged. This lack of consensus may also be due to the fact that the chrysalis of 'popular religion' studies coincides with the emergence of the post-modern moment in

7.   See also Isambert 1977: 161; Scribner 1984: 47; Kselman 1986: 24; Candelaria 1990: 13 and Berlinerblau 1993.

research universities. Given post-modernism's 'intense distrust of all universal or "totalizing" discourses' (Harvey 1990: 9), its focus on 'the unique rather than...the general' (Rosenau 1992: 8), it is perhaps not surprising that the practice of offering transhistorical, universal definitions of religion (as well as innumerable other concepts) has been forcefully problematized.[8]

Whatever the reasons might be, it is safe to say that the desire to achieve *the* universal, ahistorical definition of 'popular religion' is currently very weak. Instead, many scholars are producing what I refer to as 'local definitions'. These are constructed to conform to the unique circumstances encountered in the particular society which is scrutinized by the researcher.

While many social scientists and historians have devoted a great deal of effort to defining the term 'popular religion', research of this nature has surfaced only sporadically in biblical scholarship. Typically, one finds this term mentioned only in passing by a researcher who is concentrating on a different set of issues. Such is the case among the aforementioned students of the Israelite vow.

Curiously, even works exclusively devoted to the theme of Israelite 'popular religion' often neglect to articulate any detailed statement as to what this term connotes (see Berlinerblau 1993, 1995).[9] As already noted, this reluctance to define basic terms has had decidedly detrimental effects on the development of biblical 'popular religion' studies. Below, I shall forward my own 'local definition', one which is tailored to ancient Israel and, most importantly, to the particular textual materials which are used when studying it.

---

8.   One also notes an affinity between the tendency of 'popular religion' researchers to study marginalized social groups and the post-modern project as summarized by Rosenau:

> Post-modern social scientists support a re-focusing on what has been taken for granted, what has been neglected, regions of resistance, the forgotten, the irrational, the insignificant, the repressed, the borderline, the classical, the sacred, the traditional, the eccentric, the sublimated, the subjugated, the rejected, the nonessential, the marginal, the peripheral, the excluded, the tenuous, the silenced, the accidental, the dispersed, the disqualified, the deferred, the disjointed... (1992: 8)

9.   Some scholars have offered definitions of these terms (for instance, Vorländer 1986: 63 and Albertz 1978: 12. For a review and critique of these definitions see Berlinerblau 1993.

'Popular Religion' and 'Official Religion': Internal Heterogeneity
As the reader may have gathered from my title, this work concerns itself
with the study of 'popular religious groups'. In order to achieve a greater
degree of sociological precision this term has been chosen over the more
standard 'popular religion'. My preference for the former usage will now
be explained.

Biblical scholars who have studied 'popular religion' usually bifurcate
the religious landscape of ancient Israel into two *internally homogenous*
religious spheres: one is labeled 'official' and the other is called 'popular'.
In his article 'Popular Religion in Ancient Israel', J.B. Segal writes:

> There were two levels of Israelite religion. The one...is that of established
> sanctuaries and of established dates, a formal religion...the other is less
> easy to characterize...(1976: 1)

In a similar vein, T. Vriezen remarks:

> To what extent the religion of the 'man in the street' was affected by the
> official temple cults is a question that must be asked and can only be
> answered in quite vague and general terms. Considering what the expe-
> rience was in the time of Elijah and Isaiah, we might say that a hard core, a
> 'remnant', clung loyally to the ancestral faith in Yahweh, while the great
> mass of the people must undoubtedly have trimmed their sails to the wind
> (1967: 20).

Recent studies have, however, challenged the assumption that 'popular
religion' is a homogenous entity, comprised of one unified group, standing apart from an equally homogenous and unified 'official religion'.
Instead, researchers are beginning to notice extraordinary amounts of
heterogeneity existing *within* 'official' and 'popular' religion.

Mart Bax's research on the Dutch Brabant yields the crucial insight
that even within an 'official religion' one is likely to find competing
religious factions. Bax writes: 'the Church is not viewed as a huge mono-
lith, but rather as a complex constellation of rival religious regimes, each
striving for expansion and consolidation' (1987: 7; see also Brett 1987:
29).[10] The situation is similar, if not even more complicated, in the
'popular' sphere. Anthropologist Stanley Brandes observes: 'No matter
where we go in Europe, no matter how large or small our unit of analysis,
we inevitably discover the coexistence of several competing, mutually

---

10. One thinks of Vilfredo Pareto's observation: 'There is never, to be exact, one
elite stratum, there are only various strata which together constitute the elite' (1991:
78).

derivative systems of religious beliefs and practices' (1990: 185; compare Gramsci 1975: 420). Thus, if there is such a thing as 'popular religion', there is probably more than one manifestation of it in the society which is being studied. It is for these reasons that the term in question can be misleading. It implies that in every society there exists a single 'popular religion' comprised of one homogenous group. This assumption of homogeneity is quite at odds with the opinions of the authors of the Old Testament. As far as they were concerned, quite a few distinct religious groups lived side by side (for example, Baal worshippers, supporters of Molech, devotees of the Queen of Heaven, and so on). Accordingly, a phrase like 'the "popular religion" of ancient Israel' drastically over-simplifies the variegated sociological constitution of the society being studied.[11] Unless one wishes to suggest that these groups were colluding with one another, it may be best to speak not of one 'popular religion', but of many distinct 'popular religious groups'.[12]

'Official religion' must be approached somewhat differently. Bax's observation points to the existence of rival regimes existing within the parameters of *one* unified Church. The (antagonistic) interplay between these groups will be decisive in giving shape to the ultimate formulation of the political and theological agenda of this 'official religion'. Yet while internecine conflict is observed within the ranks of 'official religion', it nevertheless ultimately stands as a unity against others. (If it fails to do so one of the competing groups will eventually cast out the 'heretics'.) Insofar as the consolidation of antagonistic factions under one tent con-stitutes one of the major tasks—as well as the peculiar genius—of an 'official religion', it would be inaccurate to speak of 'official religious groups'.

The Relational Approach
As an area of academic inquiry the subject of 'official religion' has been somewhat neglected in recent years. Since the groundbreaking 1979

11. Here it is assumed that heterodox social movements constitute a 'popular religious group'. For a full discussion of this issue see below.

12. This emphasis on the delineation of numerous groups is, incidentally, one of the methodological hallmarks of Max Weber's *Ancient Judaism*. As David Petersen observes, Weber's ancient Israel is 'heterogenous in the extreme' (1979: 123); also see Eisenstadt (1981: 61). For an example of this approach in Weber's writing see his remarks on the 'conception of Yahweh' (1967: 133). Curiously, this work has had a minimal impact on biblical scholarship (see Fahey, 1982: 62; Holstein 1975: 159; Talmon 1987: 588; Wilson 1984: 15).

volume *Official and Popular Religion: Analysis of a Theme for Religious Studies* (Vrijhof and Waardenburg 1979) little has been said about the 'official' dimensions of religion. It would seem that many scholars are atoning for years of neglect by focusing exclusively on the issue of 'popular religion'.

From a sociological perspective, however, it is untenable to study either one of these constructs in isolation. Vrijhof observes: 'Both the terms official religion and non-official religion must not be regarded as static, substantial concepts indicating fixed, separate entities' (1979a: 238; also see Vrijhof 1979b: 670; Bouritius 1979: 156). Badone suggests that researchers should 'focus on the dialectical character of their interrelationship' (1990a: 6). Thus, 'popular' and 'official' religion must be viewed as existing in a nexus or in relation to one another; we may not fully understand either unless we examine the interrelations which exist between both (Lanternari 1982: 126).

This methodological rule of thumb is grounded in one of the most basic principles of historical sociology. It is axiomatic among sociologists that within a society groups and individuals interact with one another in an infinite variety of ways, perpetually structuring and restructuring their social world in the process. 'Society exists', wrote Georg Simmel, 'where a number of individuals enter into interaction' (1971: 23). Karl Marx placed a similar importance on social interaction, albeit on the macro-level, when he spoke of the 'relations of production' (for example, the Bourgeoisie and Proletariat in a capitalist mode of production). The same assumption may be detected in Max Weber's discussions of competing status groups, as it can in Rosaldo's statement that: 'men and women ultimately live together in the world...we will never understand the lives that women lead without relating them to men' (1980: 396; see also Elias 1978: 113).

Similarly, 'popular' and 'official' religion are, to use Pace's phrase, 'firmly intertwined...in a complex and articulated circularity' (1979: 72). To study either in isolation would be to ignore the particular manner in which each exerts determining effects upon the other. An example of this 'complex and articulated circularity' may be identified whenever an 'official religion' designates another group as 'heretics', 'apostates', and so on. In so doing, the former stigmatizes the latter, eliciting from these 'deviants' types of social actions (such as feelings of resentment, polemical literature, revolutionary activity) that would never have manifested themselves had this designation not been conferred. Needless to say the

actions and beliefs of the heretical group will exert influence upon the
'official religion' insofar as the latter will orient *their* social action against
the former (for example, when military campaigns are directed against
'heretics' and religious doctrines are formulated that demarcate the difference between what 'we' believe and what 'they' believe). As George
Herbert Mead once remarked: 'We are what we are through our
relationship to others' (1962: 379).

The student of 'popular religion' who does not employ this interactive
approach runs the risk of essentializing these *relative* sociological constructs. In his *Sociology and Philosophy* Emile Durkheim demonstrated
that no particular act *in and of itself* is criminal: 'An act, intrinsically the
same, which is blamed today among Europeans, was not blamed in
ancient Greece since there it violated no pre-established rule' (1974: 43).
When this insight is transposed into the key of religious studies it is
quickly seen why a relational methodology is necessary. There does not
exist any constellation of religious doctrines and practices that are
universally identifiable as 'official' or 'heretical'. Instead, this is a judgment which emerges as a consequence of a specific social interaction
between two groups: an 'official religion' which bestows this label, and a
'heretical group' which—unwillingly—receives it. Thus, to know what is
'popular' in a society we must know what is 'official', and vice versa.

'Official Religion'

A perusal of the research that does exist on 'official religion' (often
forwarded by students of 'popular religion') suggests that consensus as
to its definition will also not be achieved easily. In another study, I have
pointed to four themes which tend to surface in scholarly investigations
of this construct. These themes will be briefly summarized in the
following discussion.[13]

It is often suggested that an 'official religion' is comprised of and/or
represents the interests of a privileged economic class. Such an approach
has obvious affinities to materialist perspectives. An orthodox Marxist
interpretation would stress that an 'official religion'—or any religion for
that matter—is nothing but a super-structural expression of distinct class
interests. Engels's remark, 'Even the so-called religious wars of the
sixteenth century involved positive material class interests; those wars
were class wars, too' (1969: 41), nicely expresses this position (see also
Engels 1974: 57, 59). As such, an 'official religion' could be understood

13. For a fuller discussion see Berlinerblau 1996.

as an ideological system whose primary function consists of legitimating the domination of an economically privileged class.

Issues of economic class also figure prominently in discussions of 'popular religion'. By construing 'popular' and 'official' religion as relational concepts, a rather neat, albeit simplistic, definition of the former emerges. If the owners of the means of production are seen as the bearers of 'official religion' then it follows that the religion of others could be subsumed under the 'popular' category. Many researchers—whether explicitly or implicitly—view 'popular religion' as that religion (whatever its form) practiced by economically non-privileged groups. As Pace notes, a number of Italian social scientists understand 'popular religion' as 'a class phenomenon which most especially involves subaltern classes and most predominantly, though not exclusively, agricultural classes' (1979: 73).[14]

An entirely different approach emphasizes the links between 'official religion' and the process of 'rationalization' discussed by Max Weber (1958, 1976).[15] While various interpretations of this term can be found, for now Wolfgang Schluchter's term 'metaphysical–ethical rationalism' is acceptable. This is defined as:

> ...the systematization of meaning patterns. This involves the intellectual elaboration and deliberate sublimation of ultimate ends. In this sense rationalism is a consequence of cultured man's 'inner compulsion' not only to understand the world as a 'meaningful cosmos' but also to take a consistent and unified stance to it (1984: 15).[16]

Stanley Brandes suggests that the ideas of an 'official religion' are 'systematized and codified into some internally consistent, all-encompassing cosmology' (1990: 185). P.H. Vrijhof describes 'official religion' as: 'rational, coherent and coercive doctrines and rules' (1979a: 223). Thomas Luckmann writes:

---

14. See also D. Levine 1986: 4; D. Levine 1992: 10; M. Carroll 1992: 7; Isambert 1975: 196; Brettell 1990: 68; Cipriani 1976: 226, 228 and Kselman 1986: 32.

15. As Giddens notes, even though the notion of rationalization occupied a central place in Weber's thought he seems to take its meaning for granted (1992:36).

16. Let us not neglect to mention that another major part of Weber's concept of rationalization lies in 'the negation or overcoming of *simple* magic and ritual forms as the major modes by which man related to the "other" world' (Eisenstadt 1981: 55). For Weber, this 'overcoming' of magic was a salient feature of ancient Judaism (Weber 1967; see also Raphaël 1973: 51; Schluchter 1989: 166; Schiper, 1959).

The 'official' model is, of course, formulated and elaborated by the experts
and the various dimensions of the 'official' model eventually become the
subject of specialized knowledge, such as doctrine, liturgy, 'social ethics',
and so forth (1972: 74; see also Wichers 1979: 200).[17]

In this scenario, 'official religion' is distinct from 'popular' varieties
insofar as it consciously aspires to elaborate, systematize, codify and
clarify the particular metaphysical beliefs upon which it is predicated.
Such an endeavor necessitates a group of specialists who are trained in
performing the tasks mentioned above. In sociological parlance this
group is commonly referred to as 'the intellectuals'.[18]

Other researchers have called attention to a particular sexual division
of labor which characterizes religion in general. One thinks of I.M. Lewis's
observations regarding Somali pastoralists:

> this public cult is almost exclusively dominated by men, who hold all the
> major positions of religious authority and prestige. Women are in fact
> excluded from the mosques in which men worship and their role in reli-
> gion tends to be little more than that of passive spectators (1989: 65, 69).

In her study of Mexican-American women's devotion to The Lady of
Guadalupe, Jeanette Rodriguez remarks:

> The very nature of the hierarchy of the Roman Catholic church and of its
> traditional teachings has called for women to be subordinate to men, but
> this system has not precluded them from playing an active role in the
> practice of popular religiosity (1994: 59).

Thus, we could maintain that another characteristic of an 'official
religion' lies in its tendency to be administered, managed and controlled

---

17. Caution is needed when positing rationality, coherence, systematization and so
on, as unique attributes of 'official religion'. For implicit in this view lies the assumption that 'popular religion' has either less rationality or—as many earlier generations
of scholars suggested—no rationality at all (see above). Yet studies such as
Ginzburg's *The Cheese and the Worms: The Cosmos of a Sixteenth-Century Miller*
(1982) or J. Schneider's impressive study of peasant ethics, 'Spirits and the Spirit of
Capitalism' (1990), show how reflective and complex the world-views of non-official
religious groups can actually be (see also Brandes 1990: 197).

18. On the subject of intellectuals Weber remarked:

> It is the intellectual who conceives of the 'world' as a problem of meaning...As a con-
> sequence, there is a growing demand that the world and the total pattern of life be
> subject to an order that is significant and meaningful (1978: 506; see also Sadri 1992:
> 71, 61. For a different view on the roles of intellectuals in religion see Gramsci 1975:
> 340; Gramsci 1991: 190).

by men. Women, conversely, are relegated to a secondary status and thus excluded from positions of authority, power and prestige.

Power

All three characteristics of 'official religion' just mentioned—its dominant position within the ensemble of social relations, its rationalizing disposition and its tendency to be dominated by men—are at once a cause and an effect of the fact that it typically exerts 'power' over those groups with whom it interacts.[19] In paraphrasing Max Weber's famous definition of power, we could say that an 'official religion' is capable of 'carrying out its own will' against other religious groups (1964: 152).[20]

In the first analysis, power of this sort consists of the capacity to create a dominant conception of social reality—and to make it stick. As Berger and Luckmann note: 'Those who occupy the decisive power positions are ready to use their power to impose the traditional definitions of reality on the population under their authority' (1967: 121). In my opinion, the *sine qua non* of 'official religion' lies in its ability to make its *particular* theological agenda assume the status of 'orthodoxy' within a given territory. Needless to say, this entails the ability to relegate dissenters to the status of 'apostates' and 'heretics' and to make them suffer accordingly.[21]

How does an 'official religion' accomplish this feat? In order to answer this question we must examine the means by which ruling groups exert power. In Weber's well-known formulation the state is seen as 'a relation of men dominating men, a relation supported by means of legitimate (i.e., considered to be legitimate) violence'. (1958: 78). A theocratic state then, could be seen as one which effectively deploys the means of force

19. The reader might ask why 'official religion' is discussed in terms of Weber's concept of 'power' but not 'authority'. As will be seen, much 'popular religion' research concerns itself with heretics and apostates. It should be noted that among such groups there is no belief in the 'legitimacy' of the ruling order. If such groups acquiesce to the ruling powers, they do so not out of an internal belief in the validity of this particular form of rule. Instead, their submission is solely attributable to their subordinate power position.

20. For a discussion of power as construed in Weberian sociology, see Chapter 8.

21. For purposes of analysis a further distinction may be drawn between the *apostate* who abandons the Yahwistic faith for another religious system and the *heretic* who upholds 'the group's central values and goals' but offers different 'means for implementing its goal' (Coser, 1964: 70). For an excellent discussion of the sociological difference between heretics and apostates see Coser (1964: 69-72).

against its adversaries.[22]

The use of physical coercion, however, is neither the only nor the most effective means by which a ruling group wields power (Weber 1967: 78). Power which rests on force alone is a highly precarious form of social domination (Fontana 1993: 144; see also Maduro 1982: 72). As Weber recognized, power also consists of persuading women and men to obey authority *without* the application of external coercion.

A useful analysis of how power—in its coercive and non-coercive incarnations—is exercised can be found in the writings of Antonio Gramsci. In his *Prison Notebooks* the Italian political philosopher and political prisoner demonstrates that a state, or more precisely, 'a hegemonic apparatus', achieves its rule through the 'ingenious' *combination* of force and consent (1975: 310, 80 n. 45). Gramsci writes:

> the supremacy of a social group manifests itself in two ways, as 'domination' and as 'intellectual and moral leadership'. A social group dominates antagonistic groups, which it tends to 'liquidate', or to subjugate perhaps even by armed force; it leads kindred and allied groups (1975: 57; see also Fontana 1993: 144).

According to Gramsci, the hegemonic apparatus performs two distinct tasks simultaneously. It endeavors to gain the consent of as many other groups as possible (that is, 'intellectual and moral leadership') while using force against dissenters.[23]

The voluntary acquiescence of other social groups is achieved through the use of various consent-generating institutions positioned in what Gramsci calls 'civil society'.[24] These institutions function to disseminate

22. Here ancient Israel is taken as an example of a theocracy. The latter is defined by Robertson as 'union of church and state, with emphasis, however, on church autonomy' (1987: 157). See also Weber's original discussion of this issue (1978: 1158-1211).

23. Thus, for Gramsci also, an 'official religion' would be comprised of a coalition of heterogenous groups consolidated via the 'intellectual and moral leadership' of the 'directive grouping'. It should be stressed, however, that Gramsci's views on the interplay between coercion and consent are not always consistent or clear (see Anderson 1976).

24. According to Gramsci civil society refers to 'the ensemble of organisms commonly called "private"' (1975: 12). Renate Holub remarks: 'civil society, with its institutions ranging from education, religion and the family to the microstructures of the practices of everyday life, contribute(s) to the production of meaning and values which in turn produce, direct and maintain the "spontaneous" consent of the various strata of society to that same status quo' (1992: 6; see also Said 1979: 7; Scott 1977:

the ideological world-view of the hegemonic apparatus throughout the arteries of the social body. It could be said that an 'official religion' sponsors institutions whose task it is to impart its theological agenda to the population at large. This may be achieved through a variety of media such as schools, art, monumental architecture, periodic rituals and public recitations of sacred legends.[25]

For the time being—pending further research in this field—I shall define an 'official religion' in Antiquity as follows: 'the religion of an association of male-dominated and interconnected social groups[26] which exercises the greatest power (via coercion and/or consent) in its relations with other religious groups and thus comes to stand as the "orthodoxy" of a particular society'.

'Israelite Official Religion' vs. 'Official Yahwism'

In the preceding sections I presented a handful of frequently encountered interpretations of 'official religion'. For purposes of analysis I shall consolidate these criteria in order to formulate a tentative 'ideal-type' of the 'official religion' construct. As Stephen Kalberg notes: 'Rather than being endowed with the capability to "replicate" the external world or define any particular phenomenon, ideal types are constructed "utopias" that alone aim to facilitate empirical inquiry' (1994: 85; also see Giddens 1992: 141).

The criteria forwarded above are thus submitted not with the intention of describing empirical reality, but in the hope of providing some 'hypothesis-forming models' (Kalberg 1994: 92). By stating them one attempts, in the words of Erving Goffman, to establish 'common features with the hope of highlighting significant differences later' (1961: 5). The significant differences will arise once these general criteria are compared to the particular situation found in ancient Israel.

273; Bates 1975: 353, 357). For works dealing with Gramsci's view of religion see Fulton (1987); Nesti (1975) and Portelli (1974).

25. Notice how institutions of coercion and consent operate concurrently in anthropologist Talal Asad's description of the power of the Medieval Church: 'ranging all the way from laws (imperial and ecclesiastical) and other sanctions (hellfire, death, salvation, good repute, peace, etc.), to the disciplinary activities of social institutions (family, school, city, church, etc.) and of human bodies (fasting, prayer, obedience, penance, etc.)' (1983: 242).

26. For example, privileged economic strata, powerful hereditary clans, dominant priestly classes, rulers of the state/monarchy and their intellectual cadres, and so on.

'Official religion' is that religion which exerts the greatest power in its relations with other religious groups within a given territory. Co-determining this capacity to exert power are three factors. The 'official religion': is in some capacity linked to an economically-dominant group; is primarily staffed and administered by men, and via the work of intellectuals produces a rationalized world-view which (through the exertion of power) comes to stand as 'orthodoxy'.

Can this (provisional) ideal-typical schema be applied to the biblical milieu? First, a prevailing locus of power in ancient Israel would have to be identified. A plausible candidate for this role would be the monarchy/state. As Whitelam notes, the establishment of kingship in Israel entailed 'The centralisation of military, economic, political and religious power' (1989: 120). As the most dominant player in the pre-exilic social arena it can be assumed that the monarchy represented the interests of economically privileged classes. A verification of this claim can be sought in Marvin Chaney's article 'Systemic Study of the Israelite Monarchy'. There, the author extrapolates from studies of stratification in agrarian monarchies and notes that 'a ruling elite of probably no more than two percent of the population controlled up to half or more of the total goods and services' (1986: 56). Via coercion and consensual institutions such as education, art, monumental architecture (Whitelam 1989: 121, 133) and so forth, the monarchy was able to inculcate a 'royal ideology' and hence to acquire the consensus of a large part of its populace (see also Brett 1987: 29).

It can also be assumed that the important administrative and leadership roles within this religious regime were occupied by men. Such an assumption seems warranted in light of recent research.[27] Lastly, it can be maintained that intellectuals (such as scribes, court theologians, court historians and priests) employed by the monarchy were responsible for the creation, dissemination and maintenance of this 'official religion'. It also seems likely that in ancient Israel, and in the ancient Near East in general, a royal court sponsored intellectual activity of this sort (Whybray 1990: 137; Sweet 1990: 101, 107).[28]

It is at this point, however, that a significant difference arises between the 'ideal-type' posited above and the unique circumstances found in

27. See Bird 1987: 403, 405; see also Bird 1991: 108; Meyers 1988: 12 and Sperling 1986: 28-29.

28. Also see Meyers 1988: 11; Dever 1990: 123 and Whitelam 1989: 120, 121, 128, 130.

ancient Israel. This occurs when an examination is made of the relation between the Hebrew Bible and this very abstract Israelite 'official religion' which has just been postulated. In biblical research it is often held that the 'official religion' of ancient Israel largely resembles the religion presented on the pages of the Old Testament. Accordingly, an implicit correlation is made between the authors of this document and the monarchy/state (that is, the prevailing institution of power in ancient Israel); biblical Yahwism is viewed as synonymous with Israelite 'official religion'.

The methodological corollary of this assumption can be described as follows: when a scholar wishes to discuss some aspect of 'Israelite official religion' he or she points to a particular Old Testament verse. As such, various passages of the Hebrew Bible are adduced as indices of the policies of Israelite 'official religion' at some particular point (and place) in history. This approach stands as one of the most widely-held, deeply-embedded and least-discussed methodologies in biblical scholarship.

Yet if the Old Testament can be read as the literature of Israel's 'official religion' why are so many of its verses so overtly hostile to the very institutions of power which typically buttress 'official religion'? As is well known, parts of the text evince an antagonistic stance towards Israelite kings, Judahite kings and the institution of the monarchy itself.[29] This unambiguously critical approach to institutions of power makes the Old Testament unique among contemporary documents. As Morton Smith notes: 'There is nothing comparable to this in any other religious literature from the ancient Mediterranean or Mesopotamian worlds' (1987: 35). Here we have a corpus of texts which do not restrict themselves to hagiographic depictions of monarchs and adjacent institutions of power. On the contrary, the authors of the Old Testament exhibit little compunction in excoriating kings, even revered kings (for example, in 2 Sam. 12; 1 Kgs 3.2-3; 11.5-13; 15.5), and calling into question the very legitimacy of the monarchy.

The impression one receives is that those who wrote certain sections of the Old Testament, far from being loyal devotees or employees of the monarchy, actually lived in a state of high tension with this institution.[30]

29. See 1 Sam. 8; 1 Sam. 12.12-17; 1 Kgs 15.1-4; 2 Kgs 8.16-18; 2 Kgs 16.1-4; 21.1-17;19-22. See also Alt 1968: 313; Pedersen 1947: 95-101; Mendelsohn 1956; Weber 1967: 195; Brett 1987: 28 and Whitelam 1989.

30. As P. Berger notes in his discussion of Israelite prophets, in them is found a group of intellectuals 'essentially in opposition to the official institutional structure of

P. Kyle McCarter, Jr remarks: 'the biblical writers themselves indicate that the branch of preexilic religion they are embracing was a dissenting viewpoint during much of the Israelite monarchy' (1987: 137).

Such a state of affairs suggests that there should be no immediate assumption that the Hebrew Bible is a record of Israelite 'official religion'. For if 'official religion' is to be correlated with power, and if the monarchy is construed as the major power player in pre-exilic Israel, then it becomes difficult to account for the denunciations of this institution found in the Old Testament.

The Hebrew Bible, then, offers insights into either 'official religion' as it was actually practised at some particular period(s) or 'official religion' as Yawhist theocratic historians thought it *should have been* practised. An inquiry as to which of these propositions was closer to the actual situation, or at which particular periods of Israelite history either may have been true, is well beyond the scope of the present study.[31] The preceding analysis should serve only to restrain exegetes from making a facile equation between the verses of the Old Testament and the actual, real 'official religion(s)' which existed on the soil of Palestine during the pre- and post-exilic periods.

When discussing any given biblical text which discusses the vow, I shall oscillate between two somewhat distinct conceptualizations of its relation to 'official religion'. First, I shall assume that all Old Testament vow-texts may be taken as reasonably accurate reports of the votive policies of an 'official Yahwism'.[32] Second, it will be held that at various periods the latter may actually have been an 'official religion' as described above.[33] Thus, each vow-text encountered will be understood

---

Israel as represented by monarchy and priesthood' (1963: 941; see also Petersen 1979:127).

31. Any attempt to answer these questions will need to bear in mind Dever's crucial observation that the Old Testament is 'a *curated* artifact' (1991: 199). The fact that this text was 'continuously reworked' over time by various groups makes the challenge of dating its relation to 'official religion' immeasurably complex.

32. Though not *the* 'official Yahwism'. Since there is no information regarding other forms of Yahwism it should not be assumed that the Yahwism preserved in the Old Testament was always the accepted 'official' variant of Yahwism. Perhaps an 'official religion' existed which was Yahwist in nature but qualitatively different from the Yahwism described in the Hebrew Bible.

33. The question of when this might actually have been the case is left in abeyance. I assume that the post-exilic period offers some potential examples of a real Yahwist 'official religion' (for example, during the Hasmonaean monarchy) or perhaps a sort

as an expression of 'official Yahwism' and *possibly* an expression of 'official religion'. These vacillating conceptions will permit me a confrontation of the questions which are of interest to this study. Nevertheless, a more consistent stance toward this issue will need to be developed in future research.

'Popular Religious Groups' Defined

Having defined 'official religion' I shall now use the relational methodology as a means of identifying 'popular religious groups'. It should be noted that this local definition, like the one just offered, is not intended to be a permanent fixture in biblical 'popular religion' studies. Rather, it is hoped that as more Old Testament scholars address this issue, it will be continually refined, improved and discarded once its usefulness has been exhausted.

An 'official religion', as noted above, arrogates to itself the status of 'orthodoxy'. In so doing, it confers upon dissenters labels such as 'heretic' and 'apostate'. It is clear that the theocratic historians of the Old Testament acted in precisely such a manner. As far as they were concerned, the hills and valleys of Israel were inhabited by religious deviants of every conceivable type.

This much seems more or less incontrovertible. A problematic—and currently insoluble—question concerns whether or not this Yahwist party at any time had the requisite power to elevate its views to a hegemonic position and thus persecute these 'deviants'. Insofar as I have maintained that it is plausible to assume that at some point biblical Yahwism was an 'official religion', it is possible to accept that those groups singled out for scorn on the pages of the Old Testament constitute potential 'popular religious groups'.

These deviant constituencies will be referred to as 'heterodoxies'. A heterodoxy will be defined as 'any association of individuals living within the borders of ancient Israel who by dint of their religious beliefs, rituals, or symbols, are denigrated by the authors of the Old Testament'.

---

of local 'official religion' which was granted autonomy by Persian, Greek or Roman overlords. Doeve (1979), in his important discussion of Israelite 'official religion', looks at the Second Temple as a possible locus for an 'official Judaism'. In the post-exilic period, according to Doeve, the day-to-day management of such a religion was carried out by those who had executive functions within the Temple (1979: 326). Whatever the case may be, it will take the publication of several monographs to address all of the pertinent issues.

Baal worshippers living in Judah and Israel and excoriated on the pages of the Bible can be considered excellent candidates for this designation, as can those who backslide, go whoring after other gods, do what is offensive to the Lord, disobey the ritualistic precepts of Yahwism, and so on.

In another application of the relational methodology it could be maintained that the types of groups least likely to be a part of the hegemonic apparatus may be potential candidates for 'popular religious groups'. It was suggested above that 'official Yahwism' was characterized by a certain gender asymmetry. Men seemed to play a disproportionately large role in the establishment and maintenance of the cult of this deity. As Carol Meyers remarks in *Discovering Eve: Ancient Israelite Women in Context*, the priesthood 'was an all-male, hereditary group' (1988: 11). Such a state of affairs leads us to speculate that women may have practised forms of religiosity which differed in some way from the male-centered 'official Yahwism' trumpeted on the pages of the Hebrew Bible. Or, as Phyllis Bird notes: 'women's religion did represent a significantly differentiated form of religious expression within Yahwism' (1991: 108; see also Ackerman 1989: 110). It is in light of these considerations that I shall posit women as another 'popular religious group'.

In the same study, Meyers notes that the cult of Yahweh did not differ from others solely in terms of its gender configuration:

> The priestly, royal, and gubernatorial establishment was not only unrepresentative of women; it was also unrepresentative of the population as a whole. Priests, kings, officers, and bureaucrats were elite groups; as such, they were removed from the masses of the population, both male and female (1988:12).

This citation from Meyers underscores an opinion shared by many non-biblical scholars of 'popular religion': the members of 'official religion' and 'popular religious groups' are often members of different economic classes. If it is maintained that dominant ruling classes comprised the 'official religion' then, following other researchers, non-privileged economic classes can be assumed to be a 'popular religious group'.

When compared to the 'official Yahwist' party, all three of these groups share certain sociological attributes.[34] Each had little to do with the day-to-day operation of the 'official' Yahwistic cult. Baalists, women

---

34. These are not necessarily the only 'popular religious groups' which may be scrutinized. It is hoped that future researchers will delineate other groups for study.

and the poor, it seems, were never permitted to officiate at Yahwistic ceremonies or administer the rituals of this deity. Nor, it can be surmised, did they have much input into the actual authorship of the sacred literature found in the Old Testament. Further, we have little evidence which indicates that any of these groups exerted power in their relations with 'official Yahwism'.[35]

In the conclusion of this monograph I shall reassess the efficacy of 'popular religious groups' and 'official religion' as analytical tools for the study of Israelite religion. For the moment, with three 'popular religious groups' defined, I shall turn my attention to a series of crucial exegetical questions. These concern the textual materials which are used to study the votive behavior of the Israelites targeted in this study.

Towards A New Methodology: Exegetical Questions

Given that the Hebrew Bible is the product of passionate and partial 'theocratic historians'—diametrically opposed across innumerable sociological continua to the 'popular religious groups' under consideration— then how may it be trusted to furnish veridical assessments of those who differed from them?

In the following section, I shall attempt to outline a strategy for answering this question. In order to bring my own methodological approach into sharper focus, I shall delineate and then critique one of the most frequently encountered exegetical strategies employed by biblical scholars who have addressed the issue of 'popular religion'.

The Explicit Approach

This method is referred to as the 'explicit approach' and its distinguishing characteristic lies in its tendency to read the explicit statements of the biblical literati as if they were wholly accurate accounts of Israelite ('popular') religious life.

An example of this method may be found in Segal's article on Israelite 'popular religion'. Segal writes:

> When we consider practices connected with birth we note a general desire
> for children, especially for sons. Childlessness was regarded as a divine

---

35. Women and non-privileged classes are to be analytically distinguished from heterodoxies in that they are *not* categorically derided by the authors of the Old Testament. Women and indigent Israelites, unlike Baal worshippers, are occasionally shown to be exemplary Yahwists.

punishment, and some women adopted the children of their husband's concubine. The time of conception was especially momentous and the announcement of pregnancy may have been marked by a sacrifice (1976: 3).

As one reads through Segal's footnotes it becomes clear that each one of these claims is verified *solely* by a reference to a biblical verse. For example, if Genesis 16 speaks of Abram's taking of a concubine, then it is concluded that 'some women adopted the children of their husband's concubine' (Segal 1976: 3).

A similar method may be found in Hermann Vorländer's article 'Aspects of Popular Religion in the Old Testament'. Vorländer points to Jacob's vow (Gen. 35) as evidence of a 'kind of personal piety' found 'throughout the popular religion of the ancient East' (1986: 64).

Yehezkel Kaufmann also takes the explicitly-stated words of the literati at face value. This strategy is based on his belief that the Old Testament is itself an expression of the popular voice:

> Biblical faith is thus based on the popular legends. It draws on them even when it battles the people's backslidings into idolatry. The popular legends and the beliefs they imply are the common property of the folk and the authors of the Bible. They constitute the source and substance of early monotheism (1972: 132).

Accordingly, the Psalms are assumed to stem from the hands of popular poets, and the Old Testament is held to be a 'folk literature' (1972: 223). Kaufmann remarks: 'Biblical religion is therefore not an esoteric religion of a spiritual elite like the higher pagan religions, but is a growth that is rooted in and nourished by the popular religion of Israel' (1972: 133).

In these works, explicit details regarding the actions of biblical Israelites are never subjected to any type of critical interrogation.[36] Instead, all references to 'popular religious groups' or constitutive aspects of human existence such as birth, death and marriage are treated as if they were more or less veridical descriptions of Israelite 'popular religion'.

A Critique of the Explicit Approach
There are two principal reasons for casting doubts on the soundness of the explicit approach. As noted earlier, the theocratic historians who authored the Old Testament viewed the world through an optic colored by their own particular ideological presuppositions. This may have motivated them intentionally to misrepresent groups and individuals who did

---

36. For an examination of other approaches used by biblical scholars see Berlinerblau 1993.

not share their world-view or who differed from them. Thus, by basing historical reconstructions on the tale of the explicit evidence there is always the risk of, to use the old Marxist adage, sharing 'the illusion of that epoch' (Marx and Engels, 1991: 60).

In 'The "Popular Religion" Paradigm in Old Testament Research: A Sociological Critique', I called attention to a more subtle form of distortion. I referred to it as 'unintentional misrepresentation'—a process whereby the literati *inadvertently* offer erroneous information (1993). It may be the case that there were certain facts about 'popular religious groups' that the biblical authors either simply could not understand, or of which they were unaware.

As I noted in my article:

> Can highly educated litterateurs interested in chronicling the 'truths' of monotheistic Yahwism truly hear the '*vox populi*', or is it articulated in a dialect which, to them, is socially incomprehensible? Can the scribes really understand the religion of the agriculturalist, or the meaning of the Baal worshipper's rituals—what they signify *to the Baalist* and what they are really intended to do (1993: 14)?[37]

Whether the misrepresentation is intentional or unintentional, it is of tremendous methodological import to recognize that 'popular religious groups' are always *represented*. For whatever reasons, the poor, the women and the heterodox of ancient Israel never express themselves in their own words on the pages of the Hebrew Bible. As such, they are always portrayed, always depicted, and historians are always in danger of being the victims of intentional and unintentional misrepresentation.

Implicit Evidence: Tacit Assumption and Mechanisms
How then can one study the religious life of social groups and strata which Old Testament historiographers either maligned, misunderstood or relegated to obscurity? My own methodological approach begins with the conviction that, whenever possible, less reliance must be placed on

---

37. In the case of women, for example, it is possible that the male authors of the Old Testament might not have been interested in, or might not have known very much about, their female co-religionists. This 'male perspective that dominates scripture' (Meyers 1991: 50) creates innumerable difficulties for biblical students of gender. In her article on the worship of the Queen of Heaven, Susan Ackerman notes that the issue of women's religion is treated by 'The all-male biblical writers...with silence or hostility' (1989: 110). Peggy Day speaks of the 'androcentric perspective on Israelite culture' which characterizes the writings of the Old Testament (1989: 5; see also Emmerson 1989: 371; Bird 1987: 398, 408).

the explicit statements of the literati. To ignore this decree is to run the risk of understanding the Old Testament world precisely as the Old Testament authors wanted it to be understood.

In an effort to generate an alternative source of data that is less susceptible to the preceding charges, I shall make use of what I call the method of 'tacit assumption'. This approach attempts to identify a species of information which has little or nothing to do with the theological, political or social agenda of the Old Testament authors.

As a means of illustrating this method, I shall begin with an analogy. On any given day the reader of a newspaper in the United States will encounter a first-hand account regarding the proceedings of a trial. Typically, the reporter will mention that someone took the witness stand, or that the witness testified for three hours, or that an attorney fiercely cross-examined this person under oath.

The modern reporter does not need to specify that the person who took the witness stand in the preceding day's trial did so alone. Today's readers and writers simply know that in the United States witnesses do not testify in pairs or in large groups. Thus, when the journalist writes that 'the witness descended from the stand visibly shaken', he or she does not state, but *tacitly assumes* what is known to everybody: in this society witnesses testify one at a time. This analogy, I believe, can be usefully employed by the modern biblical scholar.

Embedded within every vow-text there exists a wealth of information which is entirely distinct in both form and content from the explicit details discussed above. This 'implicit evidence', as I call it, is unique in that it is not articulated by the biblical authors; it does not need to be stated, since everybody 'knows' it. Instead, it is *tacitly assumed* by authors who have much more important information (namely, explicit details) to relay to their audience.

Let me offer another example. In 1 Samuel 1 we read about Hannah's vow to Yahweh made at the Shiloh sanctuary. It is safe to say that there are many explicit details in this episode that the authors of the Old Testament want the reader to know. They want the reader to know that a pious worshipper was the beneficiary of Yahweh's kindness. They want the reader to know that the God of Israel, in all his greatness, is capable providing an infertile woman with a child. They want the reader to know that the Shiloh sanctuary run by Eli is a den of corruption, and that a great prophet of Yahweh will soon restore the sanctity of this once-sacred place.

Statements of this order are precisely the ones upon which the biblical historian must cast the brunt of his or her exegetical skepticism. For this explicit evidence harmonizes perfectly with the 'party line' of the theocratic historians of the Old Testament. In manifold ways these details sing the praises of the God they worship, and vocalize the advantages that accrue to all who steadfastly obey that God. Yet deeply inlaid within the Hannah episode there lies a rather mundane fact. It is never explicitly articulated because it is so trivial, or perhaps because it was so commonly understood by the literati and their audience, that it did not need to be stated. The authors of the Old Testament tacitly assume that Hannah makes her vow alone, as an individual.

I cannot identify a plausible connection between this detail and any ideological impulse of the Old Testament authors.[38] In other words, I find no reason to assume that the literati wanted the reader to know that Hannah makes her vow as a solitary agent. If they did, they certainly did not concern themselves with expressly articulating this fact. It is more likely that this particular detail is situated beyond the margins of their ideological agenda. Indeed, it seems so inherently banal that one wonders if the writers of the Hebrew Bible were even aware that they had furnished it to posterity.

In and of itself, this observation regarding the solitude of Hannah's vow may certainly seem insignificant. Yet as will become clear, an identical state of affairs is repeatedly (tacitly) assumed in a large core of northwest Semitic vow-texts. It is known to the writers of J, E, P and D and as the inquiry is extended to the extra-biblical data from the Canaanite world, this 'mechanism' of 'individual initiation' will again be identified.

A mechanism can be defined as a rule, standard method or normative procedural component of votive praxis. Each mechanism I uncover in the Hebrew Bible will be assumed to have operated as a norm in ancient Israel. Thus, from the point of view of the agent, the mechanism/norm provides a prescription for social action, specifically, one which defines appropriate and inappropriate ways to make a vow. To use the example already cited, it may be concluded that Israelite supplicants knew that it was perfectly acceptable to initiate their vow alone. The first part of this study will be devoted to extracting five of these tacitly-assumed mechanisms from Old Testament and northwest Semitic vow-texts. Once

---

38. This does not mean that no such impulse existed. The burden of proof, however, lies on that scholar who wishes to suggest that ideological motivations prompted the literati to place this detail within the text.

identified, these mechanisms will permit me to speculate as to the basic ground rules of the votive procedure.[39]

Accessibility

After having uncovered these tacitly-assumed mechanisms, I shall evaluate whether they served to render the votive system 'accessible' to members of Israelite 'popular religious groups'. When speaking of accessibility, I am referring to the degree to which a religious practice both attracts members of a particular group and facilitates their participation in it. Conversely, to label a practice as 'restrictive' is to suggest that some fundamental component of this religious act serves to discourage or preclude certain groups from participation.

The study of accessibility requires that the interrelations between two distinct constellations of information are studied. On the one hand, the rules that govern the particular practice which we are examining need to be known. In my study, I have referred to such rules as the 'mechanisms' of the Israelite vow. On the other hand, there must be an understanding of the normative behavioral patterns of the group in question.

Sociologists who study religion often attempt to delineate the characteristics and dispositions of social groups (for example, economic classes, status groups, professional associations). It is often assumed that for a variety of reasons members of a particular social group will incline to behave in certain ways.[40] The study of accessibility consists of an examination of the interplay between a religious practice and the normative behavioral patterns of a particular social type. Something about the

39. To what degree does a tacitly-assumed mechanism serve as an accurate indice of those votive norms known to *real* flesh-and-blood Israelites? I can only offer an indirect response to this question. The likelihood that a mechanism found in one vow-text represents an actual rule known to a genuine Israelite may be said to increase under the following three conditions. First: there must be no identifiable plausible correlation between a discovered mechanism and a particular ideological motivation of the Old Testament authors. Secondly, the more frequently a mechanism appears in vow-texts stemming from different biblical sources, the more likely it is that it constituted actual practice. Thirdly, the more often a mechanism appears in vow-texts authored in different northwest Semitic cultural settings (such as ancient Israel, Ugarit, Ammon, and so on) the more probable it is that it witnesses a general regional norm.

40. One of the most deft applications of this assumption may be identified in Weber's chapter 'Religious Groups', known to many English readers as *The Sociology of Religion*. See, for example, Weber's remarks on the ideal-typical dispositions of peasants (1978: 468, 470).

practice entices the members of a group. Yet there is something about the latter as well, which motivates them to select this particular practice.

I offer one final example. Let us assume that a certain religious act in society *X* demands that the worshipper donate one year's income to the local sanctuary. Such a practice would be categorically restrictive to members of non-privileged classes. To those in possession of tremendous wealth, however, the loss of one year's earnings would not necessarily reduce the accessibility of this behavior. In the former case there is an incommensurability observed between the demands of the practice and the fiscal capacities of impoverished worshippers. In the latter, no such incongruity may be observed and hence the practice may be seen as accessible to the wealthy.

Part II of this study will be devoted to assessing the accessibility of the vow to my three 'popular religious groups'. By examining the correspondences or conflicts between the mechanisms of the vow and the sociological dispositions of these Israelites, I shall attempt to ascertain whether or not and why the Israelite votive system was accessible to them.

The Vow and 'Popular Religious Groups'

Throughout this opening chapter I have called attention to a series of fundamental questions which confront sociologists and historians who set out to study the 'popular religious groups' of Antiquity. As a means of engaging these questions, this research will concentrate on the practice of vow-making in ancient Israel and the northwest Semitic world.

Reduced to its most basic components, a vow (נדר) is a Hebrew conditional contract that a worshipper attempts to make with a deity.[41] When making a vow the supplicant essentially says to the god(dess) in question: 'if, *and only if,* you do something for me, then I will do something for you'.[42] Or, as Cartledge notes: *'dabo si dederis:* "I will give if you will give!"'' (1992: 38).[43]

---

41. The empirical body of evidence which will serve as the basis for this study will be the frequently attested northwest Semitic triliteral root *ndr* (נדר). Appearing a total of 91 times in the Old Testament (Keller 1976: 39), 31 times as a *qal* active verb and 60 times as a masculine noun (Andersen and Forbes 1989: 373-74), this word is best translated as 'to vow', or, in substantive form, 'a vow'.

42. Throughout this research, when speaking of the vow, I refer only to the 'positive' variety. On the difference between positive and negative vows see Appendix 1.

43. See also Moore 1903: 5253; Cartledge 1989: 415; Peake 1902: 872; Westphal 1956: 835 and Heiler 1958: 62.

It is not by coincidence that I have chosen to concentrate on this particular religious practice. As one reads through those biblical passages which discuss the vow a few explicit details appear which pique the interest of the student of 'popular religious groups'. Precisely those types of Israelites discussed above solicit this opportunity to negotiate with the God of Israel; princes vow, but so do paupers; men *and* women vow; very pious Yahwists engage in this practice as do their backsliding co-religionists. In and of itself this explicit evidence does not prove that these Israelites actually made vows in ancient Israel. Rather, it places a hypothesis in our minds, one that will either gain or lose in probability when measured against the implicit evidence.

The Old Testament, regardless of its aforementioned inadequacies, is our most comprehensive source for the elucidation of the votive behavior of 'popular religious groups'. This should not be taken as an endorsement of the exceptional historical accuracy of this document. Rather, it simply means that at present we do not possess a better source, be it textual or archaeological, from which to study the phenomenon in question. Be that as it may, it is necessary to become familiar with the merits and demerits of the other sources.

The Ugaritic,[44] Aramaic,[45] Ammonite,[46] Phoenician and Punic vow-texts that are available will be tremendously relevant to this study. Nevertheless, they do not necessarily provide a more exhaustive, revealing or accurate corpus of evidence than that found in the Old Testament. In terms of quantity, this extra-biblical data is rather unimpressive. There are only a few vow-texts from Ugarit, only one written in Aramaic and one in a language that is now thought to be Ammonite (see Berlinerblau: 1991). Further, with the exception of the latter, we have good reason to surmise that the authors of these texts are every bit as susceptible to the charges of intentional and unintentional misrepresentation as their counterparts in ancient Israel.

There is an almost embarrassing quantity of Phoenician and Punic

---

44. According to Whitaker's (1956) concordance, there exist nine known vow-texts in Ugaritic (a vow-text will henceforth refer to any text in which the form *ndr* may be identified). For a more recent summation of the existing Ugaritic evidence see Cartledge 1992: 108-22.

45. This being the Aramaic Bar-Hadad inscription that will be discussed below.

46. *AS* 49 is now recognized as an Ammonite inscription. For a full analysis of this text with bibliographical references see Berlinerblau 1991.

vow-texts.[47] Yet, while there are literally thousands of stelae, these texts written in the third-century BCE and extending forward a few centuries, are temporally (as well as spatially) removed from the pre-exilic and early post-exilic Israelite periods targeted in this study. Nevertheless, this data will often be helpful in shedding light on various aspects of biblical vows.[48]

Contrary to what many scholars have claimed, there is no archaeological evidence pertaining to the Israelite vow. Researchers frequently speak of 'Israelite votive artifacts' or 'votive vessels' (for example, Dever 1990: 132). Problematically, however, we do not have any reason to suppose that the objects in question had anything to do with the votive system discussed in the Old Testament. Tony Cartledge, the first to point this out, remarks:

> like almost all stelae found in cultic contexts, [they] are routinely referred to as 'votive' stelae. However, they do not mention a vow (*ndr*), so we would argue that a more appropriate name should be found (1989: 421).

From all of this emerges a fact of extreme methodological significance: there are no extant extra-biblical documents or archaeological materials which are so accurate or detailed that they alone permit either verification or rejection of the reports of the biblical literati. While useful as an adjunct source of information, they cannot surpass the Old Testament as a resource for the study of the vow and the 'popular religious groups' who may have engaged in this practice.

Conclusion

The forthcoming inquiry is submitted as a case study in how the biblical scholar may go about studying the 'popular religious groups' of Antiquity. As a means of achieving this goal I have proposed a series of

---

47. See Beyerlin 1978: 234. Lehmann makes the curious suggestion that vow-making was an 'institution characteristic, if not a creation of the North-Canaanites or Phoenicians' and 'absent in other areas' (1969: 85).

48. Cognate evidence from Akkadian is of little use in light of Jesse Boyd's observation that 'the Akk. root *ndr* is only a homonym of *ndr*, "to vow"' (1986: 66). There is, however, textual evidence for a votive system in Akkadian as represented by the noun form *ikribū* and the verbal form *karābu*. Though, as *CAD* VII, 'I/J' notes, the term may also refer to prayer. See Cartledge 1989: 417-18 and Cartledge 1992: 74-91 for basic bibliography. For a cross-cultural collection of vow-texts see Beyerlin 1978: 32-39 and 226-42.

sociological and text-critical initiatives, all of which are of an experimental nature.

In terms of sociological initiatives, I have forwarded definitions which will permit us to analyse two interrelated layers of the religious social structure of ancient Israel. 'Official religion', in the abstract, is the religion of an orthodoxy, one which yields power against others through coercion and/or consent. These 'others' I have labeled 'popular religious groups', and in this study three such groups have been targeted for scrutiny (women, non-privileged economic classes and heterodoxies).

Yet, before parading these Israelites into the sunlight of modern scholarship specific methods are needed for extracting them from the shadowy existence to which they were consigned by Old Testament historiographers. That is, text-critical strategies are needed which permit the circumvention of the distortions of accuracy which characterize the Old Testament as a historical document. As has already been seen, those who authored the Old Testament are susceptible to the charge of distorting various aspects of Israelite religious life. Unfortunately, a categorical dismissal of the Old Testament as a source of evidence is a luxury which the biblical scholar simply cannot afford; nearly everything that is known about the Israelite vow is known through the generosity of the Old Testament authors. This creates the problematic—and paradoxical—circumstance of having to rely almost exclusively on a text whose historiographical integrity is everywhere subjected to doubt.

As a means of circumnavigating this problem, I have proposed a two-tiered division of the details relinquished by the biblical authors. First, there is what I call 'explicit evidence'. This consists of information presented in the Old Testament which the literati wanted known. These typically involve polemical claims about particular groups, precise formulations concerning 'orthodox' religious practice, tendentious historical narratives and normative statements about the way things in the universe ought to be. These details must be approached with tremendous suspicion. This does not mean that such information is useless. Indeed, it will be used throughout this study as a means of generating primary hypotheses regarding Israelite votive praxis.

Ensconced within each vow-text there exists a completely different species of detail. This 'implicit evidence' consists of information that the literati never meant to tell us, but inadvertently told us anyway. What makes such details so important is that they seem to demonstrate a certain sovereignty from the ideological motivations of the biblical literati. The sheer banality of this information makes it difficult to imagine that the authors of the Old Testament intended for it to be known. Instead, it appears that this data just 'slipped out', that its presence in Scripture was not the result of coordinated forethought and calculation.

Implicit details, however, are not to be construed as components of a 'textual unconscious'. They reveal neither profane nor sacred aspects of the votive system that the literati unsuccessfully sought to repress. On the contrary, it is their thoroughly mundane nature that accounts for the fact that the biblical authors could afford either to casually mention them or to forget that they had mentioned them at all.

Part I will undertake to tease out five basic mechanisms of the Israelite vow from the Old Testament and northwest Semitic data. In Part II the testimony of this implicit evidence will be evaluated against that of the explicit evidence. With both types of evidence at my disposal, I shall be able to assess whether the votive system was accessible or restricted to each of the three groups selected in this study.

In Part III I shall shift my attention to an examination of the nexus that existed between 'official Yahwism' (perhaps at some point synonymous with 'official religion') and votaries emanating from 'popular religious groups'. Finally, my conclusion will be devoted to evaluating the efficacy of the methodological design proposed in this chapter.

It is now appropriate to begin an examination of the vow and the 'popular religious groups' of ancient Israel. The explicit evidence hints at widescale participation in this act by those targeted in this study. The task now is to measure this explicit evidence against the implicit evidence that is about to be unearthed. By specifically searching for such information, I am attempting in some way to evade the distortions of accuracy inherent to 'theocratic history'. It is hoped that the more skeptical methods advanced in this monograph will facilitate confronting the challenge of rescuing 'popular religious groups' from 'the enormous condescension of posterity'.

Part I

THE MECHANISMS OF THE ISRAELITE VOW

Chapter 1

INDIVIDUAL INITIATION

But if we leave these speculations in regard to the future aside for the moment, and confine ourselves to religions such as they are at present or have been in the past, it becomes clearly evident that these individual cults are not distinct and autonomous religious systems, but merely aspects of the common religion of the whole Church, of which the individuals are members. The patron saint of the Christian is chosen from the official list of saints recognized by the Catholic Church; there are even canonical rules prescribing how each Catholic should perform this private cult (E. Durkheim, *The Elementary Forms of the Religious Life*).

Individual Initiation

This chapter is devoted to proving a deceptively significant fact—one that will serve as the theoretical keystone of this research: in the Old Testament a vow is almost always initiated by an individual supplicant.

This observation, in and of itself, is by no means a novel insight. As early as 1858 Weiss could speak of 'The sacrifices vowed by individuals' (1858: 193). Plumptre refers to vows as a component of *'men's* personal religion' (1898: 147; emphasis mine). In commenting on Hannah's petition (1 Sam. 1.11), Kittel avers: 'her prayer is a purely personal, individual affair' (1922: 410). Von Rad speaks of the vow as 'a quite personal union of the individual with God' (1972: 286). And more recently, T. Cartledge remarks: 'The making of vows clearly played a significant role in the cultic life of Israel and seems to have been especially prevalent in the domain of individual piety' (1988: 999; also see Noth 1965: 162; Klinger 1987: 301).

While I generally agree with these remarks, the following caveat is in order: a few northwest Semitic texts seem to suggest that a petition could be made by more than one person. I will refer to these as 'group vows', defined as: 'any vow initiated by more than one person'. These persons are situated in the same time and space and they request an end from the deity (or deities) that serves to directly benefit all members of the vowing group.

A good example of such a phenomenon (in the non-Israelite milieu) is recorded in Caroline Brettell's study of priest/parishioner interaction in modern Portugal. Brettell writes:

> in the region of Portugal where I carried out fieldwork there is an annual pilgrimage in early June to the shrine of Santa Luzia located at the top of the hill that overlooks the provincial town and county seat of Viana do Castelo. This pilgrimage dates back to 1918 when the Spanish flu devastated the population of this region. It was initiated in the form of a collective vow or promise (*promessa*) by all the villages in the region to give thanks for the disappearance of this disastrous epidemic (Brettell 1990: 58; also see Bossy 1989: 73-74).

My own research suggests that in ancient Israel such group vows were much less frequent than petitions initiated by individuals. The evidence presented will demonstrate that the latter were the norm, while the existence of the former is very difficult to substantiate.

I shall also attempt to show that a recent argument in favor of a Ugaritic group vow (Miller 1988) is at best problematic and at worst impossible to verify. In so doing, I shall be able to lend greater credibility to the view that the vast majority of vows in northwest Semitic Antiquity were 'individually initiated'—that is, they were made by a single agent.

The Pre-exilic Sources of the Old Testament
There is little doubt that the supplicants in the epic vows[1] are acting alone. Hannah (1 Sam. 1.11), Jepthah (Judg. 11.30) and Absalom (2 Sam. 15.7) all make their vows individually. Jacob, the fleeing patriarch, does so as well. His individual petition reads as follows:

---

1. The term 'epic vow' will be used to refer to the five biblical and the two Ugaritic vow-texts in which we are privy to the full spoken text of the vow. That is, we hear the vow *as pronounced*—in the alleged words of the votary. The five instances of epic vows in the Old Testament are Gen. 28.20-22; Num. 21.2; Judg. 11.30-31; 1 Sam. 1.11 and 2 Sam. 15.8. In the Ugaritic sources we may point to *KTU* 1.14 IV 36-44 and *KTU* 1.22 II 16-21. Cartledge refers to these as 'narrative vows' (1992: 143).

Gen. 28.20

וידר יעקב נדר לאמר
אם־יהיה אלהים עמדי
ושמרני בדרך הזה אשר אנכי הולך
ונתן־לי לחם לאכל ובגד ללבש

21

ושבתי בשלום אל־בית אבי
והיה יהוה לי לאלהים

22

והאבן הזאת אשר־שמתי מצבה
יהיה בית אלהים
וכל אשר תתן־לי
עשר אעשרנו לך

20   Then Jacob made a vow, saying,[2] 'If Yahweh Elohim is with me,[3] protects me on this journey that I am making, gives me bread to eat, and clothing to wear[4]

21   And[5] I return safely to my father's house,[6] then Yahweh shall be my God.

22   And this stone which I have set up as a stele[7] will be God's abode,[8] and all that you will give to me, I will tithe it to you.'[9]

2.   For the opinion that vv. 20-22 are an appendage to the original text see Westermann 1981: 458; Richter 1967: 42-53 and Otto 1976.

3.   I prefer to use the conditional conjunction 'if' only once throughout the body of the vow. While most translators use it repeatedly, Jacob, it must be stressed, does not. This repetitive use of the conditional conjunction yields an overly-polite petition and detracts from the sense of bargaining, negotiation and cajoling that I believe to be constitutive of the votive process.

4.   Speiser offers an equivalent translation: 'just enough to subsist on' (1964: 218). Westermann writes: 'There is no mention of food and clothing in the promise in v. 15; one explanation is that it too was typical of a vow' (1981: 459). Though, against Westermann, it should be noted that no other votary in our register of northwest Semitic petitions makes such a request.

5.   Many commentators take this verse as an insertion (see Speiser 1964: 218; Clamer 1953: 368; Gunkel 1917: 321; contra Westermann 1981: 459; Bennett n.d.: 284). See also the verse division proposed by Spurrell (1896: 254). Delitzsch (1889: 166) suggests that the apodosis begins here.

6.   On this term see Wolff 1981: 182, 214; Meyers 1991. For a sociological treatment, see Weber 1967: 15 as well as Gottwald's discussion (1985: 285-92).

7.   Many commentators translate מצבה as 'pillar' (for example, Speiser 1964: 218; Westermann 1981:451; von Rad 1972: 283; Delitzsch 1889: 166; Bennett n.d.: 283; Ryle 1921: 296; Driver 1909: 267; Murphy 1873: 386; König 1925: 598; Sarna 1989: 200), but I prefer the translation 'stele' (de Vaux 1965: 285; Clamer 1953: 368; see also Sarna 1989: 201). I favor this translation because of the appearance of a cognate in other inscriptions where it denotes not a pillar, but a stele (see Dupont-Sommer 1958: 17 l. 6). A more dramatic parallel can be found in the ninth-century Bar-Hadad inscription to be examined below. Of course, the question still remains as

In 1 Sam. 1.21 it is reported that Elkanah has gone up with his family to Shiloh in order to offer Yahweh 'the annual slain offering as well as his vow' (את־זבה הימים ואת־נדרו). The Masoretic Text makes reference to 'his vow', את־נדרו, and as such it should be emphasized that the author is tacitly assuming the making of an individual petition.[10]

This brings us to Num. 21.1-3, a passage that would initially seem to feature a group vow. Yet the text itself, contrary to what nearly all exegetes have maintained, testifies to the primacy and indispensability of individual initiation in the votive process. This passage, utterly disjointed from its surroundings,[11] places the Israelites in the Negeb. When attacked by the king of Arad, an unnamed Israelite makes a vow:

to what the basic function of the stele actually was. On this issue see Graesser's excellent article for suggestions (1972); also note Palmer's (rather dated) use of anthropological evidence (1899: 84-85). The most recent and comprehensive treatment of this issue is offered by de Pury, who suggests that the stone is perceived as a witness which represents the supplicant, 'pierre témoin' (1975: II.409).

8.   For a comprehensive discussion of this term see de Pury who suggests that בית אל and בית אלוהים have nothing to do with one another (1975: II.429). See also Fitzmeyer 1967: 90, who translates 'bethels'—an object performing a function similar to a stele. For evidence both for and against the existence of a deity by this name see Hyatt 1939.

9.   A few scholars have maintained that in ancient Israel there existed a 'votive tithe'. Accordingly, Jacob is viewed as a model for would-be votaries who will come to the temple and offer tithes as did their patriarchal ancestor. Kaufmann writes: 'The votive tithe of Jacob in Genesis 28 was archetypal for the later Israelites who followed Jacob's example when petitioning God' (1972: 190). Von Rad notes: 'When those who came later brought the tithe to Bethel, they shared somewhat in Jacob's vow' (1972: 286; see also Haran 1978: 16 n. 4; Fohrer 1972: 209; G. Anderson 1987: 85 *passim*). It should be emphasized, however, that tithing appears in only one northwest Semitic vow-text (namely, Jacob's vow). Nor is it mentioned in relation to vows in any of the priestly texts as is often alleged. Sarna has noted that tithes are usually only offered 'to a king or to a sanctuary with an established clergy' (1989: 201). Lastly, Cazelles has shown that in Ugaritic ʿšr often refers to the unction of a stone: 'Moreover, the tradition which is the basis of Gen. 28:22 is also favorable, because the title which is announced recalls the unction of the oil made by Jacob on the sacred stone of Bethel' (1951: 133). As such, we may need to reevaluate the translation 'tithe', as well as the association between the latter and the vow.

10.   The literati do not tell us anything about the actual initiation of this vow. Only its fulfillment is recorded here. See Chapter 6 for exegesis.

11.   Scholars have had great difficulty in discerning the placement, dating and motivations of this passage. As Ehrlich remarks: 'Der Text ist hier nicht in Ordnung' (1909: 189). Since this passage is separate in theme from the narrative that proceeds

2   וידר ישראל נדר ליהוה ויאמר
                                                 אם־נתן תתן את־העם הזה בידי
                                                      והחרמתי את־עריהם

2   And Israel made a vow to Yahweh saying: 'If you deliver this
         people into my hand, then I will proscribe[12] their towns.'

What makes this text so curious, and simultaneously so germane to our
discussion, is that although 'Israel' makes the vow, the petition is clearly
initiated by an individual. The unidentified supplicant makes use of first-
person suffixes both with the verb החרמתי and with the substantive בידי.
This immediately raises the following questions. Why does only one
person speak for an entire community as it faces a crisis? Why is there no
report of all Israel petitioning and praying together for their deliverance?

Most exegetes translate this verse with the first-person plural as opposed
to the form attested in the text (the first-person singular). Thus, they
avoid posing such questions. Wendel, for example, renders this passage
as 'If you deliver these people into our hands, we will proscribe their
town' (1927: 130; emphasis mine).[13] Milgrom attempts to smooth out
the difficulties presented by the first-person singular form by making the
ingenious suggestion that 'For the vow to be effective it had to be taken
by every soldier' (1990: 172; see also Coats 1976: 185).

Cartledge, who draws attention to the use of the singular, also con-
cludes that this is a group vow. In defending this interpretation he notes:

> Israel *corporately* makes a vow…The singular nature of the verbal forms
> in this text is not just an unconscious use of the standard vow formulation.
> Rather, it serves as a remarkable statement of unanimity and trust in
> Yahweh (1992: 163; see also 164 and 145).

and follows, many have rightly identified it as a parenthetical insertion (also see Coats
1976: 183; Heinsich 1936: 81; Noth 1968: 154). Most exegetes, however, have
assigned this text to either J or JE (Gray 1906: 272; Noth 1968: 154; Strack 1894:
425). But also see Eissfeldt who assigns it to L (1965: 195), or Cross, who discusses
it within the context of priestly writings (1973: 316), or Baentsch who sees it as a later
gloss on an earlier tradition (1903: 573-74).

   12. On the relation between the חרם and the vow see Gottwald 1985: 544 and
1964. See Miller 1988 who draws a parallel between this and a Ugaritic text to be
examined below (see also Pedersen 1963: 15).

   13. But see Wendel's later study 1931b: 113 where the proper translation is
given. For more instances of the first-person plural translation see Steuernagel 1901:
77 and Milgrom 1990: 172.

Cartledge suggests that an Israelite community plagued by internecine strife banded together by making a group vow. The use of first-person singular forms is taken as a symbolic act demonstrating the capacity of the beleaguered Israelites to unify via faith in Yahweh. But Cartledge has yet to explain why first-person singular forms would be any more indicative of 'Israel's corporate faith' than plural forms (1992: 164). The author(s) of this text could have illustrated Israel's 'unanimity and trust in Yahweh' just as convincingly by employing the first-person plural.

The fact remains that in this vow, as in all of the other epic vows, the petition itself is articulated by an individual supplicant. The writers who created or re-animated this tradition did not depict their protagonists as corporately initiating a petition to Yahweh. Rather, the text—which has more important explicit details to relate to us—implicitly assumes the opposite: a vow is made by an individual.[14] Even in a situation where a crisis confronts the community, a vow is made by one person.[15]

The Legislative Material
In the legislation of the Old Testament, there is a nearly identical state of affairs, albeit rendered in a different literary idiom. Here, there are a series of laws and regulations from D and P that attempt to regulate the proper procedures for the payment of vows.

These laws may be justifiably adduced as evidence for individual initiation. Most of them make use of singular forms when discussing the rules of votive recompensation. That is, their hypothetical subject (namely, the votary who enters the sacred precincts in order to pay a vow) is typically—although occasionally not unequivocally—an individual.

In Num. 30.3-4 there are two laws that are prefaced by the phrase כי אשה איש, 'when a man (or woman) makes a vow'. The votive legislation in this chapter tacitly assumes that the supplicant is an individual,

14. It must also be noted that in Num. 21 and Judg. 11 an individual makes a vow in order to secure an end for a group. In other epic vows, the individual makes the vow solely to secure an end favorable to himself or herself. Thus, two distinct votive modes may be identified: vows made for personal gain, and vows made for the good of the group. Of course—and this is crucial—in both cases the vow is initiated by an individual.

15. I would like to point out that in the Neo-Punic archives there is also an instance of a vow made by one person on behalf of a group. In *KAI* 164 a woman named ʾAKBRT makes a vow for the community (להגו). While no other details are given, the drawing of parallels is compelling (see also *EH* 24 for a discussion of the reading of this word).

whether a man (v. 3), an unmarried woman (v. 4), a married woman (v. 7), a divorced woman or a widow (v. 10). This same third-person singular address can be found throughout Leviticus 27. Once again it is presupposed that the priest is to receive payments for vows from individuals. The legislation also makes use of the phrase אִישׁ כִּי (vv. 2, 14), as well as third-person singular forms. Nowhere in this chapter is there to be found any regulation that instructs the priests as to the proper procedure for the administration of goods vowed by more than one supplicant.

The vow-text of Lev. 7.16 speaks of an individual's right to consume the votive offering until the third day after it is offered as a sacrifice. Deut. 23.19 and 23.23 are again unambiguously (and tacitly) directed at individual votaries. It can be inferred from the previously-cited texts that the payment of a vow (and therefore the making of a vow) is performed by a single supplicant. In these there is no law that reads 'when some persons make (or fulfill) one vow'.

Not all the vow-texts, however, demonstrate individual initiation with such clarity. Some chapters in the Old Testament contain laws which utilize both singular and plural forms when discussing the would-be votary.[16] Such ambiguity may be detected in Lev. 22.23, though this law is clearly directed to an individual. This can be surmised from the use of the verb תַּעֲשֶׂה, conjugated in the second-person singular. In v. 21 it is also the case that an individual is addressed with the characteristic formula אִישׁ כִּי.

Earlier in the same chapter, however, v. 18b makes curious use of a plural form, לְכָל נִדְרֵיהֶם.[17] The use of the third-person plural pronominal suffix on the substantive (that is, 'their vows') cannot be taken as evidence of a regulation concerning a group vow, since this verse commences with the phrase אִישׁ אִישׁ 'when any man' and makes use of singular verb forms.[18] The employment of the third-person plural pronominal suffix can be explained by the fact that this instruction is not directly intended for the ears of the Israelites. Rather, it is meant for the sons of Aaron (v. 18) who are to administer 'their (namely, the Israelites') vows'.

---

16. Milgrom notes, 'The frequent change of person in the direct address to Israel is characteristic of the priestly style' (1990: 119).

17. The inconsistent usage of singular and plural forms, as well as the general lack of thematic unity in this chapter has been noted elsewhere (Noth 1965: 163; G.B. Gray 1906: 168).

18. For a discussion of this term see Chapter 5.

In Numbers 15 votive regulations are again phrased in singular as well as plural forms. Verses 2-3 read:

> Speak to the Israelites and say to them: 'when you [pl.] enter the land which I am giving you [pl.] and will present [pl.] an offering by fire to Yahweh from the herd or flock, be it a burnt offering or sacrifice in fulfillment of a *special vow*[19] or freewill offering, or at your [pl.] fixed occasions producing an odor pleasing to Yahweh...

I find it highly unlikely that this passage constitutes evidence for a non-individual vow. The verse that immediately follows (v. 4) qualifies this law by speaking solely in the first person. In v. 8, a clause that fully develops the contents of v. 3, singular forms are once again used. Accordingly, the rather vague legislation of v. 3 would again seem to be addressing all the Israelites. In so doing, stylistic conventions demand that plural forms be used. When v. 3 is fully explained in vv. 4-10, however, it is clear that the lawmakers know only of vows made by individuals.

At this point I should like to make an observation which is of great significance to this discussion. The frequently encountered statement that 'they fulfilled their vows' or 'fulfill [pl.] your vows' or 'bring your [pl.] vows', can be interpreted in many ways. Most plausibly, it can be speculated that the lawmaker is instructing all the individual members of the community to fulfill all their individual commitments, even though these have been made apart from one another and at different times throughout the year.

What cannot be assumed, however, is that a number of people made one unified group vow to Yahweh. For in order to advance such a hypothesis there would have to be a formulation such as 'they paid (or made) their *vow* [singular]', or 'fulfill [pl.] your vow [singular]'. Only if such a statement were to surface could it feasibly validate the existence of non-individual votive initiation.[20]

Deuteronomy 12 is yet another text in which a fluctuation in the style of address can be perceived. While vv. 17 and 26 tacitly assume that an individual will make a votive payment at a site sanctioned by Yahweh, vv. 6 and 11 do not. Here, the Israelites are urged to bring 'your [pl.] vows' to a centralized location. Once again, the use of such a form is

---

19. See Excursus 2 for a discussion of the troublesome phrase פלא נדר.

20. As noted above, in Num. 15.3 such an instance actually does occur. However, it is most improbable that this cryptic text is referring to group vows.

undoubtedly due to the fact that the author is addressing the entire community. The same logic applies to Num. 29.39 and Lev. 23.38, where even though a plural form is encountered, it seems certain that the individual vows of all the community members are being discussed.

It has been shown that legislation regarding the vow is mostly phrased in language that addresses an individual supplicant. In texts that address the votary in plural terms, it seems most probable that a group vow is not being discussed. Instead, the author is referring to *all* the vows that *all* of the members of the community have made—individually and apart from one another. While evidence of this nature is certainly not as convincing as that gleaned from the epic vows, it is significant that not one explicit instance of a vow made or fulfilled by more than one person can be identified.

Individual Initiation in the Prophets

In the prophetic sections of the Old Testament there are five references to votive activity. In Mal. 1.14 the prophet curses the 'cheater' who is unscrupulous in his or her votive behavior. In Isa. 19.21 it is mentioned that Yahweh will make himself known to the Egyptians and that they too will serve him with vows. Yet this does not stand as an example of a group vow made to Yahweh. As Cartledge notes: 'when the Egyptians come to know Yahweh, they will demonstrate their allegiance by worshipping Him with sacrifice and burnt offerings (cultic responsibilities as a part of the community) and by making and performing vows (individual piety)' (1988: 999).

In Jer. 44.25 the prophet mockingly exhorts a clan of expatriate Judaeans living in Egypt to 'fulfill your [pl.] vows'.[21] It should be stressed once again that Jeremiah did not say 'fulfill your [pl.] vow'.

The literati's unfamiliarity with group vows is again witnessed in Nah. 1.14 (MT 2.1). In the aftermath of the passing of the Assyrian menace the prophet exclaims: 'Celebrate your feasts[22] oh Judah, fulfill[23] your vows' [imperative]. חגי יהודה חגיך שלמי נדריך. As Smith, Ward and Bewer note: 'The many vows that have been made in the effort to win the favour of God for the afflicted people are now due' (1974: 304). Had the writer of this story known of a system whereby the nation

---

21. See Chapters 3 and 7 for a discussion of this vow.

22. On חג meaning 'to celebrate a feast', see Ward 1962: 405.

23. Here and throughout this study שלם will be translated as 'to fulfill' and not 'to pay'. See Excursus 3.

corporately made one desperate, group vow to Yahweh, it stands to reason that we would have encountered something like: 'Oh Judah, fulfill your *vow*'.

Finally, this brings us to the highly unusual vow-text of Jon. 1.16. A detailed analysis of this passage will be offered in chapter two. The text reads ויזבחו־זבח ליהוה וידרו נדרים, which I translate as 'they offered a slain offering to Yahweh and paid their vows'. What is most interesting about this passage is that while all the men make *one sacrifice* (slain offering) to Yahweh, they nevertheless pay their *vows* (pl.). In other words, the sacrifice is communal, all the sailors participate in this act together. The making of vows, on the other hand, is not a corporate venture; each sailor pays an *individual* vow to Yahweh (contra Cartledge 1992: 27).

The Wisdom Literature and the Psalms
In the wisdom literature and the Psalms there is also ample evidence of individual initiation. In Prov. 7.14, an (individual) adulteress (?) is portrayed as having just made a vow.[24] Prov. 31.2 reveals that the mother of King Lemuel had made a vow prior to his birth. In Prov. 20.25 a warning is issued to the man (אדם) who pledges a sacred gift rashly. In Eccl. 5.3-6 the potentially unscrupulous votary is again addressed in the singular. And in Job 22.27 Eliphaz points out to Job that Yahweh will indeed listen to his vows.

In the Psalms there again seems to be little doubt that the supplicant is an individual. The fact that the votary is a solitary agent is tacitly assumed in Pss. 22.26; 50.14; 56.13; 61.6,9; 66.13 and 116.14.[25]

In sum: in the Old Testament the overwhelming majority of evidence points towards vows being made by people as individuals. While some of the data does not directly attest to the practise of individual initiation, it must be remembered that neither does it lend any solid evidence for group vows. While I do not wish to exclude categorically the possibility that a group of prisoners could jointly initiate a vow, I would note that evidence for this practice is currently lacking in the Old Testament.

---

24. See Chapters 6 and 7 for a full discussion of this passage.

25. Ps. 76.12 speaks in the plural and exhorts its listeners to 'make [pl.] vows and fulfill them'. Insofar as the verse does not read 'make [pl.] a vow and fulfill it', it cannot be used to prove that the literati knew about group vows. It can, however, be read as a call for many separate individuals to make many vows.

The Extra-Biblical Data

In the cognate northwest Semitic literature the situation is similar. In both of the Ugaritic epic vows individual protagonists (namely Keret and Danel) make vows to various deities.[26] Thus, in the entire northwest Semitic register there are seven reports of vows that permit access to the literati's perception of what a petition sounds like when it is made (that is, epic vows).[27] In each case, an individual approaches the deity with some sort of tangible request.

Recently, Patrick Miller, Jr. has forwarded a translation of a Ugaritic ritual text (*KTU* 1.119) which seems to feature something quite different— a group vow. Miller remarks:

> The king and people are instructed in appropriate petition to Baal of Ugarit when an enemy has come up against the city. The petition is essentially a vow to sacrifice and visit the temple if the deity delivers (1988: 148).

In another contribution Miller calls attention to structural similarities between this alleged vow and those found in the Old Testament:

> The prayer is formally a vow, not unlike what one finds in Num. 21.1-4 and Judg. 11.30-32, where vows are uttered in situations of military conflict seeking divine help against the enemy. The deity is promised sacrifices if the enemy is repulsed (1987: 62).

Miller's assessment has been endorsed by Simon Parker (1989: 71). Other scholars, writing before Miller published his findings, have almost unanimously agreed that a vow of sorts is being depicted in this text (see de Moor 1976a: 930; de Moor 1987: 173; Herdner 1973: 694; Xella 1978: 133).

I should like to re-evaluate Miller's translation and analysis of this passage. I shall argue that there is good reason to doubt that not only a group vow, but any vow, is being referred to in these verses. I shall begin my critique with a translation of the relevant section of the text.[28]

---

26. Keret's vow = *KTU* 1.14 IV 36-44. Danel's vow = *KTU* 1.22 II 16-21 (see Chapter 3).

27. These include the five epic vows from the Old Testament (discussed above) as well as the two vows from the Ugaritic literature just mentioned.

28. Here following Miller's reading except where indicated.

26 *kgr ʿz.t̠g̱rkm.qrd*	When a fierce (foe) attacks your gates, a warrior[29]
27 *ḥmytkm. ʿnkm.lbʿl tšun*	your walls, raise your eyes to Baal[30]
28 *ybʿlm. [a]l.*[31]*tdy ʿz lt̠g̱rn*[32]	'Oh Baal, please drive out the fierce (foe) from our gate[33]
29 *y.qrd [l]ḥmytny.ibry*	Indeed, the warrior from our walls[34] A bull
30 *bʿl.nšqdš.md̠r bʿl*	(to) Baal we shall consecrate a gift (?)[35] (for) Baal
31 *nmlu*	we will remit...'

29. On *gr* see *BDB*, גור; see also Xella (1978: 132 n. 22) where the translation 'attaccare' is suggested. De Moor translates ʿz as 'a strong one' (1976a: 930; 1987: 173). Baruch Levine, in an unpublished paper given at the November 1989 SBL meeting in Anaheim, translates *gr* as 'a fierce foe'; For *qarradu* see *CAD* XIII 'Q'. See also Miller (1988: 146) for biblical parallels.

30. See de Moor (1987: 173) for relevant biblical passages. See also Jer. 13.20; Ezek. 33.25 and Isa. 51.6.

31. Based on a private communication with Dennis Pardee, Miller (1988: 139-40) reads an *m* instead of the *l* read by Herdner (1973: 694) and *KTU*. De Moor (1987: 173) translates the word ʾl, as a vocative particle, as I do. My reasons for rejecting Miller's reading are made clear above.

32. Miller (1988: 146) reads *lt̠g̱rny* here. With Levine, I prefer to read *lt̠g̱rn* followed by the vocative particle *y*.

33. De Moor (1987: 173 n. 18) has pointed out that the use of the *Pluralis Majestias*, *tdy* is probably cognate with Akkadian *nadu* 'to knock down'. See *BDB* נדה for potential cognates and examples from Hebrew.

34. The *ny* ending of *ḥmytny* can possibly be explained as a first-person dual pronoun (see Segert 1984: 48; also Ginsberg 1946: 43). Jean Michel de Tarragon has noted the rarity of the term *ibr* in Ugaritic ritual texts (1980: 37).

35. While I would not categorically rule out the possibility that *md̠r* is a variant of the Semitic root *ndr*, for the reasons mentioned I am not as confident as other scholars have been in positing this relationship. For example, Herdner writes:

> The word *md̠r*, 1.13—where the ringing ancient Semitic interdental is, quite oddly, maintained—is most likely related to a root *nd̠r* 'to vow' which might exist alongside the form *ndr*, more widely attested and of the same meaning. Thus, we have in Ugaritic, in all probability, the same doublet as in Hebrew where *nzr* (with a *z* representing the ancient interdental *d̠*) exists alongside *ndr* 'to vow' (1973: 695).

For a similar opinion see Miller (1988: 147). Boyd (1986: 64-65) also believes *md̠r* to be a dialectical variant of *ndr* (see also de Tarragon 1980: 66; Xella 1978: 133). However, with Levine I prefer to translate this word as 'gift' as opposed to 'vow'. As I shall demonstrate, if this word did signify a vow it would testify to a type of votive initiation that has never before been encountered. This should not rule out the possibility of an etymological relationship between *md̠r* and *ndr*, but it should be noted

Miller's translation reads as follows:

26   When a strong one has attacked your gates, a warrior
27   your walls, your eyes to Baal you shall lift up:
28   O Baal, *if* you will drive the strong one from our gates, the
          warrior from our walls, a bull, O
30   Baal, we shall consecrate, a vow, O Baal,
31   we shall fulfill… (1988: 142; emphasis mine)

Miller has argued that this text stands as a 'prescriptive ritual'[36] that instructs the entire population to make a vow when threatened by an enemy.

This analysis hinges on the reading of the word *hm* in v. 28. (*hm* is the conditional conjunction found at the opening of all seven Ugaritic and Old Testament epic vows).[37] Following Dennis Pardee's private communication, Miller accepts this reading whereas most earlier commentators have inclined to read *[a]l*.

After assuming that the form *hm* testifies to the initiation of a vow, Miller then translates vv. 30 and 31, as 'a vow (*mdr*), O Baal, we shall fulfill' (1988: 142). Opinions differ, however, as to the correct translation of the *hapax legomenon*, *mdr*. While many have maintained that it is but a variant of the root נדר, the paucity of etymological data makes the classification of 'dialectical variation' at best a conjecture (Boyd 1986: 65: also see Cartledge 1992: 118 n. 3). It should be recalled that forms of the root *ndr* appear at least nine times in the Ugaritic lexicon, while this is the only example of *mdr* at our disposal. Neither does the appearance of the verb *ml'* strengthen Miller's argument. Nowhere in the northwest Semitic record is this term used as the verbal form governing the noun נדר.

Philological difficulties aside, the most pertinent criticisms of Miller's theory arise when the 'vow' of this text is compared with those found in the Hebrew Bible. There are considerable structural incongruities between

that the latter form is attested at least nine times in the Ugaritic lexicon while the former only appears here. It is clear from the discussion above that the mechanics of vow-making as we know them do not apply to the still misunderstood mechanics connected with *mdr*. Thus, I prefer to take *mdr* as a possible cognate, albeit one that describes the giving of some type of ritualistic gift.

36. Levine defines a 'prescriptive ritual' as one where a text 'set[s] down the manner in which rites were to be performed' (1963: 105-11).

37. The first of these letters is essentially unreadable, while the second can be identified as either *m* or *l* (see *KTU* 1.119).

the former and the latter. Leaving aside the fact that no group vow is to be found anywhere in the Old Testament, it also seems curious that no other *prescriptive* ritual regarding vows is known. Vows, as Cartledge notes, 'grow out of specific needs and thus are tailored to fit particular circumstances, making them intensely personal' (1992: 26). A pre-scripted ritual, that dictates when and how a vow will be made, departs radically from this pattern.

Another difficulty in Miller's translation arises from his taking the conditional conjunction *hm* in v. 28 as evidence that a vow is being initiated. Even if this highly contested reading were accepted, there are problems in drawing parallels between this vow and those biblical vows cited by Miller (1988: 150-52). This is because the protagonists in the epic vows never refer to the fact that they are making a vow once they begin their petition. According to Miller, in v. 30 the supplicants tell the deity they are going to consecrate a vow to him. Yet in the other vow-texts, the participant never relays such information to the deity—there is no self-conscious acknowledgment that a vow is being made. Typically, the votary—in a business-like manner—simply lists the amenities which he or she will offer the deity should the request be granted.

With all these considerations in mind, it is extremely difficult to utilize *KTU* 1.119 as evidence of a group vow or for that matter as evidence for any type of vow. While it should not be ruled out that some type of etymological connection exists between *mdr* and *ndr*, this hypothesis has yet to be firmly established. The 'vow' in this passage is made commu-nally and the element of spontaneity so frequently found in other vows is contradicted by the prescriptive nature of this ritualistic text. Finally, the supplicants take the unprecedented step of referring to their vow-making activity. These various anomalies make it very difficult to accept that this text portrays the initiation of a vow, group or otherwise.

The only early Aramaic vow-text is a good deal more forthright in illus-trating the mechanism of individual initiation. The Bar-Hadad inscription, which, on the basis of tenuous paleographic and historical evidence is dated to the middle of the ninth century BCE,[38] serves as written

---

38. There is basic accord among exegetes as to the correct dating of this inscription. Albright suggests the year 850 BCE or thereabouts (1942: 27), as do Levi Della Vida 1943: 30, Cross 1972: 42 and Shea 1979:173. A few scholars have slightly digressed by placing the date at 860 (see Gibson 1975: 1; Jespen 1952–1953: 317), although some earlier commentators have argued for a later date (Dunand 1939: 76; Herdner 1946–1948: 329).

testimony to the monarch's (the biblical Ben-Hadad) payment of his
otherworldly debts.

1	נצבא זי שם ברה
2	דד בר טברן[מ]ן בר [חז]ין
3	מלך ארם למראה למלקר
4	ת זי נזר לה ושמע לקל
5	ה

1   The stele[39] which Bar-Hadad
2   son of Tobrimmon son of Hezion[40]
3   king of Aram, set up to his Lord, Melcarth[41]
4   to whom he made a vow;[42] and Melcarth heard his voice

Scholarly attention to this inscription has preponderated toward the
proper reading and translation of line 2. Following Albright's association
of the name found here with that of biblical Ben-Hadad, researchers
have aimed either to verify or reject his reading.[43] For our purposes,
however, what is immediately relevant is the fact that this ancient
Aramaic example clearly depicts an individual whose particular circumstances impelled him to make a request to the deity.

Unfortunately, the evidence from neighboring countries during the
pre-exilic period is so scarce as to be almost non-existent. With the
exception of a very interesting Ammonite inscription, made by a certain

39. Here we encounter the word נצבא, which is cognate with מצבה, encountered
above in Jacob's vow. Most commentators translate 'stele', though see Gibson's
translation 'statue' (1975: 3). As pointed out in *KAI* 201, שם is related to the root
שום/שים.

40. The proper reconstruction of this phrase has provided the basis for most
scholarly work on this text. See Gibson's alternative reading (1975: 3) as well as the
review by Shea (1979).

41. See G. Levi Della Vida for some astute observations on the god Melcarth
(1943; see also Albright 1942: 29).

42. As *KAI* 201 notes in relation to זי, 'wohl nicht auf Barhadad, sondern auf
Melqart zu beziehen' (204; however see Sukenik's remark reported in Dunand
1942–1943: 44 n. 5). In a now famous article, philologian H.L. Ginsberg theorized
that the word נזר in l. 4 was not to be translated 'he vowed' but 'he prayed'.
Ginsberg's conclusion was based on his belief that the roots נזר and נדר are both
derived from proto-Semitic *ndr* (1945: 160). Insofar as his analysis was based on a
proposition which is most likely erroneous (see Appendix 4) this complicated
argument need not be detailed here.

43. See Albright 1942, Cross 1972 and Shea 1979, for the history of this
controversy.

individual named Abinadab, there is no other textual documentation regarding vows made in this period.[44]

There remains the abundant, albeit somewhat redundant, core of vow-texts from the Punic and Phoenician sources. If ever any doubt were to exist as to the prevalence of individual initiation as against group initiation it would be immediately dispelled after an examination of this evidence. There are literally thousands of stelae that do not stray too far from the type of formula witnessed in the following text.[45]

1	לאדן בעל חמן
2	נדר אש נדר עזמלך הקרת
3	כשמע קלא ברכא[46]

1	To the lord Baal Hammon
2	a vow that AZMLK the QRT[47] made
3	For he heard his voice, he blessed him

Occasionally, however, there are instances of group vows in the Punic and Phoenician sources. An extremely rough estimate leads me to suggest that group vows appear one time for every one hundred votive stelae which are encountered. Such a state of affairs may suggest that individual initiation was the rule; group vowing, while not unheard of, was the exception. An interesting example of the latter is encountered in *KAI* 47 which reads:

1	לאדן למלקרת בעל צר אש נדר
2	עבדך עבדאסר ואחי אסרשמר
3	שן בן אסרשמר בן עבדאסר כ שמע
4	קלם יברכם

1	To our Lord, to Melcart, Lord of Tyre
2	this is what your servant ABDASR and his brother ASRSMR
3	the two sons of ASRSMR son of ABDASR vowed. For he heard
4	their voice, may he bless them.

---

44. *AS* 49; for textual analysis see Berlinerblau 1991.

45. Beyerlin notes, 'we have knowledge of several thousand votive inscriptions on stelae from the Punic empire of Carthage' (1978: 234).

46. *EH* 94.

47. For the personal name AZMLK see Benz 1972: 165-67. On the term QRT see *EH* 80.

Conclusion

In this chapter I have demonstrated that the literati of various northwest Semitic cultures tacitly assume that the vow was initiated by an individual. Conversely, it was concluded that the group vow, (that is, a vow initiated at one point in time and space by more than one person) was quite rare.

I do not wish to dismiss completely the possibility of the latter phenomenon. Innumerable details regarding the religious life of ancient Israel are missing from the pages of the Old Testament. Every possibility exists that clues regarding group vows have simply not been saved for posterity. For the time being, however, there is little evidence which suggests that individual initiation was not the norm in ancient Israel or the northwest Semitic world; everywhere we look, this type of initiation is tacitly assumed by the literati.

Vows are initiated by one person even when the entreaty is of interest to a group. As has been seen, the Israelites in the Negev faced a situation of communal crisis, as did the elders of Gilead (Judg. 11.4-11) who were at war with the Ammonites. Nevertheless, in both cases, the literati depict an individual making a vow on behalf of others in order to secure an end favorable to that group (Judg. 11.30-31; Num. 21.1-3). Why is this so?

I would argue that this portrait of individual initiation is given because it reflects a rule of votive praxis well known to the authors of the Old Testament. I cannot identify any particular political or theological motivation that may have prompted the literati to downplay the importance of group vows in favor of solitary petitions. Rather, I believe that the literati knew, as did everyone in their society, that a vow was usually made by a person acting alone. Accordingly, in their sporadic writings on this subject, they unknowingly reveal to us the widespread norm (mechanism) of 'individual initiation'.

With this said, I should like to qualify my previously cited definition of 'individual initiation'. It would be indicative of a profound sociological naivete to conclude that the vow is an 'individual' affair, or something which an 'individualist' does. For religion, as Durkheim argued, 'is something eminently social' (1965: 22). A *homo religiosus* is not some sort of psychological monad, but an individual member of a human society. It is from this society that the individual receives the necessary cultural knowledge by which to hunt, speak, make vows, bury family members, and so on. In one of his brilliant digressions on the concept of culture, the great German sociologist Georg Simmel observes:

> The labour of countless generations is embedded in language and custom, political constitutions and religious doctrines, literature and technology as objectified spirit from which everyone can take as much of it as they wish to or are able to, but no single individual is able to exhaust it all (1990: 449).

The Israelite vow is 'individual' insofar as it is uttered by *one person*. This does not mean that the votary in question is some sort of non-conformist, participating in a 'distinct and autonomous religious system(s)' (Durkheim 1965: 61). Rather, this particular technique was borrowed from a vast storehouse of cultural knowledge whose origins in time extend much further back than the life of the individual supplicant.

It is not surprising then, that those 'canonical rules' mentioned by Durkheim are found in the votive process. While the content of the individual's vow varies from case to case, in the epic vows at least, the elementary structure of these petitions does not. Our supplicants seem to be following unwritten rules of votive behavior. So, while Hannah, Jephthah and Jacob all ask for and promise Yahweh different items, they all make their vows alone, they all employ structurally similar petitionary forms (see Richter 1967; Cartledge 1992: 137-61), they all promise to give the deity something in return, and so on. Thus, while the practice is individually initiated, there exist distinct cultural patterns of votive behavior that have been absorbed by every member of the community.[48]

With this said, our first mechanism of the votive procedure has been extracted. In the next chapter I shall point to another related mechanism, that of 'privacy'.

---

48. A skeptic might argue that a redactor decided to homogenize votive accounts so that nothing is portrayed but portraits of individual votaries making their vows in nearly identical (that is, Yahwistically-approved) ways.

Chapter 2

PRIVACY

The Vow and the Temple: Privacy

Many scholars have suggested that in ancient Israel all vows had to be
initiated within the confines of a sanctuary. Simon Parker has observed:

> Keret comes to a sanctuary of the goddess, and 'there' makes his vow.
> ...Hannah had gone up to 'the house of Yahweh' in Shiloh with her
> family—her prayer is uttered 'in the presence of Yahweh'. *Both contexts
> are surely reliable reflections of actual practice*. The vow was made in the
> sanctuary, and was addressed to the deity of the sanctuary. The deity's
> response was gratefully acknowledged by the fulfillment of the vow also in
> the sanctuary (1979: 694-95; see also Parker 1989: 77; emphasis mine).

Following Parker's lead, J. O'Brien writes:

> As also seen in the biblical accounts, the vow is a matter of public concern.
> Deut. 12.5-6, 17-18 and 26 indicate that the vow is made in the sanctuary,
> is addressed to the deity in the sanctuary and is completed in the
> sanctuary... The fulfillment of the vow, while an individual obligation,
> nonetheless involves public display and perhaps also public participation
> (1987: 281).

Albert de Pury opines: 'the vow is a religious act which, just as with the
wave offering, has its "Sitz im Leben" in the sanctuary' (1975: II, 437-
38). And Claus Westermann remarks: 'It is common to *all vows* that
they are pronounced at a sanctuary (temple)' (1981: 459; emphasis
mine).[1] To use the terminology employed in this research it could be
said that for these scholars there existed a mechanism of 'temple-
centered initiation' in ancient Israel.

As will be seen below, Parker has also suggested that the making of a
vow required the presence of a member of the cultic apparatus. Parker

---

1. Also see Haran where a similar assumption, though never directly stated, can
easily be detected (1978: 33, 306).

seems to argue that the latter was responsible for observing or blessing or validating the vow as it was being made. If this were indeed the case an essential component of votive initiation would consist of interaction in the form of a mandatory encounter between the votary and a representative of the cultic apparatus. The activities of the latter would, in some way, serve to authorize the supplicant's petition. I shall refer to this as 'supervised/interactive initiation'.

In this chapter, I shall argue that there is little evidence to support the existence of the mechanisms of 'temple-centered initiation' and 'supervised/interactive initiation'. As regards the former, the aforementioned scholars are not entirely incorrect. The explicit evidence clearly shows that vows were made in such places as sanctuaries and temples. I believe, however, that they have overstated their case. While the vow-texts seem to indicate that most vows are to be *paid* in a sanctuary, they certainly do not maintain that 'all vows', or even most vows, are *made* in sanctuaries, temples, in front of altars or in the presence of Yahwistic personnel. Nor, it should be added, does the implicit evidence support such a view.

Further, the explicit evidence does not substantiate the claim that the assistance, regulation or scrutiny of a priest was necessary upon the making of a vow (that is, supervised initiation). On the contrary, a close reading of the sole vow-text that offers a glimpse of this situation (1 Sam. 1) suggests that cultic personnel played a completely inconsequential role in votive initiation.

In this chapter a re-examination of the biblical evidence will permit me to challenge those claims that argue in favor of 'temple-centered initiation' and 'supervised/interactive initiation'. In so doing, I shall attempt to build a case for the mechanism of 'privacy'. A definition of this term will be provided following the forthcoming discussion.

'Temple-Centered Initiation?': The Vow of the Seaborne Sailors
In the entire Old Testament there is only one instance where a vow is specifically made within a sanctuary (1 Sam. 1.11).[2] The argument that this solitary example illustrates 'actual practice' becomes even more unlikely when it is taken into consideration that there is one unequivocal case of a vow that was not made in a temple (Jon. 1.16; see below). Vows made on the battlefield are also attested. To this end, four more

2.   Jacob's vow in Gen. 28.20 is not made in a sanctuary or temple *per se*, rather it is made in a place where the patriarch feels Yahweh's presence (Gen. 28.16-19).

petitions that were not pronounced in a sanctuary can be identified (namely, Judg. 11.30-31; Num. 21.2; Pss. 56; 61; see Gottwald 1964: 300; Gottwald 1985: 544; Wendel 1931a: 121). Perhaps most important is that nothing is known about the spatial setting of any other Old Testament vow.[3]

These considerations make it difficult to accept the proposition that all vows were made in temples or at 'official' cultic sites. In looking purely at textual examples it can easily be recognized that the Old Testament furnishes many more instances of vows made outside the sanctuary or in unidentified places than within the confines of a cultically-sanctioned holy site. Of much greater importance is the fact that the literati's *perception* of the votive procedure is not consonant with the belief that temple-centered initiation is compulsory; they never emphasize that this constitutes proper Yahwistic behavior.

A vow that was certainly not initiated in a temple will illustrate these points. Jonah 1.16 reads:

וייראו האנשים יראה גדולה את־יהוה
ויזבחו־זבח ליהוה וידרו נדרים

The men greatly feared[4] Yahweh, they offered a slain offering[5]
to Yahweh and *paid* their vows.

Most commentators have opined that the sailors are now making, that is, initiating vows.[6] Others have gone so far as to suggest that the sailors have made their vows on shore. Stuart, in commenting on the זבח and thus the נדר which occurred simultaneously, notes:

> This could hardly have occurred on board the ship, denuded of its cargo. The transportation of edible animals on ocean-going ships was as infrequent in ancient times as in modern. The sacrifice would have taken place

---

3. While there are a few verses of legislation that specify where a vow should be *paid* (see below), not a word is heard about where vows should be initiated.

4. The translations 'feared greatly', 'a great fear', 'une grande crainte', 'große Furcht', seem to capture correctly the mood of the sailors after their ordeal (Deissler and Delcor 1961: 281; Weiser 1959: 216; Bruno 1957: 84; Riessler 1911: 156; Horton n.d.: 207). Snaith views את־יהוה as an addition (1945: 23), though see Almbladh 1986: 24.

5. For an invaluable study of the term זבח see B. Levine 1974: 115-17.

6. See Deissler and Delcor 1961: 281; Riessler 1911: 156; Bruno 1957: 84; Wolff 1977: 83; Horton n.d.: 207; Weiser 1959: 216 and Cartledge 1992: 64.

on shore, for another simple reason. In all the religions of the ancient Near East, as far as the evidence is known, sacrifices took place at shrines or temples. One could not simply sacrifice wherever one felt like it...At any rate, the sailors in all likelihood went to an already established Yahwistic shrine or temple to offer their sacrifices of gratitude... (1987: 464).

I disagree with Stuart's claim in two ways. I have great difficulty with accepting that in this verse: (1) a vow was *made*, and (2) that this vow was made in a sanctuary. Let me begin with an analysis of the former proposition.

A vow usually originates when a supplicant requires some specific thing from the deity (Cartledge 1992: 26). He or she initiates the petition in order to obtain this object or condition. Vows are often (though not always; see Berlinerblau 1991) invoked in times of distress (Wendel 1931a: 17; Cartledge 1992: 12). The supplicant petitions the god in order to alleviate some troubling situation. Now, if the sailors are indeed *making* vows in Jon. 1.16, what is the purpose of their vow ? The sea is calm, the immediate danger has passed—why are they petitioning Yahweh?

H. Wolff is one of the few scholars who has addressed this issue. He offers the following solution: 'The vow is probably indicative of a lasting bond of trust with Yahweh' (1977: 98). Wolff's suggestion, however, is susceptible to the criticism that we know of no precedent, be it in the Old Testament or the extra-Biblical world, for a vow made in order to insure a 'lasting bond of trust'.[7] Wolff's analysis is reminiscent of that of many theologians who claim that the heathen sailors had converted to

---

7. Wolff has offered Ps. 61 as a precedent for this type of vow. It seems quite clear, however, that the vows referred to in Ps. 61.9 correspond to the vows referred to in 61.6. These have to do with Yahweh's rescuing of the protagonist from danger. Verse 9 refers to paying the many vows that this supplicant made while in distress and not to the formation of a special union between humanity and Yahweh. Thus, in my opinion the votary is simply remitting a vow; A. Schenker has made the perceptive observation that the verb שלם is not used here, and hence 'fulfill the vow' is not a legitimate translation (1989: 87). In defense of Schenker, when the noun נדר is the object of the verb נדר it usually refers to making vows. Even with these considerations in mind, I still think that the evidence cited above favors the interpretation that the sailors in Jonah 1:16 remitted vows. As B. Levine has noted, נדר is 'a term which applies both to the original pronouncement of a "vow" as well as to its subsequent fulfillment or payment' (1974: 42 n. 108; see also Coppes 1980: 557). That is to say, the term can be used to refer either to the making of the vow or to the fulfillment of the vow. For example, payment is referred to in 1 Sam. 1.21, but the same word refers to the making of vows in Num. 21.2, Gen. 28.20 and Eccl. 5.3.

Yahwism (for example, Deissler and Delcor 1961: 281; Horton n.d.: 207; Weiser 1959: 219). Needless to say, such an outcome is not suggested by the biblical author, who would not have hesitated to draw attention to such a detail.

Another alternative would be to suggest that the men's 'great fear' of Yahweh motivated them to make vows. R.J. Thompson observes:

> Jon. 1.16…where the heathen sailors offer sacrifices and vow vows, after the pacifying of the storm, could be also understood as a thanksgiving, but the fact that the men 'feared Yahweh with a great fear' seems to favour a propitiatory sense (1963: 225).

It should be noted, however, that the invocation of a vow as a means of making a conciliatory gesture is also unprecedented. A vow is essentially a bargain with the god(s), initiated by a supplicant who has a concrete need and thus makes a request. Therefore, the making of a vow (that is, asking the deity for a favor) would not appear as a particularly efficacious means of appeasing an angry deity.

The notion of thanksgiving, of paying a vow, that Thompson suggested but eventually rejected, may provide the most logical solution to this problem. Clearly, the moment of distress in this chapter is marked by the raging sea storm, not by the reverential fear that the sailors feel once the storm has passed. It seems a good deal more logical, as well as consistent with the attested usage of this practice, to conclude that the vows were made during the storm by the sailors. It is possible, then, that verse 16 refers not to the making of vows but to a process of thanksgiving, of paying back Yahweh for saving their lives.

Following this line of reasoning, the original vows were made during the storm, then in v. 16 the sailors thank Yahweh for rescuing them by first offering a slain offering (ויזבחו זבח) and then by paying back their vows. It would certainly be curious and perhaps even a bit impolite if after offering the זבח in order to thank Yahweh, the rescued sailors were to impose more demands on him by making new vows.

Nor can we assume, as Stuart does, that the vows were made in a temple. There is no mention of a visit to any port of call, much less a Yahwistic shrine. The action in the preceding verses (1.3-15) takes place at sea, as does the narrative in the verse that immediately follows (2.1). The text simply does not permit the conclusion that there has been a change of locale such as that suggested by Stuart and others.

While the reader may want to accept or reject my theory that v. 16 refers to the payment of a vow, according to either scenario it is certain

that the sailors have made vows. That is, whether they made or paid
their vows in verse 1.16 is irrelevant insofar as *they must have initiated
their vows at sea*. For as just noted, all the narrative action takes place
on the deck of the ship and therefore the vow was initiated there. Thus,
in a text that most commentators date as post-exilic, there is a clear
instance of a vow made, and perhaps even paid, away from the temple.[8]

Implicit Assumptions
I now turn to the implicit evidence. Psalms 56 and 61 provide us with
more reasons to doubt the likelihood of the mechanism of 'temple-
centered initiation'. In these texts an individual appears, who reports
being in a situation of great distress. In both instances the protagonist
notes that thanks to Yahweh's intervention the danger has passed; it is
now time to pay back the deity. Psalm 56.13-14 reads:

13	עלי אלהים נדריך
	אשלם תודת לך
14	כי הצלת נפשי ממות

13   Your vows are upon me[9] Oh God, I will fulfill thank offerings to
       you[10]

14   For you saved me from death

It is interesting to note that both here and in Psalm 61 the votaries find
themselves in situations that would not seem conducive to a visit to the
temple. In the latter, the supplicant calls to Yahweh 'from the ends of
the earth' (61.3: מקצה הארץ אליך אקרא). The supplicant in Psalm 56 is,
if this chapter's introduction is to be believed, a captive of the Philistines.

The accuracy of these accounts is perhaps not as important as the
writer's failure to pinpoint a temple or approved holy site as the sole
legitimate locus of votive initiation. Surely, if a visit to such a place were
known or assumed by the author to be a prerequisite for the initiation of
vows, or if temple initiation were of great concern to the literati, such a

---

8.   On the late dating of this passage see Deissler and Delcor (1961: 266);
E. Levine (1984: 238); Payne (1979: 3); contra Landes (1982) who argues persuasively
for a pre-exilic setting.

9.   Anderson has offered a similar translation and noted the sense of 'moral
obligation' connoted by the term עלי (1972: 423; also see Briggs and Briggs 1907:
33; Oesterley 1953: 288; Schmidt 1934: 168; Kraus 1961: 407).

10.   Though noteDahood's translation which reads these verses as the pronouncement of a vow in itself (1968: 41).

portrayal of Israelites petitioning Yahweh from battlefields, raging seas and 'from the ends of the earth' would be unlikely. It is quite surprising that the literati do not model initiation of a vow to be—as with compensation of a vow—a practice reserved exclusively for the temple.[11]

It has been shown that the explicit and implicit evidence indicate that vows were not exclusively made in shrines, temples, cult installations, and similar places.[12] I shall close this section by noting that Adolf Wendel, a distinguished student of the Israelite vow, presaged this conclusion more than sixty years ago:

> By the Israelite period the shrine or temple might have been the right place for the making of pious vows. Hannah makes hers at the temple 'in front of Yahweh'. As with prayer in ancient Israel, however, it was, generally speaking, not made in a fixed place; the vow can be made in other places as well. Thus, one vows on a ship during a storm, Jephthah makes his on the battlefield.

'Supervised/Interactive Initiation'

Jephthah in the Field

In the previous section, I attempted to refute the claim that the literati believed that *all* vows must be made in a sanctuary. I shall now turn to another assumption regarding the vow which needs to be re-evaluated.

It was noted earlier that the Old Testament offers examples of vows made on the battlefield. In such instances it would be hard to argue that initiation took place in a temple. One immediately thinks of the vow Jephthah made prior to his defeat of the Ammonites (Judg. 11.30-31). If Jephthah did come to the temple to make this vow then it is certainly not indicated anywhere in the text (contra Haran 1978: 33). Simon Parker has suggested that the exigencies of this particular situation required that the temple come to Jephthah:

---

11. On this issue see Chapter 8.

12. It should not be forgotten that vows *can* be made in temples, shrines, sanctuaries, and cult sites. The point to be noted is that while the supplicant is not legally bound to initiate vows in any of these places, should he or she decide to do so this alternative always remains open. B. Levine has suggested that those who did utilize this option may have done so out of the conviction that the temple is a place where their prayers will be most clearly heard (private communication with Dr Baruch Levine; see also Levine 1974: 45 n. 117; Bird 1991: 101).

It is unnecessary to propose, as have some commentators, that Jephthah's vow was in fact made at a sanctuary, or even that the text of the vow should be moved elsewhere to make that explicit. The presence of cultic functionaries (priests, prophets) on military campaigns, well attested in Israelite historiographic literature, provides for the proper observance of religious acts and utterance of religious pronouncements during military expeditions without benefit of a sanctuary (1989: 80).

Parker maintains that even though this vow was not made in a temple, it is merely an exception to the rule. Further, he argues that 'proper observance' of a vow necessitates the services of cultic functionaries. According to this view a typical vow is made at a sanctuary and requires the assistance, or at least the presence, of members of the cultic apparatus. For Parker, Jephthah's vow is procedurally correct since he interacts with the proper cultic personnel upon the pronouncement of his petition.

In addition to the passage cited above, Parker has elsewhere assumed that cultic functionaries are present during votive initiation. In commenting on the use of third-person forms in the apodosis of the votive formula, Parker remarks:

The shift to the third person for the actual promise probably implies *a direct address to the personnel of the sanctuary, who serve not only as witnesses of the vow but also as its immediate beneficiaries on behalf of the deity.* To state the matter in the opposite way: the presence of the cultic personnel as witnesses and eventual beneficiaries of the promise prompts the individual to address them directly at this point, and therefore to refer to the deity in the third person (1989: 86; emphasis mine).

From these two citations it may be surmised that for Parker the initiation of a vow is an interactive and supervised process. The interaction occurs between the petitioner and members of the priesthood, who seem to serve in some regulatory capacity. It is, apparently, the function of the latter to bear witness to the vow and thereby validate the request.

However, there is no evidence anywhere in the northwest Semitic data for the type of worshiper–priest interaction envisioned by Parker.[13] Keret's vow (*KTU* 1.14 IV 36-43), for example, is almost certainly made

13. Parker notes that in the protasis of the vow, Yahweh is addressed in the second person and in the apodosis the supplicant (sometimes) shifts to the third person. Accordingly, he theorizes that in the apodosis the supplicant's terms of address have shifted on account of the fact that he or she is now addressing temple personnel. However, as acknowledged by Parker, this pattern does not hold in all of our epic vows. It should also be mentioned that this third-person address does not in any way prove that the supplicant is now speaking to a priest.

in the shrine of Asherah. Yet at no point does the text allow the inference that a member of the cultic apparatus was present during the King's petition. Jacob makes a vow in what is *soon to become* the Bethel sanctuary (Gen. 28.20-22). But here again, there is absolutely no basis for concluding that a religious functionary, or for that matter any human being, accompanied him.

In Num. 21.2, an epic battlefield vow, we have no reason to suspect that priests were in attendance. In the curious vow of Aqhat's father, Danel, the petition made in the 'holy palace' seems to be an individual affair; if anyone else was present we certainly do not hear about it in the text.[14] Nor does the Jephthah passage make mention of cultic functionaries.

It is difficult to identify any explicit textual support for the claim that a cultic functionary or priest is stationed with the votary. There exists, in fact, only one vow-text in which such a scenario may be plausibly identified. But as we are about to see, even when a priest is physically present at the making of a vow, he (according to the literati's portrayal) plays absolutely no role in its proper initiation.

Eli's Interference

In the entire northwest Semitic record there is only one instance in which a cultic functionary is present upon the initiation of the vow. This is Hannah's petition, made in front of Eli the priest at the Shiloh sanctuary. In 1 Sam. 1.11 we read:

11
$$\text{ותדר נדר ותאמר}$$
$$\text{יהוה צבאות אם־ראה תראה בעני אמתך}$$
$$\text{וזכרתני ולא תשכח את־אמתך}$$
$$\text{ונתתה לאמתך זרע אנשים}$$
$$\text{ונתתיו ליהוה כל־ימי חייו}$$
$$\text{ומורה לא־יעלה על־ראשו}$$

11   So she made a vow saying:[15] 'Yahweh *ṣb'wt*,[16] if you will take
       into consideration the affliction of your maidservant,[17] remember

---

14. See Chapter 3.

15. McCarter connects v. 11 with v. 10 and thus offers the translation: '[10] From the bitterness of her heart she invoked Yahweh and, weeping greatly, [11] made the following vow' (1980: 49). In light of Richter's demonstration that the epic vows have been artificially inserted into the narratives that surround them, I should prefer to separate the actual vow from the narrative based on the traditional verse division (Richter 1967: 21-52). For an examination of the overall structure of this vow see van Zyl 1984.

16. Commentators usually fall into three camps when translating the term יהוה צבאות. First, is the somewhat dated 'Lord/Yahweh of Hosts' translation (Klein 1983:

me and not forget your maidservant,[18] give to your maidservant the seed of men[19] then I will give him to Yahweh for his entire life and never shall a razor touch his head'[20]

My major interest here lies not in scrutinizing the contents of Hannah's vow, but in examining her 'interaction' with Eli the priest. A detailed analysis of her actions may serve to underscore a tacit assumption of the biblical literati: a vow—even if uttered in public—could be made privately, without the assistance or regulation of a member of the cultic apparatus.

In commenting on this passage H.W.F. Saggs observes:

> Though Hannah's prayer was at the cult place it was neither in nor through the cult. That no cult ceremony was in progress is clear from the fact that the priest Eli was merely watching the pilgrims (1978: 174).

Saggs is correct in noting that Hannah's behavior retains no interactive dimension; she is clearly not coordinating her actions with any other human being or set of social activities. Hannah's physical and psycholo-

---

1; Hertzberg 1964: 22; Ackroyd 1971: 22). Second, is the attempt to read a specifically militaristic tone into this term. Hence, 'Iahve des armées' (Pirot and Clamer 1955: 352; Dhorme 1910: 21; Bruno 1955: 12; Tsevat 1965: 55; see also Weber 1967: 111). The most compelling reading, however, takes the name 'Yahweh ṣb'wt' as the appellative of a deity which was specifically associated with and worshipped at Shiloh (Ross 1967: 79).

17. On the term עני, A. van Zyl comments:

> Whenever the exegete comes across the word עני (misery) in a psalm of lament, he should remember that it is the word in which all the emotions of the sufferer created by his or her unfavourable situation are concentrated: isolation, humiliation, indignity, impotence, worthlessness, depression, resignation, disappointment, grief, self-deprecia-tion, loss of self confidence, loss of motivation, and even a loss of any interest in life and living as such because his or her life is thrown into the primordial chaos (1984: 156).

18. Klein has noted the switch from second to third person and, following Stoebe, observed 'The sudden switch from 2nd (you) to 3rd person (to Yahweh, v. 11) in her prayer may connote a special kind of festival solemnity' (1983: 8; contrast Parker's view, above); See McCarter for the discrepancies between LXX and MT (1980: 53) and more generally Stanley Walters' article 'Hannah and Anna: The Greek and Hebrew Texts of 1 Samuel 1' (1988).

19. The literal translation 'seed of men' is more plausible than the more intuitive translation 'a male child'. The latter is advocated by scholars who have argued that Hannah has explicitly vowed for a son (H. Smith 1899: 9; Hertzberg 1964: 25; Pirot and Clamer 1955: 352; Klein 1983: 2).

20. Compare this with the LXX version which adds 'and he shall drink no wine nor strong drink'.

gical separation from her surroundings brings to mind an observation made by McCarter. He offers the following translation of v. 9: 'After she had eaten, Hannah arose *privately* and presented herself before Yahweh' (1980: 49; emphasis mine). In defence of this translation McCarter writes:

> MT has *bšlh*, 'at Shiloh', and the versions offer nothing substantially different. The mention of Shiloh seems oddly repetitious here...In the present passage the original reading was *bšly* 'privately, quietly', exactly as in 2 Sam. 3.27. This was misread as *bšlw*, 'at Shiloh', *w* and *y* being easily confused in the scripts of many periods (1980: 53).

McCarter's translation seems substantiated by the overall description of Hannah's vow. For she does in fact remain alone throughout the entire process. She sits (or possibly stands) by herself and 'pours out her heart' (v. 15) to Yahweh (Ap Thomas 1956: 227-28). Her vow is private and uninterrupted: Eli's interference and consequent rebuke, occur *after* the vow has been completed.[21] In order to prove these assertions I shall focus on Eli's activities.

Eli does not demonstrate any desire to regulate Hannah's vow. Presumably, he has watched her enter since he is described as sitting near the מזוזת (v. 9 reads: ועלי הכהן ישב על־הכסא על־מזוזת היכל יהוה, 'and Eli the priest was sitting on the seat near the doorpost of the temple of Yahweh').[22] There is no account of him rising, advising or 'registering' the incoming supplicant. Instead, he is passively perched at the doorpost, presumably at some distance from the worshipper.

Verse 12 states that Eli is watching the mouth of Hannah, ועלי שמר את־פיה. Some scholars have surmised that this particular act serves as a means of validating the vow of the supplicant. By watching her mouth Eli lends Hannah's request a sort of cultic approval. The very efficacy of the vow, then, hinges not on unmediated, vertical discourse between supplicant and deity, but requires the mediation of the priest. Weisman has written:

> Accordingly, in the story of Hannah's vow (1 Sam. 1.1) the validity of the vow is confirmed by the fact that 'Eli watches her mouth'; and indeed the story of her vow also ends with Eli's words 'Go in peace, and may the God of Israel grant what you have asked of him' (1967: 216).

---

21. In fact, as we shall see below, Eli's actions have little or nothing to do with Hannah's vow.

22. As Driver has noted 'The ptcp. [ישב] describes what Eli *was doing* at the time when Hannah appeared where he was' (1913: 12).

Against Weisman's interpretation, S. Zalevsky has suggested that Eli's observance of Hannah's mouth, as well as his eventual blessing, have nothing to do with the process of validating the vow:

> From the writing 'and Eli watched her mouth' one cannot conclude that this expression has any connection with the vow of Hannah. It is more logical to assume that this expression describes the duty of the priest in the temple. As part of his function as supervisor of the normal procedures of the temple... Eli was obliged to prevent the lingering of desecrators in the temple. Therefore it is not surprising that by moving her lips (but) with her voice (remaining) inaudible, Hannah evokes in Eli—who is 'watching her mouth'—the suspicion that she is drunk...If the intention was to confirm her vow, it would seem more likely that this expression would appear at the end of Hannah's vow. Meaning at the end of v. 11 or preceding it (1978: 309).

It seems to me that Zalevsky is quite correct in his assessment of Eli's reasons for watching Hannah's mouth. In v. 13 there is an account of Hannah's actions during her prayer. Although her petition was inaudible, her lips continued to move. This seems to have struck Eli as extremely peculiar, for in v. 13 he is led to the conclusion that Hannah is intoxicated and in v. 14 he actually confronts the worshipper, telling her to 'sober up' (*JPS* 418).[23]

Eli's interference, then, was motivated by the fear that Hannah's behavior was wantonly inappropriate for the sanctuary. He perceives some type of impropriety in her behavior that he equates with drunkenness.[24] Accordingly, the priest disrupts what he imagines to be an impious act on the part of the supplicant. Yet are any of Eli's aforementioned actions truly indicative of a cultic functionary who is regulating a vow? Upon closer scrutiny, this possibility seems highly unlikely. For in looking at Eli's remarks in vv. 14 and 17 it becomes obvious that

23. What was it in Hannah's behavior that led Eli to question her sobriety? Ahlström notes:

> A quiet, tranquil or silent prayer would certainly not have been mistaken for drunken behavior. On the other hand, Eli's misconception may well have been the result of his seeing Hannah in a state of intense prayer (v. 12) which was accompanied by heightened emotions and perhaps by bodily movements (1979: 254).

There are many variations on these themes in the scholarly literature (see Klein 1983: 8; Eslinger 1985: 78; Garsiel 1985: 36; Hertzberg 1964: 25; Keil and Delitzsch 1880: 24; Pirot and Clamer 1955: 352; Polzin 1989: 28).

24. Apparently, this phenomenon was not altogether alien to the hallowed confines of the temple (Hertzberg 1964: 25; see also Zalevsky 1978: 309; H. Smith 1899: 10).

he has little or no understanding of what exactly it is that Hannah is doing. In v. 17, after having received an explanation from Hannah, Eli offers her his blessing, saying לכי לשלום ואלהי ישראל יתן את־שלתך אשר שאלת מעמו. The point to be noted here is that *Eli has never heard the content of Hannah's vow*. He gives her his blessing without any knowledge of what she is asking to receive. Garsiel has accurately described the incident:

> All the same, he replies, 'Go in peace, and may the God of Israel fulfill your request which you have asked of him' (1: 17). He too speaks in general terms, without any reference to her detailed petition—which reinforces the impression that he has no knowledge of the specific cause of her grief—although he assumes that she must have asked for something, and therefore gives her a general blessing for a granted prayer...he functions here merely as a mechanical device to transmit a blessing of whose exact nature he himself is ignorant (1985: 37; see also Eslinger 1985: 80).

Given that Eli does not know the subject matter of the vow, can it be said that he was in the process of regulating this practice? As Zalevsky has concluded, had Eli actually heard Hannah's petition, he certainly would not have mistaken her for a drunk (1978: 310).

Seen in this light, none of Eli's actions can be held as indicative of a priest's role in regulating votive initiation. His interruption of Hannah is based on what he perceives as a slight to the dignity of the sanctuary but not as an affront to some standard procedure for making a vow. It cannot be inferred that his rebuke is a consequence of Hannah's violation of the precepts of a standardized vowing procedure. Nor can it be assumed that Eli heard something within her petition that he did not like. Eli proceeds to bless Hannah without any knowledge of the contents of her vow. It is also significant that *he never requests to hear them*; it is only upon Hannah's payment of the vow in v. 27 that Eli is informed as to what Hannah had done (Willis 1971: 289).

Interaction between votary and cultic functionary does not seem to be part of the votive process as adumbrated in 1 Samuel 1, although I would caution against reading too much into these explicit details. The concern of this 'anti-Elide narrative' obviously lies in articulating the incompetence and corruption of the current Shilohite regime. As Willis has noted: 'Chs. 1–3 contain a strong polemic against the syncretism practiced at the Shiloh sanctuary, and against the Elide priesthood which officiated there' (1971: 306-307).

Nevertheless, this is the only instance we have of a priest being present upon the initiation of a vow. The only conclusions possible from this text are that the priest's role in the vowing process is minimal: he sits far off, near the doorpost; the supplicant makes no effort to 'check-in' with him or to solicit his assistance; he only interferes when he perceives that a gross violation of temple etiquette has occurred; he does not know that a vow is being made; he does not ask to know the contents of the vow and he is only informed of the supplicant's vow at the time of payment (see below, pp. 80-81).

If forced to draw conclusions from this one passage it could be said that votive initiation did not require any supervision or interaction. Instead, the practice appears to be carried out privately.

Cultic Mediation

As has been seen, the authors of the Old Testament do not place any particular emphasis on where and how a vow is to be made. They do, however, go to great lengths to articulate where and how a vow should be paid. Whether through legalistic commands, Psalmatic modeling, or portraits of pious Yahwists such as Hannah, there is little doubt that the literati believe that the votive process is consummated in the presence of cultic personnel. Initiation of the vow may be referred to as vertical and unmediated, insofar as a direct line of communication may be established between the supplicant and the deity. Payment of the vow must be described in different terms. It is mediated through the cultic apparatus; there is, according to the Old Testament authors, no direct and unmediated means of reimbursing Yahweh. To this latter theme the literati devote a significant number of explicit details.

With the possible exception of Jon. 1.16 (see above), as well as those texts that fail to mention the precise location of the vow's payment, it seems certain that the literati want us to know that good Yahwists fulfill their vows within a temple, shrine or sanctuary.[25] Absalom, for instance, is adamant about returning to the sanctuary in Hebron in order to fulfill his vow (2 Sam. 15.7-8; see Haran 1978: 34). Elkanah and Hannah in 1 Samuel 1 both go back to the Shiloh sanctuary to follow up their votive promises.

Once again, the case of Hannah is interesting in that it offers the sole example of a priest attending to the fulfilled vow of a supplicant. Unfortunately, the various versions of this text are not in agreement and

---

25. Though never at a solitary altar (Haran 1978: 16). Some texts do not yield any information as to the location of a vow's fulfillment (for example, Jon. 2.8-10; Judg. 11.30-31 and Num. 21.3).

no particular source seems definitive. Thus, it may be best to examine the most basic of Hannah's actions in this sequence.

In vv. 24 and 25 Hannah returns to Shiloh with a three-year-old bull (see Speiser 1938: 16-17), apparently a very expensive offering (Klein 1983: 10; Hertzberg 1964: 28). She also offers an *ephah* of flour and a skin of wine. These offerings, it should be noted, seem to bear no relation whatsoever to Hannah's original vow; they are not mentioned in her original petition.

The fulfillment of the vow proper most certainly begins in vv. 26 and 27. In brief, the encounter can be summarized as follows:

1 entrance into the temple with the item promised (v. 24);
2 vowed item is brought to Eli (v. 25);
3 respectful salutation, explanation of contents of vow, with
    acknowledgment of Yahweh's fulfillment (vv. 26 and 27);
4 restatement and affirmation of her promise (v. 28);
5 bowing down to Yahweh (v. 28).

While it is impossible to know if this itinerary represents 'actual practice', I would speculate that steps 3 and 4 might be the most realistic aspects of this description. One can well imagine, given the private and individual nature of votive initiation, or given the sheer volume of supplicants, that a priest would not know the content of the vows uttered by those who come before him. Accordingly, it seems feasible that before paying back a vow a supplicant would be expected to restate the terms of the deal. In this manner, the priest would be apprised of exactly what it was that his sanctuary would be receiving. It might also have been the case that in doing so, the priest could retroactively regulate the contents of the transaction—perhaps suggesting to a votary that the item offered may not be as well calibrated to the item desired as the supplicant might originally have believed. However, this is only speculation.

Thus, the first chapter of the book of Samuel reiterates the importance of temple-centered payment. This same demand may be identified across all sources and in nearly all descriptions of fulfilled vows. In the legislative sections, for example, payment of the vow at a cultically approved site is often implied and occasionally directly stated. The laws of Leviticus 27 and Lev. 22.17-25 clearly assume that a priest will be on hand to administer the vowed item. Similarly, Lev. 23.37-38 seems to suggest that, as with the other offerings mentioned in the chapter, vows are typically 'brought' to Yahweh. Deut. 23.19 maintains that 'whore's fees' should not be brought into the 'House of Yahweh' (בית יהוה).[26]

Deuteronomy 12, however, does not merely imply that vows are to be paid in the temple. In accordance with the 'centrist theology of the Deuteronomist' (Cartledge 1992: 13, 34), it demands that vows, as well as other offerings, be paid strictly to Yahweh and solely at the site that he chooses (Deut. 12.4, 11, 26). It does not demand, as O'Brien has erroneously suggested, that a vow be *initiated* in a sanctuary (1987: 281). Rather, the legislation is quite specific in insisting that it be *paid* there. Verse 6 reads, 'And you shall bring them there, your burnt offerings, your sacrifices, as well as your tithes and contributions and your votive offerings and your freewill offerings and the firstlings of your herds and flocks'.

In the Psalms there is more evidence supporting the proposition that vows were paid in a temple, although in these instances it is specifically the Jerusalem Temple that is posited as the location in which public compensation takes place (see for example, 22.26; 65.2; 66.13 and 116.14).

In brief, it seems certain that the literati want us to know that remuneration takes place in a temple. Nor is it a coincidence that the Old Testament authors persistently emphasize the importance of temple-centered payment. As Morton Smith has noted, the priests 'derived their income' from precisely such practices (1987: 134).

Conclusion

In this chapter, I have delineated the mechanism of 'privacy'. I began by arguing against the widely-held view that all vows were made at official cult sites. As has been seen, the *explicit evidence* simply does not support the existence of a mechanism of 'temple-centered initiation'. In fact, the texts that we have at our disposal explicitly and implicitly assume that vows may be made in many different places. As far as the literati are concerned, there is no particular location in which a vow must be uttered.

The authors of the Old Testament are far less taciturn on the subject of how and where a vow should be *paid*. They offer very precise details regarding the proper procedures for votive remittance. Further, they repeatedly and explicitly maintain that vows should be fulfilled in a setting where Yahwistic personnel are present. This emphasis on issues concerning payment leads us to wonder why the literati are so indifferent to

26. For a discussion of this passage see Chapter 4.

the issue of votive initiation. This question will be answered in Chapter 8.

I have also suggested that even when a vow is made in a temple, nothing indicates that the cultic apparatus plays any significant role in its initiation. As such, it would be very difficult to prove that the process of initiation was cultically supervised and interactive as Simon Parker has suggested.

Looked at together, the lack of legislation regarding vow-making, the implicit assumption that vows may be made anywhere, and the apparent lack of interaction and supervision inherent to initiation all suggest that a mechanism of 'private initiation' may have existed in ancient Israel. I cannot point to any explicit or implicit detail which suggests that if a worshipper so desired, he or she did not have the right to make a vow outside of a Yahwistic cult site. Nor does any vow-text demonstrate supervision or interaction as a component of the initiation process.

Thus, when I speak of the mechanism of private votive initiation, I refer to the fact that the making of a vow is an individual (as opposed to interactive) practice, that does not require the presence, assistance, or scrutiny of any other human being, even if the petition is made in a public setting (such as the temple).

Chapter 3

SPOKEN INVOCATION

Spoken Invocation

As one reads through the Israelite and northwest Semitic votive literature, one particular mechanism of the votive process reveals itself with unusual clarity and consistency: the vow is *spoken* to the deity. Verbs denoting speaking and listening activity abound in Old Testament and extra-biblical vow-texts. As will be seen, supplicants typically speak, cry, call out or even scream to the god(s). In this chapter, I shall present evidence in support of the mechanism of 'spoken invocation'. This mechanism, found throughout the northwest Semitic votive literature, will be compared with a disparate mechanism encountered in the east Semitic milieu. The latter would seem to make the vow far less accessible to members of the 'popular religious groups'.

The Ugaritic Sources

It might be understating the case somewhat to claim that Ugaritic epic vows feature supplicants who speak and gods who listen. In one of the two vow-texts that we have at our disposal there appears *a deity* in the act of speaking, even screaming at an unscrupulous votary. In the other, the supplicant is depicted as not merely talking to the gods, but giving them commands.

In KTU 1.15. III the goddess Asherah becomes enraged at King Keret. The text informs us that she screams at the monarch—*w tšu.gh.w**[tṣḥ]*, 'She raises her voice and [screams]' (l. 27). As will be seen in Chapter 8, her rebuke and eventual punishment of Keret is attributable to his apparent refusal to pay back his vow.

In a somewhat homeless fragment of the Aqhat epic[1] Danel prefaces

---

1.   *KTU* 1.22 = AQHT 4 frag. C (see de Moor 1987) = *UT* 123 = RP 3AB (see Virolleaud 1941). R = *CTA* 22. The relation of this fragment to the main body of the Aqhat epic is not entirely clear. For the most part, scholars have maintained that these fragments are thematically related to the epic itself. Thus, some have attempted to link

his vow by screaming '*šmᶜ atm*', 'listen!', to the *Rephaim*.[2] The use of the imperative as a means of gaining a deity's attention is attested frequently in the Ugaritic literature.[3] As Loewenstamm has noted, the language employed in these instances is predicated on the type of verbal interaction demonstrated 'in plain everyday conversation' (1980: 123). Thus, it must be emphasized that Danel's address is not inherently respectful, nor is it couched in an idiom of petitionary obsequiousness. Instead, he addresses the *Rephaim* as if they were his social equals.[4]

His vow reads as follows:

16 *ydr. hm. ym* *[*lk*[5] ?]	he vows: 'If[6] [my son] *will rule*
17 '*l.*[7] *amr. yu**[*ḥd.*	over Amurru, seize [*the ks'* mlkh?[8]

the narrative in this fragment with that of the epic in general (see Caquot 1960; Caquot, Sznycer and Herdner 1974: 466). Dijkstra and de Moor note that the fragment was written by the same scribe who authored two other installments of the main epic (*CTA* 17-19; 1975: 171). In another article Dijkstra offers the possibility that '*KTU* 1.20-22 formed part of the sequel of our legend' (1979: 209). A similar opinion is expressed by Sapin who suggests that these fragments belong to 'la même oeuvre littéraire' (1983: 166 n. 45), whereas Gibson hesitantly opines that this text concerns itself with the eventual resurrection of Aqhat (1978: 27 n. 2). My own opinion is that no relation can be found between this fragment and the rest of the Aqhat epic. I agree with Parker who observes: 'There is no comparable connection between the structure of the narrative, so far as it can be traced, in any of the so-called *Rephaim* tablets…and that in any of the *Aqht* tablets' (1989: 134).

2.   This brings us to the thorny question of who exactly the *Rephaim* are. Unfortunately, there exists no consensus regarding this issue, nor does it seem likely that one will emerge in the near future. For the present it will be assumed that they are incarnations of dead Ugaritic kings (see Levine and de Tarragon 1984). For a history of scholarship on this subject until 1960 see Caquot 1960. For more recent discussions see de Moor 1976b; Good 1980; Horwitz 1979; Talmon 1983; Dietrich, Loretz and Sanmartín 1976b.

3.   On the uses of the verb *šmᶜ*, see Loewenstamm 1980.

4.   This tendency to command the *Rephaim* to appear has also been noted in other texts (Levine and de Tarragon 1984: 657).

5.   This reading is based on *KTU*. Readings in square brackets signify possible reconstructions. I have included only those reconstructions that I feel are most plausible. Virolleaud originally reconstructed *ymlk* here (1941: 13; see also Caquot 1960: 91). The reading *ymlk* is rejected by Gibson (1978: 136) and Gordon (1949: 102).

6   I read *hm* as the same conditional conjunction form that introduces the content of all the epic vows (see Richter 1967: 22-24; see also Segert 1984: 184). Attempts at reading *hm* as a third-person object pronoun seem unlikely (Aistleitner 1964: 85 translates '…gelobt er ihnen…'; also see Gordon 1949: 102).

7.   *KTU* reads '*ṣ* here, as does Gibson 1978: 136. But the use of '*l* 'over' (also

throne of his kingship]

18 *nḥt.*[9] *kḥt. dr**[*kth*[10]?] the seat of the throne of his dominion,[11]

19 *aṣḥ. rpim**[ ] I will call the *Rephaim* [ ]

20 *b qrb. hk**[*ly…*] to the midst of my palace [ ]'

21 *tdd. aṯrh**[ ] hasten,[12] to his holy place![ ]

This fragment, as well as the Keret episode, gives the impression that Ugaritic deities and votaries are on somewhat familiar terms. Above, it has been noted that the goddess Asherah did not hesitate to reprimand Keret personally. In the Danel passage the supplicant does not seem unduly over burdened by the demands of protocol either, as he implores the gods to listen to him and to accept his open invitation to his palace. The *Rephaim*, for their part, are not radically transcendent deities. Instead, they linger above the palace, seemingly amenable to making an unplanned visit.

The Old Testament Sources

In the sphere of votive activity Yahweh is far less immanent than these Ugaritic deities. He is never shown to upbraid his delinquent votaries: this task is left to the prophets and lawmakers.[13] Nor does Yahweh often come down to earth and speak with his subjects. And it goes without saying that we never see him making impromptu visits to his supplicants' quarters either.

Israelite votaries are also portrayed differently from their Ugaritic counterparts. The southerners are indeed more polite; nowhere in the Old Testament would a supplicant command Yahweh's attention by employing the imperative form, שמע. As Hannah's vow indicates (1 Sam. 1.11-

suggested by *KTU*), makes for a more logical reading.

8. This reconstruction was suggested by Virolleaud based on a probable parallel with V AB, D 47 (1941: 13). *yḥd* is seen as deriving from *'ḥd* 'to seize', 'to take hold of' (Gordon 1955: 235).

9. *KTU* reads *nzt* here.

10. On *drkt* as 'rule', 'authority', see Segert 1984: 184.

11. *kḥt*, literally, 'chair'. Segert traces this word back to Hurrian *kešḥi* (1984: 189). Perhaps a more provocative reading of *nḥt* would take it as cognate to Akkadian *neḥtu* 'peace', 'security' (*CAD* 'N' 150).

12. For a discussion of the root *ndd*, see Tropper and Verreet 1988: 345. Their analysis of the meaning of this root as 'fliehen', 'entwischen', 'weggehen', is consonant with the general scholarly consensus that the *Rephaim* are being told to 'hasten' to the palace (see also BDB 622).

13. See Chapter 8.

18) this deity is to be approached with the utmost respect. Unlike Danel, who employs the imperative, Hannah uses the infinitive absolute form of the verb ראה.[14] She also emphasizes her lowly position, referring to herself as Yahweh's 'maidservant' three times in her opening verse (1 Sam. 1.11).

The evidence is certainly too sparse to permit the drawing of definitive cross-cultural comparisons. Nevertheless, it seems clear that the Ugaritic sources display aspects of votive invocation that are either alien to, or have been censored by, the Old Testament literati. Yet, the Ugaritic and Israelite sources are in accord over one basic mechanism of the votive process. In both sets of vow-texts it is clear that a vow is spoken to the deity. In the pre-exilic data this point is verified by the fact that in the introductory formula of each epic vow the verb אמר 'to say' is present (that is, in Gen. 28.20; Num. 21.2; Judg. 11.30; 1 Sam. 1.11; 2 Sam. 15.7).

In the Ugaritic materials a similar emphasis is placed on the importance of speaking. This may be inferred from an examination of the narrative voice in the Keret epic. Prior to the King's visit to the sanctuary a long description of his actions is rendered in the third person (KTU 1.14 I-IV 35). As he enters the sacred precincts in order to utter his vow, however, the narrator suddenly shifts to a first-person account; the reader is permitted to hear the king speaking in his own words (KTU 1.14 IV 36-43). Immediately after the petition is spoken by the monarch the author returns to third-person narration. Thus, the vow is portrayed as being spoken by Keret whereas all his other actions to this point are related from the point of view of the narrator. In undertaking this dramatic change of narrative voice it would seem that the author of this text either wants to stress or implicitly assumes that supplicants *vocalize* their requests to Asherah.

This emphasis on the spoken nature of the vow may have had some sort of internal significance for the literati of Israel and Ugarit. They seem to subscribe to an ethos which maintains that a spoken obligation to a god was to be taken with the utmost seriousness. An example of this is the conversation between Jephthah and his daughter that ensues after his vow has been fulfilled. Upon seeing his daughter emerge from his home in Mizpah (Judg. 11.34) Jephthah suddenly realizes the terrible fate that is about to befall her: in accordance with the terms of his vow

---

14. Thus yielding the very polite 'If you would please see...', as opposed to a command form, like 'See! (or "take note of!") the suffering of your maidservant!'

(Judg. 11.30-31) she must be sacrificed as a burnt offering (?).[15] Understanding the irreversibility of the situation, he cries:

35c   ואנכי פציתי־פי אל־יהוה ולא אוכל לשוב

35c   'For I opened my mouth to Yahweh and I cannot retract'

To which his daughter replies:

36a   אבי פציתה את־פיך אל־יהוה
                   עשה לי כאשר יצא מפיך

36a   'Father, you opened your mouth to Yahweh, do to me as you said.'[16]

Jephthah's remorse seems predicated on his realization that he actually spoke to Yahweh, that with his mouth he made a promise. As such, the situation appears to be hopeless and irreversible, for one cannot—as his daughter seems well aware, and as the literati are explicitly demonstrating—renege on a spoken commitment made to Yahweh. In his intensive study of this passage, *Jephthah and his Vow*, David Marcus observes: 'Both Jephthah and his daughter represent the point of view, common among the Israelites, that a vow is a sacred obligation which must be fulfilled under all circumstances' (1986: 29; see also Pirot and Clamer 1955: 242; O'Brien 1987: 281; Cartledge 1992: 29).

The literati's depiction of votive initiation as both vocalic and binding once spoken, is not confined to the pre-exilic literature. Rather, this portrayal persists throughout *all* strands of the Old Testament. In the prophetic writings there appears a similar view of the vow. Jeremiah castigates a clan of Judaeans living in Egypt, reminding them that they made illicit vows to the Queen of Heaven; these were spoken with their mouths (ותדברנה בפיכם; Jer. 44.25).

In v. 17 of the same chapter the votaries are depicted as defiantly saying that they will steadfastly perform all the ritual acts they have promised to this goddess. Once again, they make reference to words literally leaving their mouths (v. 17: כי עשה נעשה את־כל־הדבר אשר־יצא מפינו, 'For we shall certainly perform everything that has gone forth from our mouths'). To which the prophet ripostes by mockingly quoting the pledge made by this heretical faction.

Yet his recital of their words is not exact, as he makes one crucial substitution. In v. 17 the ex-Judaeans cry 'we shall certainly perform

---

15. For a discussion of this issue see Marcus (1986).

16. On the expression פצה את פה, Wendel notes 'In the Bible, to open the mouth is repeatedly found as an expression for vowing' (1931a: 95).

everything that has gone forth from our mouths...' (כי עשה נעשה את־כל־הדבר אשר־יצא מפינו) but in v. 25 the prophet paraphrases these sentiments by saying עשה נעשה את־נדרינו אשר נדרנו, 'we shall certainly perform *the vows which we made'*. Here then, the authors reveal that in Jeremiah's dialect making a vow is synonymous with words leaving a person's mouth. Hence, the association between the form נדר and actual speech may have assumed the status of an idiomatic expression in Jeremiah's dialect (see Carroll 1986: 740).

In Deut. 23.24 we again receive evidence of this idiomatic association between spoken words and the making of vows. The verse reads:

24
מוצא שפתיך תשמר
ועשית כאשר נדרת ליהוה אלהיך נדבה
אשר דברת בפיך

24   You will perform the utterance of your lips and you will do that
      which you voluntarily vowed to Yahweh your God; (that) which
      you spoke with your mouth.[17]

This one verse demonstrates two important aspects of a vow: a vow is an act which requires speech, and once uttered to the deity it is a binding obligation that must be fulfilled.

Both these points are reiterated in the Priestly source. In Num. 30.3 it is stated that once uttered a vow must be remitted; all that went out of the mouth of the supplicant must be fulfilled (ככל־היצא מפיו יעשה). G.B. Gray has remarked: 'An intention only becomes binding when it has been embodied in speech, and so gained an independent existence;

---

17. The verse is extremely problematic. The use of מוצא and אשר דברת בפיך שפתיך in one verse seems somewhat redundant. Many commentators have maintained that the latter is a gloss, with the former being the original component of the verse (G. Smith 1950: 275; Steuernagel 1900: 87). If מוצא שפתיך were to be eliminated, however, the verse would still make sense and essentially have the same meaning. Accordingly, it is hard to tell which of the two is actually the gloss. As a means of resolving these difficulties, I would tentatively propose a new division of the verse. First, the writer urges the supplicant to 'perform the utterance of your lips', here taking תשמר in the sense of faithfulness to a verbal utterance (cf. 1 Kgs. 2.43). The next clause is introduced by ועשית 'and fulfill that which you voluntarily vowed to Yahweh your god'. Notice that I take נדבה not as 'freewill offering' (as do Craigie 1976: 303; H. Robinson 1907: 176; G.A. Smith 1950: 275; Buis and Leclercq 1963: 158), but as an adverb (cf. Hos. 14.5; see Driver 1903: 268; Schultz 1859: 576; Steuernagel 1900: 87; Oettli 1893: 83). The last part of the verse serves as a sort of redundant afterthought: '(that) which you spoke with your mouth'.

consequently stress is frequently laid, as here, on the *utterance* of the vow' (1906: 415; see also Snaith 1967: 321).

A similar emphasis on the importance of the spoken word, and the gravity of its betrayal, can be found in the later wisdom traditions, for example in Eccl. 5.3.[18] The Psalms also abound with references to the vocalic dimensions of this religious act. In Ps. 22.25 the supplicant reports that Yahweh listened to him when he cried out. In Ps. 66.14 the worshipper again emphasizes that vows are made with the mouth: אשר־פצו שפתי ודבר־פי בצר־לי. Psalm 116.4 presents us with a troubled supplicant who invokes the name of the deity: ובשם־יהוה אקרא. In Ps. 56.10 the same verb, קרא 'to call out' is employed in a vow-text.

In the Phoenician and Punic sources the fact that a vow is initiated by audible utterance has now almost become taken for granted. There are hundreds of votive stelae containing the rather trite assertion that the deity in question has 'heard the voice', שמע קלא of the worshipper.[19]

Listening/Granting

A corollary of the principle that a vow must be spoken to the deity is that the god actually 'listens' (שמע) to the entreaty of the worshipper. This usage functions as an idiomatic expression: when a deity has 'heard' or 'listened to' the demand of a votary it always means that the former has in fact *fulfilled* the supplicant's request. As Schult notes: 'From God it is asked and declared that he "listen" (that is, help, rescue, forgive, etc.)...'

References to Yahweh's 'hearing' are relatively rare in the biblical epic vows. It is only in Num. 21.3 that the reader is told that 'Yahweh heard the voice of Israel' (וישמע יהוה בקול ישראל).[20] Accordingly, the remaining part of the verse indicates that the terms of the petition have been granted (that is to say, the Israelites have defeated the Canaanites). Similarly, in the Bar-Hadad inscription the king reports that he has made a vow to Melcarth, and that the latter consequently 'heard his voice' (וישמע לקלה). Or, to put it less metaphorically, the king received what he asked for.[21]

The Psalms also place special emphasis on the fact that Yahweh is the

---

18. See Chapter 8.

19. With slight deviations this expression may be encountered frequently (for example in *KAI* 47, 63, 66, 68, 84, 88, 98, 103, 104, 105, 106, 107, 108).

20. The reference to the 'voice' of Israel is further evidence of spoken invocation.

21. See Chapter 1 for a discussion of this vow.

one who hears or grants votive requests (see Pss. 22.25; 61.6; 65.3; 66.18; 116.1). In Job 22.27 we encounter another reference to vows being heard and petitions granted:

27   תעתיר אליו וישמעך ונדריך תשלם

27   You will pray to him, and he will listen to you, and you shall
        fulfill your vows

Finally, there are scores of Phoenician and Punic votive texts that conclude with the formulaic expression כ שמע קלא, 'For he heard his voice'. In each of these texts, this brief coda serves as testimony to the fact that the original request has been granted.

The above discussion demonstrates that the literati of various northwest Semitic cultures, writing at different times and in different places, depict the fundamental components of votive initiation in a nearly identical manner. It is everywhere assumed that the worshiper must speak aloud to the deity, making use of his or her mouth and lips. As Davies notes, the term *ndr* itself 'suggest[s] the spoken word, the promise, or the "outgoing from the mouth"' (1962: 792).

The Old Testament sources explicitly relate that a vow made in such a fashion is binding and must be fulfilled by the worshipper. It is also assumed that a god may be listening to the worshipper as he or she speaks. For the deity to grant the supplicant's request is essentially to suggest that he or she 'heard' it upon its utterance. For a deity not to 'listen', must mean that the request made in the vow was denied. While it stands to reason that this occurred quite frequently, the Old Testament literati do not offer any evidence of such divine inattentiveness (Keller 1976: 40).

The East Semitic System: 'Written Invocation'
It should not be assumed that the mechanisms of the northwest Semitic vow are representative of ancient Near Eastern vows in general. The neo-Sumerian and Old Babylonian archives, for example, exhibit a completely different species of votive initiation. As a means of underscoring the radical accessibility of the northwest Semitic votive system I shall now briefly examine a somewhat distinct votive practice found in the east Semitic world.

The neo-Sumerian sources display vows that were not originally spoken to the deity, *but written down*. W. Hallo has studied a corpus of neo-Sumerian 'letter prayer' vows in which the supplicant initiated the votive procedure via written, as opposed to audible, petition:

> And the typical purpose of private votive objects (as of royal ones) was to forward to the deity the prayer which doubled as the name of the object by leaving the object, with its inscription, on permanent deposit in the cella of the temple, close to the niche which held the statue of the deity. Such inscribed votive objects were, then, considered as taking the place of the suppliant, and relieving him of the need to proffer his prayer in his own person, orally and perpetually (1968: 75; see also Cartledge 1992: 74).

In this system the votary is responsible for the placement of a written text near the statue of the deity. Accordingly, contact with the god(s) is not direct, vertical and private. Rather, it is indirect, and mediated through the cultic apparatus. The latter, assumedly, would have little difficulty monitoring the contents of the votive inscriptions deposited in their sanctuary.

Votive approach by inscription is also witnessed in the Old Babylonian sources. As R. Harris has proven, vows were often worded in language typically used to refer to temple loans. A corpus of texts containing the expression *šalmu balṭu* often depicts the plight of a worshipper who is ill and who promises to pay back the deity what she or he 'owes' upon regaining her or his health. To some, these texts indicated that an individual, while ill, had merely taken out a temple loan (Scheil 1916). As early as 1923, however, Koschaker and Ungnad expressed doubts that issues of credit were actually being described:

> On the contrary, it must concern a vow to the god of the temple...The votary promises a sum of money in return for his recovery from illness. In our case...the votary masks it in the form of a loan, thus it concerns an apparently fictive loan. So here the votary may have vowed to Samas the sale price of his field. For this conception can be made valid as long as the vow is masked in the form of a written obligation (1923: 46-47).

This conclusion was solidified by Harris, who noted that even though these texts were formulated as loans, the debtor borrowed not 'money or barley...as is the case with loans, but rather objects, ornaments made of precious metal and having religious significance' (1960: 135). Harris concluded that these texts were not pure loans but vows. Thus, there existed a mechanism whereby an ill supplicant claims to 'owe' a sun disk, which he or she will place around the neck of the god when he or she recovers (1960: 135). In reality, however, the supplicant has vowed that if he or she recovers this religious artifact will be donated to the temple.

Harris's identification of such a practice with the process of vowing is reinforced by the appearance of the *šalmu balṭu* clause in a text containing the word *ikribū*, the Assyrian noun-form for 'vow' (CAD 'I/J', 62). The relevant section of this text reads: *i-nu-ma ba-al-ṭú u ša-al-mu ikribīšu ana (d)Sin PN inaddin*, 'when he is physically well and solvent PN will give his votive offering to Sin' (Harris 1960: 136; see also Scheil 1916: 129).

To this point the mechanisms of 'spoken invocation' (northwest Semitic) and 'written invocation' (east Semitic) have been discussed. While the latter practice is certainly not indicative of all east Semitic vows, it confronts us with a type of votive initiation heretofore unattested in the northwest Semitic data.[22] In Chapters 5, 6 and 7 I shall show how the oral northwest Semitic system rendered the making of vows accessible to the 'popular religious groups' under consideration. It will be argued that a written votive system, such as the one seen in the east Semitic world but not in the northwest Semitic milieu, may have rendered the vow highly restrictive to 'popular religious groups'.

Conclusion

In this chapter it has been demonstrated that the Israelite votary is allowed to vocalize his or her petition to the deity.[23] This state of affairs is evidenced in the overwhelming majority of northwest Semitic vow-texts. The likelihood that such a mechanism actually existed increases when it is taken into consideration that northwest Semitic authors, writing in different times and places, all seem implicitly to acknowledge this aspect of the votive procedure.

It might legitimately be asked whether this data actually constitutes implicit evidence. The fact that vows are vocalized to the deity is, after all, explicitly mentioned by the literati. It is significant, however, that such information is repeated over and over again, in nearly the exact same way, in almost every northwest Semitic vow-text examined. It appears to have had little resonance for the biblical author insofar as this reference to vocalized petitions is never commented upon. Further, like all good implicit evidence, it appears to have absolutely nothing to do

22. In a somewhat similar vein, H.L. Ginsberg noted that Israelite forms of public acknowledgment to the deity were generally verbal, whereas as non-Israelite forms were 'very often epigraphic' (1945: 169).

23. For further evidence see Cartledge's discussion of Hos. 14.2 (1992: 49).

with the theological agenda of the Yahwist party. It is the repetitive, uncontroversial and mundane nature of this evidence which leads me to label it as implicit.

To this point then, three mechanisms have been identified: individual initiation, privacy and spoken initiation. Taken together they go a long way towards explaining why this practice may have been accessible to the 'popular religious groups' of ancient Israel. As will be seen in Part II, these mechanisms are essential ingredients in a recipe for radical votive autonomy. And as will be seen in Part III, these same mechanisms served to create tremendous frustration for the religious authorities.

Chapter 4

AUTONOMOUS REGULATION

> Private prayer went well with a *gift*. The princes offered temples, precious objects, cultivated lands, etc., and used this occasion to invoke the god for the salvation of their dynasty, their people, their armies. The poor brought small objects, beads, shells, cornaline, lapis, sandstone, etc....(V. Scheil, 'La promesse dans la prière babylonienne').

In this chapter I shall call attention to two more mechanisms of the Israelite vow. Each of these permitted supplicants to exert an extraordinary degree of control over the petitions that they made to their deities. For in the Israelite votive system *the supplicant*, as opposed to the cultic apparatus, determines not only what is to be promised to Yahweh, but also when the promise is to be paid. An understanding of these two mechanisms will go a long way towards explaining why this practice may have been accessible to the 'popular religious groups' targeted in this study.

Autonomous Regulation of Content

Variance of Items
What types of items did Israelites demand from Yahweh? What types of items did they promise to pay the deity should he grant their requests?

When examining these issues most scholars have drawn their conclusions solely from the contents of vows made by those Israelites who appear on the pages of the Old Testament. Roland de Vaux remarks: 'A vow (*neder*) is a promise to give or to consecrate to God a person or thing, e.g. a tithe (Gn 28.20-22), a sacrifice (2 S 15.8), plunder taken in war (Nb 21.2), a person (Jg 11.30-31; 1 S 1.11)' (1965: 465). McFadyen writes: 'The thing vowed was very frequently an animal, but it might also be money, a house, land or a person' (1928: 655).

A more detailed, albeit similar, explanation is offered by Wendel:

> As far as the positive vow of the Israelite period is concerned, it consisted, in this time, generally of traditional animal and vegetable sacrifices. Thus, קרבן, שלמים, עלה, זבח, can be the object of a vow. But one also vows the erection of a temple, or money will be promised (e.g., as the worth of a man)...Drink offerings and incense offerings are mentioned once. One can vow a child as a temple servant, or even, in the ancient period, as a sacrifice.

When looking at the types of *requests* which supplicants make, Simon Parker notes:

> Thus there appear to be three types of vow preserved in Old Testament narrative literature, concerned with and conditional upon 1) safe return from abroad, 2) military victory, and 3) the getting of a family. (1979: 699; see also Parker 1989: 86-87; McFadyen 1928: 656)

These observations, based on explicit evidence, are certainly accurate descriptions of what Israelites in the Bible demanded from and promised to Yahweh. Perhaps inadvertently, the aforementioned remarks foster the impression that these were the *only* promises and requests made by Israelites to the God of Israel.

If the items just mentioned were the only ones that Israelites could include in their petitions, then it stands to reason that the votive system would have been quite restrictive to the 'popular religious groups' targeted in this study. Could most Israelites be expected to offer to erect a sanctuary to Yahweh? to proscribe a town? to offer their children— potential economic assets—as gifts to the temple?[1] Initially, a glance at the demands and promises made by biblical Israelites would suggest that the votive system was not accessible to the non-biblical Israelites investigated in this study.

Yet a different approach to this data will help us to arrive at precisely the opposite conclusion. In beginning this analysis, I refer the reader to the following chart. It summarizes every demand and offer that appears in the Old Testament.

---

1.   Another question must be asked: is safe return home from exile, or the need for a military victory, a typical dilemma that faced most Israelites? For a discussion of these issues see Berlinerblau 1991.

TEXT	ITEM DESIRED	ITEM OFFERED
2 Sam. 15.8	return to Jerusalem	to worship Yahweh
Judg.11.30-31	defeat of the Ammonites	a burnt offering of whatever comes out of the door to meet him[2]
Jer. 44.25	?	burning of incense and pouring of libations to the Queen of Heaven
Mal. 1.14	?	sacrifice of a blemished animal[3]
Lev. 27.1-8	?	the 'equivalent' for a human being[4]
Lev. 27.9-12	?	an animal brought to Yahweh as an offering
Lev. 27.14-15	?	a house
Lev. 27.16-21	?	land, during or after the Jubilee year[5]
Num. 21.2	defeat of the Canaanites	proscription of their towns
Gen. 28.20-22	God to remain with Jacob, protect him on his journey. Food and clothes, safe return to father's home	worship of Yahweh setting up of an abode for Yahweh setting aside of a tithe for Yahweh

2.   For an excellent analysis of the terms of Jephthah's vow see Marcus 1986.

3.   As I point out below, this text acknowledges that both a blemished or unblemished animal may be offered to Yahweh in fulfillment of a vow. A stigma is attached, however, to the individual who initially vows the blemished animal although capable of affording the unblemished one. This is extremely interesting in light of the legislation in Lev. 22.21-25 which categorically excludes blemished animals from being offered in fulfillment of a vow.

4.   Or 'fixed equivalent'. For an explanation of this term and a discussion of this text see Chapter 5.

5.   But see Cartledge, who argues that the items discussed in Lev. 27.9-21 should not be considered as related to the votive process (1992: 137).

1 Sam. 1.11	The seed of men	dedication of child to Yahweh
Ps. 76.12	?	tribute (?)
Lev. 7.16	?	sacrifice of an animal
Lev. 22.17-20	?	burnt offering of a male animal without blemish
Num. 15.8	?	animal from the herd
Deut. 23.19	?	the fee of a whore or male prostitute[6]
Ps. 56.13	?	thank offerings
Nah. 2.1-14	defeat of enemies (?)	?[7]
Prov. 31.2	a son	?
Jon. 1.16	?	?[8]

An analysis of the five Israelite epic vows in the above list reveals three distinct types of demands and five different promises made to Yahweh. The latter statistic is of extreme importance: within the five vow-texts in which we actually hear the supplicant utter the petition there are five completely different items that the votary will offer the deity.

When the inquiry is extended to all twenty of the vow-texts on the list there is still this high rate of variance in demands and promises. In all, The Hebrew Bible proffers seven different reports of 'items desired' by supplicants. As can be gleaned from the chart above, three of these concern the defeat of enemies, two are for male offspring, and two are for safe return home.

The Scriptures are a good deal more generous in offering us data on the items that worshippers have promised their deities. Out of twenty cases, twelve distinct types of compensation can be identified. These are: pious devotion to Yahweh; incense and libations; a burnt offering; a house; land; the proscription of a town; the erection of a temple; the payment of a tithe; devotion of children; tribute; the 'equivalent' of a human being; a 'whore's fee'.[9]

6. For an analysis of this verse see below.
7. For a discussion of this text see Chapter 1.
8. This is perhaps the most cryptic vow in the entire Old Testament. My explanation as to what exactly is being asked for can be found in Chapter 2.
9. Though see my analysis of this term below.

Before offering a theory on the relevance of this variability of promised items, I shall examine some of the requests and demands revealed in the extra-biblical sources.

UGARIT TEXT	ITEM OR PERSON DESIRED	ITEM OFFERED
KTU 1.14 IV 36-43	Lady Hurriya	Twice her [weight] in silver and three times her [weight] in Gold[10]
KTU 1.22 II 16-21	Kingship for his son	To invite the *Rephaim* to the palace[11]

With the addition of these Ugaritic petitions there are now seven epic vows. In each the supplicant offers a different inducement to the deity or deities in question. Additionally, at least four different types of requests are made of the gods. It does not take an advanced statistical analysis to reveal that if more textual examples of vows were available, still more distinct types of demands and promises made by would-be supplicants would probably be found.[12]

When the parameters of the investigation are widened to include the Aramaic, Punic and Phoenician data, the sheer variety of items which humans might consider vowing to their deities can be envisioned.

ARAMAIC TEXT	ITEM DESIRED	ITEM OFFERED
Bar-Hadad	?	a stele (?)[13]

---

10. *KTU* 1.15 III 20-30, where apparently sons and daughters were requested by the king, could also be included.

11. See Chapter 3.

12. This extra-biblical evidence demonstrates that the Old Testament does not offer an exhaustive account of votive praxis. For in these Ugaritic texts there appear two completely new demands and promises that supplicants would make. Nowhere in the biblical record is there a request for a son to be king. Nor is there—though I imagine the practice might have been quite common—an instance of a man vowing for the hand of a woman.

13. However, it seems highly unlikely that only a stele was offered to the deity. It is probable that the king would have left a more significant gift for his god. The stele's primary function is probably to commemorate the situation. Unfortunately, there is no way of ascertaining what the real compensation actually was. For exegesis and a discussion of the use of stele in general see Chapter 1.

ELEPHANTINE

| Cowl. 72:18 | ? | 2 'KLWL' (?)[14] |

SAMARIA

| Sam. 15 | ? | 9 of some quantity X[15] |

PHOENICIAN AND PUNIC
(random sample)

KAI 40	?	statues[16]
KAI 64	?	stele and 2 חנוטמם[17]
KAI 66	to be healed	a bronze altar[18]

14. *Cowl.* 72:18 = *CIS* 2/1 no. 146.

18   25...לכיחך זי הו ב
2...יומ לנדר לשרתא קל ולן

18   ...the 25th of *KYHK*, which was the day of a vow, for dinner 2 *KLWL*

According to Grelot, this text is written by the overseer of a wine cellar who wants to '...justify his administrative expenditures to his master' (1972: 101). Grelot also speculates that the quantity vowed here (2 *KLWL*) is quite large and comparatively expensive (1972: 100-101; see also Cowley 1923: 182-183).

15. For the original publication of this text see Sukenik 1933: 155. This reading follows Birnbaum 1957:

1   נצבא זי נדר אח
2   9...

1   This stele was vowed *AH*
2   9 X

Birnbaum theorized that the numerals found on this jar probably represented a sum of money (1957: 29). He dates it to 300 BCE plus or minus two and a half centuries. In a private communication, Professor Andre Lemaire has suggested that this may have been a training text for a student.

16. In this text from Idalion dating from the mid-third century, 'these statues' הסמלם האל, are vowed. See also Cooke 1903: 77-78.

17. This text stems from third-century Sardinia and in it 2 חנוטמם are vowed. Though the meaning of this word is still uncertain (see *KAI* 12:1 and Cooke 1903: 108).

18. Another Sardinian inscription. In this one the suppliant apparently requested to be healed (רפיא). In exchange he offers a bronze altar (מזבה נחשת).

KAI 105	?	a human sacrifice[19]
		in perfect condition (?)
KAI 110	?	a lamb (?)[20]

It emerges from all of this that votaries had the freedom to ask for and offer their gods many different things. The evidence clearly indicates that the items that were offered varied greatly; from an animal sacrifice to a human sacrifice, a vow of land to a vow of physical devotion to the deity, or from the payment of some mundane quantity to a costly promise of precious metals.

The point to be underscored is that the textual sources indicate that the content of the votive petition varies from person to person and from situation to situation. Even the Old Testament sources taken alone evince a remarkable degree of variability in the types of things which biblical Israelites promise and demand. What is not found, however, is the existence of any one item that is repeatedly asked for or promised. The biblical literati then, have tacitly relayed that they did not know of a circumscribed set of items from which each supplicant was to choose when formulating the terms of a vow. Additionally, it must be assumed that such a state of affairs never impelled a redactor—who was well positioned to note this heterogeneity of promises and requests—to initiate a process of homogenizing the contents of petitions made to Yahweh.

Thus, the definitions of the vow offered by the scholars noted above need to be re-qualified. A vow cannot be defined solely in terms of the three or four items that the Old Testament tells us Israelites promised Yahweh. Given the wide variance of demands and promises observed in such a limited sample, it would be more accurate to envision the vow as a practice permitting supplicants to offer many different items to the deity.

As will be seen, the astonishing flexibility that the votive system permitted its patrons created all sorts of difficulties for the cultic apparatus.

---

19. Here following *KAI*'s reading of מלך אדם בשערם בתם as 'A human sacrifice of his (own) child in perfect condition' (see also *KAI* 103, 104, 106, 107). The literature that addresses the issue of child and human sacrifice in the biblical world is far too copious to be reviewed here. I would point the reader to Weinfeld's contribution (1972a) where he criticizes the reading of *KAI*. See also Picard's article in which the history of the archaeological study of votive child sacrifice is reviewed (1991).

20. Here taking אמר as meaning 'lamb', though *EH* 56 reads it as a divine name.

'The Cheater'

In looking at the Old Testament data I have come to the conclusion that the contents of the vow varied from situation to situation. The high degree of variability found in a small sample suggested that a more comprehensive record would have verified the contention that the range of items demanded and promised was quite wide.

At this point, I should like to offer a hypothesis to explain why this variability is witnessed. I believe that this state of affairs is due to the fact that the votary had the freedom to decide exactly what item would be offered and requested from the deity. This votive autonomy is co-determined by two factors. As noted in Chapters 1 and 2 respectively, a vow may be initiated individually and privately. This means that no one can regulate or monitor the contents of the supplicant's negotiation with Yahweh. Left to their own devices, Israelite votaries were free to regulate autonomously the 'terms of the deal'.

I shall now turn to an examination of three texts in which this mechanism of 'autonomous regulation of content' is tacitly assumed. Malachi 1.14 reads:

וארור נוכל ויש בעדרו זכר
ונדר וזבח משחת לאדני

Cursed[21] be the cheater! For he has an (unblemished) male in
his flock— yet vows and sacrifices a blemished one to the Lord.

Many commentators have been quick to note that this particular verse is not directed to priests but to the layperson.[22] Plausibly, it would seem to indicate the existence of a practice which the literati believed was so widespread amongst the laity that it apparently deserved a place in this diatribe directed against the cultic apparatus.

The individual addressed is the נוכל, of which O. Isopescul notes 'Cheater, Pt. Qal from נכל, deceitful, fraudulent-acting' (1908: 59). The 'cheater' has been designated as such because he offered Yahweh a משחת, a 'faulty and unsuitable animal' (Keil 1868: 441)—the very antithesis of a זכר.

It is essential for the reader to note that the 'cheater' has *originally*

21. H. Brichto, in his study of the curse in the Hebrew Bible notes that the curse here is more indicative of a 'pronouncement of doom' than a 'wish' (1963: 82).

22. See Renker 1979: 70; R. Smith 1984: 310; Glazier-McDonald 1987: 63; Deissler and Delcor 1961: 638; Elliger 1950: 188; Riessler 1911: 280 and Driver n.d.: 307 contra Farrar n.d.: 149.

vowed a blemished animal, even though he had an unblemished one at the moment of initiation. This nuance is often missed by exegetes. They assume that the supplicant originally vowed an unblemished animal only to substitute a blemished one for it at the time of payment. Such an interpretation can be seen in Riessler's 'And cursed is a cheater, who has in his herd a male animal and vows it, but then sacrifices to me an inferior female animal' (1911: 277) or Glazier-McDonald's 'Accursed is the cheat who has a male in his flock, but who, having made a vow, *then* sacrifices a spoiled thing to the Lord' (1987: 45; see also Driver n.d.: 308; emphasis mine).[23]

This translation rests on a rather awkward division of the verse in which the clause ויש בעדרו וכר ונדר is separated from וזבח משחת אדני. This rendering is highly unlikely since the verb נדר is left, uncharacteristically, without an object (leaving the incomprehensible literal translation: 'For he has an unblemished male in his herd and he vows'). Instead, the verse should be broken up more logically by equipping the verb נדר with its object משחת (see text above).[24]

The importance of this verse lies not only its content—the fact that blemished and unblemished animals alike could be vowed to Yahweh—but also in the mechanism of autonomous regulation it tacitly reveals. For at the moment of initiation the supplicant has decided to offer a faulty animal *even though he or she had an unblemished male in the flock*. This suggests that the decision as to what will be vowed to Yahweh, rests solely with the person making the vow. It also bolsters my hypothesis that members of the cultic apparatus need not be present when a petition is being initiated. Apparently, the votary sets his or her own terms—he or she alone regulates the contents, and notably the expense, of what will be offered to Yahweh.

The individual and private nature of votive initiation makes cultic intrusion into this arena close to impossible. As such, there is little that the cultic apparatus can do other than cursing the נוכל.[25]

---

23. Or as Cartledge writes: 'Mal. 1.14 accuses certain "swindlers" of vowing to give an acceptable sheep as a sacrifice, but then offering a blemished one in its place' (1992: 49).

24. For translations similar to mine see R. Smith 1984: 308; Deissler and Delcor 1961: 638; Keil 1868: 441; Renker 1979: 68; Bruno 1957: 179 and Wendel 1931a: 19.

25. For a detailed examination of this point see Chapter 8.

A Woman's Private Vow

The supplicant's right to self-regulate the contents of the vow (and the priesthood's inability to do anything about it), is again tacitly assumed in Numbers 30. This chapter addresses the conditions under which a woman's vow may be annulled. According to the lawmaker, if a woman's father finds out about the content of the vow and 'restrains her' (Num. 30.6: כִּי־הֵנִיא אָבִיהָ אֹתָהּ) then the vow may be invalidated. The same is true if she is married and her husband objects to her vow (Num. 30.9).

For our present purposes one essential point must be delineated. There is no mention of a priest or cultic functionary knowing anything about the woman's vow; it is the husband or father who is tacitly assumed to be the first person to learn about its contents.[26] As in the example from Malachi, the initiation stage of the vow, (that is, when the vow is made) is shown to demonstrate a determined resistance to penetration by priests and religious officials.

This state of affairs has undoubtedly contributed to the variance of items witnessed above. For the cultic personnel do not seem capable of effectively regulating the individual, private interaction with the deity that occurs in the request–promise stage of the vow. With the ecclesiastical authorities unable to monitor the initial dialogue with Yahweh, the supplicant finds herself in the position of vowing what she wants to the cult, though not necessarily what the cult wants.[27]

'The Whore's Fee'

In Deut. 23.19 we receive yet another glimpse at the remarkable degree of autonomy which supplicants exhibited in deciding what they would offer Yahweh. Additionally, the literati apprise us of the abuses inherent to a religious practice which is regulated by laypersons as opposed to the cultic authorities:

26. Thus, the annulment of vows is the unique prerogative of a *layperson* (namely, the father or spouse of the woman) but not a member of the cultic apparatus. Delitzsch was the first to arrive at this insight. He writes:

> But there is no evidence that the priests had the power of releasing from vows. Individual cases in which a husband can dissolve the vow of his wife, and a father the vow of his daughter, are enumerated in Num. 30. (1877: 289)

27. The fact that the Old Testament acknowledges the possibility of the husband or father *not* objecting to the woman's vow (Num. 30.5, 8) confirms the notion of variance discussed on pp. 24-101. For this verse suggests that the male could be confronted by many possible types of inducements offered by his wife or daughter to Yahweh. To some of these he would not object, though to others he certainly would.

לא־תביא אתנן זונה ומחיר כלב
בית יהוה אלהיך לכל־נדר
כי תועבת יהוה אלהיך גם־שניהם

You shall not bring the fee of a whore or the wage of a *dog*[28] to
the temple of Yahweh your God for the payment of any vow. For
both of them are an abomination[29] to Yahweh, your God[30]

Most commentators have maintained that v. 19 is contextually related
and contingent upon v. 18. This conclusion has been reached owing to
the fact that the latter articulates a prohibition against cultic prostitution
in Israel. This has led some to speculate that v. 19 refers to a prostitute,
paying his or her vows with the revenue accrued through some form of
cultic prostitution. G. von Rad, in commenting on both verses, has noted:

> This section has to do with a religious phenomenon alien to Western man,
> but all the more dangerous to early Israel, namely sacral prostitution, which
> was firmly embedded in the fertility cult (Ishtar–Astarte) of the whole
> ancient East from Cyprus to Babylon. Women especially offered them-
> selves to sanctuaries in consequence of a vow (Herodotus I, 199). In addi-
> tion cult prostitutes of both sexes were available at the sanctuaries, which
> acquired money by this means (1966: 147).

28. Opinions vary as to the status of a כלב in ancient Israel. Thomas identifies the
כלב as a respected member of the cultic apparatus, a temple servant, who is faithful as
a dog. Though, in his view this otherwise respectable and commonplace cultic servant
was excluded from the confines of the temple by the Deuteronomist (1960: 426; also
see Mayes 1979: 320). Margalith rejects the metaphorical reading of כלב suggesting
that there is a 'כלב 1' meaning 'dog,' and a 'כלב 2' meaning 'slave or servant'
(1983: 494; but also see Zipor 1987). More recently Brunet has cited Deut. 23.19 as
the sole instance where כלב refers to a human and he opts for the translation 'chien'
(1985: 485-88). Against Thomas, it seems possible, given the tone of the verse, that
the כלב is being referred to pejoratively. The מחיר כלב is again a metaphorical usage,
perhaps functioning meristically. The sense would be: 'be it the fee of a whore or the
wages of a male prostitute' (see below).
29. The phrase תועבת יהוה serves as a relatively indisputable example of what
Weinfeld calls 'Deuteronomic phraseology' (1972b: 323). Yet, while most scholars
are willing to accept the D classification (Driver 1897: 72; Eissfeldt 1965: 224), not all
are in accord with Weinfeld's view that the phrase retains links to the wisdom literature
(1972b: 274). Some are inclined to view the themes found in this section as ancient
ones which were reshaped by the hand of D (Eissfeldt 1965: 224).
30. For a discussion of the phrase גם־שניהם which aims to re-establish the relation
between v. 18 and v. 19, see Merendino 1969: 284-87.

A similar position is espoused by Buis and Leclercq who see a connection between v. 18 and v. 19. The latter verse is viewed as directly expressing the priest's concern that a vow may be paid to the temple with money acquired unscrupulously:

> The law does not only prohibit Israelites from prostituting themselves (v. 18) but also from using sacred prostitutes, even foreign ones; the most likely sense of 'to bring the salary of a prostitute' (v. 19) is, in effect: 'to hire oneself a prostitute'. The ritual Yahwist rejects this custom (Buis and Leclercq 1963: 157)[31]

All of these scholars have predicated their analysis on the belief that 23.18 and 23.19 constitute one legalistic unit. Yet there would seem to be good reason for doubting that v. 18 and v. 19 are directly related to one another. Steuernagel, who was perhaps the first to notice this, remarks:

> The two verses stem from different sources; whereas in v. 18 Israel is spoken of in the 3rd person, in v. 19 it is directly addressed. Verse 18, if taken literally, is superfluous and that is the reason why it is certainly not originally written as a continuation (1900: 86).

G. Boström has pointed out that v. 18 has already forbidden the practice of institutionalized cultic prostitution by Israelites (1935: 111). Who, then, is being referred to in v. 19? Those who wish to see vv. 18 and 19 as parts of one law must come to the following conclusions regarding the meaning of v. 19: while the very existence of cult prostitutes (קדש/קדשה) is forbidden (v. 18), the harlots of v. 19 (כלב/זונה)—whose activities are not expressly forbidden—are simply being told that they may not utilize money acquired through prostitution in order to pay back vows.[32] Could the spirit of this legislation actually concern such a highly specific, and rather unusual, circumstance? Is it possible that this

---

31. See also de Vaux 1965: 466; Driver 1965: 264; Carmichael 1974: 190; Oettli 1893: 83; Bertholet 1899: 73; Schultz 1859: 574; Clamer 1946: 660; G.A. Smith 1950: 275; for the opinion that this verse concerns popular prostitution see van der Toorn 1989: 200.

32. On the term קדשה see Mayer Gruber's article where it is concluded that this term refers to 'a prostitute with no cultic function' (1986: 146). Further, Gruber has convincingly shown that the Akkadian and Canaanite sources do not support the view that the cognate form should be translated as 'a prostitute, cultic or otherwise' (1986: 146). Thus, even if v. 18 and v. 19 are parallels, as most have maintained (but is refuted above), it would be difficult to attach any cultic significance to the זונה and כלב of v. 19.

law has been placed here to prevent prostitutes from paying back their vows with money accrued through their illicit labor?

It seems more likely that v. 18 and v. 19 bear only a superficial relation to one another. As such, the קדשה of v. 18 is distinct from the זונה of v. 19. As Boström has noted:

> The difficulties are only avoided if one sees v. 18 and v. 19 as different cases. Verse 18 speaks about actual temple prostitution. Verse 19, on the other hand, [refers to] 'payment of anyone's vow', that is, it concerns the occasional Aphroditic vow (1935: 111).

The exigencies of Boström's aphroditic cult theory notwithstanding, it seems likely that v. 18 and v. 19 are two distinct laws which have become entangled due to their external thematic similarities (Craigie 1976: 301; 1977: 159). Accordingly, it might be more accurate to examine v. 19 on its own merits and not necessarily as concerning temple prostitution.

It is my opinion that the legislation of v. 19 is targeting a general audience and not only prostitutes. Many of the commentators discussed above have assumed that the 'whore's fee' refers to an actual payment made to a prostitute. Yet the word used in v. 19, אתנן, does not connote tangible, concrete payments or forms of revenue. Rather, אתנן is almost always employed metaphorically. In Ezek. 16.31, 34, and 41, Jerusalem is cast in the role of a metaphorical harlot, so utterly decadent that she pays fees in order to prostitute herself. In Mic. 1.7 we once again learn that Samaria's wealth was symbolically amassed through harlot's fees.[33] In Isa. 23.17 the soon-to-be-resurrected trading port of Tyre will have its fees consecrated to Yahweh.

The point to be noted is that the term אתנן is typically used as a metaphor. It symbolizes wealth that is worthless in that its beneficiaries were not faithful to Yahweh. Nowhere in the Hebrew Bible does it stand as a representation of a tangible sum to be used in mundane commercial transactions.[34] Most importantly, it never refers to the activities of real prostitutes; the Old Testament never tells us that real harlots collect 'whore's fees'.

It is in light of these considerations that I should like to reinterpret Deut. 23.19. It is improbable that the אתנן signifies actual funds earned through prostitution. Rather, in keeping with the figurative usage

33. For a discussion of this phrase in the Micah passage see Loretz 1981: 134-35.
34. For a discussion of this term in Ugaritic see Dietrich and Loretz 1980: 163 and Loretz 1981: 134-35.

discussed above, the writers seem to be scolding any Israelite who promises and pays items to Yahweh which are not sufficiently valuable. They are making reference to the inadequacy of offering Yahweh any item *worth* a 'whore's fee',—votive payments that are in some way inappropriate. Apparently, when setting their own terms many supplicants vowed items that were so base, either in spiritual or economic value, that the religious authorities were forced to respond with this legislation.

In this section the following peculiarities have been observed in the vow-texts. First, biblical Israelites are shown requesting from and offering to Yahweh many different items. This suggests that no fixed set of requests and promises existed from which each supplicant was forced to draw. The wide variance in items, observed across a small set of samples, led me to speculate that many different types of demands and promises must have been made by Israelites.

This point seems to be verified by the three texts discussed above. In each I detected evidence of the literati's belief that supplicants were vowing improper items to Yahweh. This means that there existed no means of controlling or regulating the contents of a vow upon its initiation. Israelite supplicants, I argued, were in complete command of what would be offered and promised to Yahweh. The individual and private nature of votive initiation apparently permitted Israelites to call their own terms and to ask and demand from the deity nearly anything they wanted.

Autonomous Regulation Of Compensation

The capacity of the supplicant to exercise autonomy is not limited solely to the moment of initiation. Votive behavior may be independently controlled right up to the moment of compensation. For, as will be seen, it is solely the supplicant who decides *when* the vow will be paid to Yahweh.

Delayed Compensation (Pious Procrastination)

An examination of the implicit Old Testament evidence indicates that the interval between Yahweh's fulfillment of a vow and the votary's subsequent payment has not been fixed or regulated by the cultic apparatus. Instead, the precise moment of compensation seems to be left to the discretion of the supplicant.

In 2 Sam. 15.7 there appears Absalom's vow, allegedly made while in exile in Geshur. Absalom recounts that he vowed for safe return to

Jerusalem. In 2 Sam. 14.24 it is reported that he did return to the capital. And in 2 Sam. 14.28 it is mentioned that while there, he managed to avoid the King for two years. Thus, a gap of at least two years between his return to Jerusalem and his decision to apprise the king of the contents of his vow can be surmised.

When Absalom did finally get around to fulfilling his vow, a considerable amount of time had elapsed. Simon Parker has remarked:

> More striking, in view of what has already been said about the fulfillment of vows, is the delay of several years between God's fulfillment of the condition of the vow and Absalom's present proposal to fulfill his promise. Here it is necessary to remember the larger narrative context. The request for permission to fulfill his vow is in fact Absalom's pretext for getting excused from Jerusalem to go to Hebron to pursue his seditious purposes. The delay in fulfillment does not arouse David's curiosity or suspicions (1989: 82; also see Cartledge 1992: 33).

That Absalom's vow may have been a fabrication or motivated by desires that were 'not wholly pious' has been noted (Mauchline 1971: 270).[35] For present purposes, however, this text should be viewed as implicitly assuming yet another mechanism of the votive process: the supplicant pays back the deity solely when he or she is ready to do so. As David's reaction indicates, Absalom's delay does not seem out of the ordinary. Nor does the author of this text place any particular emphasis on the importance of remitting vows immediately.

Similarly, Jephthah does not feel obliged to fulfill immediately his obligation to Yahweh. In Judg. 11.37 his daughter requests *an extension* of two months before being sacrificed as a burnt offering (?). In v. 38 the fabled judge *grants* his daughter this period of clemency (לכי). What is most striking in this passage is that it is again the supplicant who decides when Yahweh shall receive his compensation.

It could be argued, however, that the ideological impulses of the literati have surfaced in these passages. Jephthah and Absalom are not perfect Yahwists and thus a depiction of their belated compensation may serve as a means of underscoring their lack of proper piety. Accordingly, the argument could be raised that this is not implicit evidence but explicit evidence serving the polemical ends of the authors of the Old Testament.

This argument is neutralized by the fact that Hannah engages in pre-

35. See also Fokkelman 1981: 171; Pirot and Clamer 1955: 520; Keil and Delitzsch 1880: 416; H.P. Smith 1899: 341; A.A. Anderson 1989: 196 and Parker 1989: 83.

cisely the same behavior. In 1 Sam. 1.22 Hannah decides to wait until her child is weaned before paying back her vow to Yahweh.[36] Scholars have been quick to point to 2 Macc. 7.27 as evidence that this process could conceivably take as long as three years.[37] The beloved matron, mother of the renowned prophet Samuel, can certainly not be considered to be breaching any cultic regulations. Accordingly, it is doubtful that the literati have explicitly placed this mechanism in the text. In 'delaying' the payment of her vow Hannah is not breaking any rules. For neither Hannah, *nor the literati*, knows of a law which requires that vows must be paid back immediately.

Of especial interest then, is the conscious act of self-regulation witnessed in the cases of Hannah, Jephthah and Absalom. Each decides to postpone the payment of the vow until the moment when it is convenient for them. Further, neither seems to entertain any fear of being punished for delaying the moment of compensation. It would seem that this 'delayed compensation' is another aspect of the votive procedure that the cultic authorities cannot or will not regulate.

Regulated Compensation?

In the later, legislative sections of the Old Testament there is further affirmation of the fact that the cultic apparatus does not regulate the time of votive payment. For while there are many regulations about the manner in which vows should be paid and many regulations about the specific time when various other sacrifices are to be paid, it is impossible to identify any rule that specifies when a vow should be paid back to the deity.

In Numbers 29 and Leviticus 23 there is detailed legislation which aspires to regulate the precise moments when certain public sacrifices are to be offered to Yahweh. Numbers 29 informs us that offerings are to be made on the first day of the seventh month (Num. 29.1), the tenth day of the seventh month (Num. 29.7-11), and so on. In v. 39, the last verse of the chapter, the following 'subscript' appears (Milgrom 1990: 249):

36. As opposed to paying the vow with Elkanah at his yearly trip to Shiloh (1 Sam. 1.22).

37. Thenius 1842: 6; Hertzberg 1964: 28; Klein 1983: 10; Keil and Delitzsch 1880: 26; van Zyl 1984: 160; or see H. Smith (1899: 12) who, on the basis of Arabic parallels, suggests a weaning period of two years.

39   אלה תעשו ליהוה במועדיכם
                                                    לבד מנדריכם ונדבתיכם לעלתיכם
                                                  ולמנחתיכם ולנסכיכם ולשלמיכם

39a   These you shall offer to Yahweh at the stated times
39b   *aside from* your votive fulfillments and your freewill offerings,
          be they your burnt offerings your grain offerings your libations
          or your *šlmym* offerings

Verse 39a takes as its antecedent all the sacrifices to be offered on the
specific days mentioned in the first 38 verses of this chapter. Yet 39b
addresses a wholly different religious act. This verse is prefaced with the
preposition לבד מ, which most commentators have translated as 'apart
from', 'besides' (McNeile 1911: 161; Greenstone 1939: 311; Kennedy
n.d.: 357), 'indépendamment' (Clamer 1946: 432), 'abgesehen von'
(Baentsch 1903: 647). Thus, the phrase לבד מנדריכם sets the votive (and
freewill) offering apart from all of the other sacrifices mentioned earlier
in this chapter.

This distinction is certainly merited since the נדר and the נדבה, unlike
the sacrifices mentioned in vv. 1-39a, need not be offered on any particular, cultically-appointed day. As Gray has noted, the votive and the
freewill offering '*may* be offered on the same days' referred to in the
rest of the chapter (1976: 412; emphasis mine). Yet here, as in the nearly
identical legislation of Lev. 23.38, regulations mandating that vows must
be paid back on a specific day are not to be found. The author seems to
be suggesting that these offerings can be paid back on *any* of the aforementioned dates, amongst others, 'if found more convenient' (Greenstone
1939: 311; see also Cartledge 1992: 29 n.1).

Thus, in a text that mandates specific times at which offerings are to
be presented, the literati do not demand that votive compensation take
place at any particular moment. This absence of legislation regarding
when a vow should be paid again indicates that the supplicants themselves decided when they would fulfill their vows.

Conclusion

Temples, children and ill-fated towns are not the kinds of commodities
that most people are capable of offering, or are likely to have any reason
to pledge, to their deities. If the Old Testament vow-texts were to be
read explicitly an inevitable conclusion would be that the majority of
Israelites simply could not afford to participate in the votive system. It

has been a methodological initiative of this study, however, to avoid taking the explicit statements of the literati as accurate portrayals of Israelite religious life. In my introduction, I suggested that there exists an abundance of relevant information about the votive system that is not directly reported by the literati. This data comprises a part of their assumptive world and hence is not directly stated. For these reasons I did not concentrate on what Hannah or Jacob offered Yahweh since I believe that the authors of the Old Testament had very good reasons for wanting their readers to know this information.

When taken together the biblical vow-texts demonstrate that Israelites promised Yahweh very different items. The tremendous diversity of incentives made to Yahweh (witnessed across only twenty cases) led me to conclude that there existed no circumscribed set of promises and demands that Israelites were required to draw from when making a vow. Instead, I theorized that supplicants were free to self-regulate the contents of their petitions to Yahweh. By the same token, this evidence suggests that the literati did not know of a votive system in which just a few items were permitted to be promised to the deity.

This state of affairs is undoubtedly a consequence of the individual and private nature of votive initiation. Since the initiation stage could not be easily monitored or controlled by members of the cultic apparatus, very little prevented the Israelite supplicant from offering Yahweh nearly anything he or she saw as appropriate. Of course, from the point of view of the religious authorities such incentives were often worth nothing more than a 'whore's fee'.

That the cultic apparatus had little control over the supplicant's demands and promises was illustrated in the three passages examined above (namely, Mal. 1.14; Num. 30; Deut. 23.19). Each case served to prove that for whatever reasons—individual dishonesty, inefficient administration or ineffective means of social control given the private and individual nature of votive initiation—the supplicant, and not the priest, decides what will be offered to Yahweh. It is this right to 'set one's own terms' that I refer to as the mechanism of autonomous regulation of content.

In the preceding section, it was shown that the interval between Yahweh's fulfillment of a request and the subject's compensation varies from case to case. This would seem to suggest that there existed no 'time limit', or standardized 'deadline' for paying back a vow. The texts examined in this chapter attest to the fact that the precise moment of compensation is to be decided by the votary. A vow is paid when the worshipper, as opposed to the cultic apparatus, deems it convenient. The supplicant's right to decide independently when the deity will be compensated is referred to as the mechanism of autonomous regulation of compensation.

Part II

THE EXPLICIT EVIDENCE AND ACCESSIBILITY

Chapter 5

INCLUSION AND ECONOMIC ACCESSIBILITY

> Thus, in summary, one can say that no restrictions existed as regards the kind of person making the vow. Everyone can vow, from a child to an old man, from a higher-up to a slave, men and women (Adolf Wendel, *Das Israelitisch-Jüdische Gelübde*).

Inclusion

In earlier chapters I have analysed various Old Testament and extra-biblical vow-texts with an eye towards extracting what I refer to as 'mechanisms'. In order to identify these mechanisms I have scrutinized various passages for information which the literati never directly articulate, but tacitly assume. It has been maintained that this implicit evidence retains a certain degree of independence from the ideological statements of theocratic historians.

There is also an entirely different species of evidence preserved in the Old Testament. It consists not of unwritten assumptions but of explicitly stated 'facts', specifically, facts which the Yahwistic literati wanted their readers to know. As noted in my introduction, the accuracy of 'facts' served up by theocratic historians is always susceptible to question. This explicit information cannot be accepted at face value. Instead, it must be contrasted and juxtaposed with the implicit evidence which has been wrested from the text.

In the next three chapters I shall concentrate on this explicit evidence and attempt to analyse it in light of the tacitly-assumed mechanisms discussed in Part I. With both explicit and implicit evidence at our disposal, the conclusion of each of the these chapters will be devoted to a discussion of the accessibility of the Israelite vow.

'*Anyone*'

What types of supplicants did the literati have in mind when they discussed vows? Was the votive procedure they wished to present only reserved for exemplary Yahwists such as Hannah, patriarchs such as Jacob, children of royalty like Absalom, or great warriors of the stature of Jephthah? Or do they furnish the reader with a portrait of a highly inclusive votive system, one that invited the participation of any person, regardless of their wealth, prestige, power, lineage or social esteem?

In v. 18b of Leviticus 22 there is a legislative passage which goes a long way towards answering all these questions:

18b	איש איש מבית ישראל ומן־הגר בישראל
	אשר יקריב קרבנו לכל־נדריהם
	ולכל־נדבותם אשר־יקריבו ליהוה לעלה
19	לרצנכם תמים זכר בבקר בכשבים ובעזים

18b　　When anyone of the house of Israel or of the strangers in Israel
　　　　presents his offering for any of their vows, or any of their
　　　　freewill offerings that they offer to Yahweh as a burnt offering—

19　　　to be acceptable in your favor[1] it must be a male without blemish
　　　　from the cattle, sheep or goats

In this legislation from the Holiness Code there appears the intriguing idiomatic expression, איש איש, translated by most commentators as 'anyone'.[2]

A cross-textual examination of this phrase, which appears nineteen times in the Old Testament (eleven times in the book of Leviticus alone), generally bears out this interpretation. In most of its appearances this construction retains a meaning similar to the one found in Lev. 17.10: 'And if anyone (איש איש) of the house of Israel or of the strangers who reside among them partakes of the blood...' This same meaning is undoubtedly intended in other texts where the phrase appears (Lev. 17.3, 8, 13; 18.6; 20.2, 9; 24.15; Num. 5.12; 9.10; Ezek. 14.4, 7). In some cases, however, a translation of 'any man' might be more appropriate (see Lev. 15.2; Num. 5.12).

When viewed through a sociological optic the audience addressed by this law is theoretically unlimited. The use of the term איש איש suggests that this legislation takes as its subject all the manifold social elements that may be encompassed by this sociologically imprecise pronoun. As Heinsich has noted:

1.　For a discussion of the term לרצנכם see Levine 1989: 6.
2.　Snaith 1967: 148; Chapman and Streane 1914: 122; Noth 1965: 158; Heinsich 1935: 100; Clamer 1946: 165; Baentsch 1903: 410; Hoffmann 1906: 110 and Elliger 1966: 294.

This law, in its contents as well as its title, addresses not only the priests but all Israelites—indeed even the resident alien who wanted to make a sacrifice to Yahweh (1935: 100).

In Leviticus 27 there is a late Priestly document which also portrays the votive system as open to a broad spectrum of social elements:

1   וידבר יהוה אל־משה לאמר:

2   דבר אל־בני ישראל ואמרת אלהם
         איש כי יפלא נדר בערכך נפשת ליהוה

3   והיה ערכך הזכר מבן עשרים שנה ועד בן־ששים שנה
         והיה ערכך חמשים שקל כסף בשקל הקדש

4   ואם־נקבה הוא והיה ערכך שלשים שקל

8   ואם־מך הוא מערכך
         והעמידו לפני הכהן והעריך אתו הכהן
         על־פי אשר תשיג יד הנדר יעריכנו הכהן

1   Yahweh spoke to Moses, saying:

2   'Speak to the Israelites and say to them: "When *any man* makes
         a *special vow*[3] to Yahweh for the [fixed] equivalent of a human
         being,[4] the following scale shall apply:

3.   For a discussion of this term see Appendix 2.
4.   Speiser identifies the final ך as 'a pronominal suffix that became fossilized
and thus absorbed in the nominal stem' (1960: 30). Following Speiser, Levine has
shown that this bound form, which literally means 'your equivalent', is best translated
as 'equivalent' (1989: 30, 193). Levine has also identified the phenomenology of the
practice at hand:

> In the commutation system of Leviticus, chapter 27, the object was to secure silver for
> the cultic establishment to be expended on various needs. The objects actually devoted
> were not being actively sought...It is therefore proper to translate 'erekekā as: 'the
> equivalent', since this term refers to the imputation of value according to another
> standard or unit. It was apparently traditional in biblical society that one intending to
> make a contribution to the temple and cult would state that he was devoting his
> possessions, or himself, to the service of Yahweh, and not merely a specified amount of
> silver (1974: 96-97; but see Wenham's interesting suggestion that the prices quoted in
> vv. 3-7 actually refer to the aforetime price of slaves [1978: 264]).

I have opted for a slightly more nuanced translation of this term as '[fixed]
equivalent'. This is based on A. Gianto's analysis of a similar phrase in the Mulk
inscription of Nebi Yunis. Gianto notes:

> The word '*arakōt* (plural of the unattested singular 'rk of Hebrew '*ērek*) is a technical
> term for officially fixed sums or valuations—not free contributions—to be paid off...
> The sum or valuation corresponds to a certain obligation, such as a tax, a fine, or a

3   If it is a male from twenty to sixty years of age then the [fixed] equivalent is fifty shekels of silver by the sanctuary weight

4   If it is a female then the [fixed] equivalent is thirty shekels

8   But if one cannot afford the [fixed] equivalent he shall be presented before the priest and the priest shall assess him—according to what the vower can afford[5] (the priest shall assess him)"'.

Of interest here is the phrase כי איש which some translators have rendered simply as 'man'.[6] Others have offered a somewhat different interpretation that seems to capture more accurately the author's intent. Thus P. Heinsich translates: 'When any person vows the estimated value to Yahweh... (1935: 123). Among English-speaking translators, B. Levine also recognized this nuance in translating 'When *anyone* explicitly vows to the Lord... (1989: 193; emphasis mine; see also Clamer 1946: 201 and Bertholet 1901: 97).[7]

In Numbers 15 the proper procedure for remitting a burnt offering or sacrifice as a payment for the vow (or freewill offering) is explained (15.3-16). As with the two previously cited texts, the authors have made use of language directed at the widest possible section of the populace. In v. 13 the term כל אזרח, 'all native born [Israelites]' appears. (See

vow...Lev. 27, which lists various kinds of valuation ('*ērek*) corresponding to various vows (*neder*), points to such a practice. (1987: 400; see also Delavault and Lemaire 1976: 576)

Thus, it seems likely that the 'equivalent' in Lev. 27 was *fixed* in correspondence to the person or object vowed. While it is difficult to make sense of this passage, it seems that the equivalent is based on a conversion from the original item promised by the supplicant. As such, this does not threaten the notion of autonomous regulation of content. Insofar as this passage knows of different items which are originally vowed and *later* (that is, at the time of payment) converted to the fixed equivalent, it still seems likely that when formulating their petitions supplicants were naming their own terms.

    5.   תשיג יד from the root נשג. Levine has noted that the phrase literally means 'Which the hand of the vower can reach' (1989: 194).

    6.   See Snaith 1967: 174; Chapman and Streane 1914: 151; Noth 1965: 202; Kennedy n.d.: 177; Kalisch 1872: 614 and Kellogg 1891: 542.

    7.   There is, however, ample reason to suppose that this expression simply means 'any man', and not 'any one'. See Milgrom 1990: 250 and Greenstone 1939: 313 for rabbinic evidence suggesting that this term does not refer to women and minors. As will be seen in Chapter 7, it is likely that this particular passage refers specifically to men.

Noth 1968: 112; Budd 1984: 165; McNeile 1911: 80; Greenstone 1939: 155; Heinisch 1936: 61). Like איש איש, discussed above, this expression refers to an extremely broad social constituency.

However, this legislative section does not confine itself solely to addressing the אזרח. In vv. 14-16 it is made clear that the same laws are applicable to the גר (the stranger). In other contexts the combination of the two terms גר and כל אזרח (that is, 'all native born [Israelites]' and 'strangers') frequently designates that a law is binding upon everyone.[8] For instance, Lev. 17.15a reads וכל־נפש אשר תאכל נבלה וטרפה באזרח ובגר, 'Any person, whether citizen or stranger, who eats what has died or what has been torn by beasts...' (see also Josh. 8.33; Lev. 16.29; 18.26; 24.22). Hence, it is safe to conclude that when גר and כל אזרח are used together they function as a merism, connoting the entire Israelite populace—citizen and stranger, rich and poor, male and female, and so on.

This same theme of inclusiveness—of the vow being accessible to all human beings—is reiterated in a different literary environment. Psalm 65.2-3 reads:

2	לך דמיה תהלה אלהים בציון ולך ישלם־נדר
3	שמע תפלה עדיך כל־בשר יבאו

2	To You praise is fitting[9] Oh God in Zion and vows shall be fulfilled to You
3	You who hear prayer, all humanity comes to you

The term used in v. 3, כל בשר, carries various meanings, such as 'all creatures', 'all living beings', 'all humanity' and 'all flesh'. In his comprehensive study of this usage, however, A.R. Hulst has noted: 'To God comes *kol baśar*, says 65.3; it is men that are being referred to' (1958: 51). As in other legalistic texts, this poetic–liturgical selection portrays the making of vows as something which 'all humanity' may engage in.

---

8. For a similar occurrence in a vow-text see Lev. 22.18.

9. The term דמה seems best translated by the notion of praise 'being fitting' for Yahweh. A.A. Anderson has noted that this connotation can be identified in talmudic texts (1972: 465; for similar translations see Oesterley 1953: 310; Schmidt 1934: 121; Wutz 1925: 161). Some have argued for a similar translation, albeit one based solely on context, since the etymology of this root is apparently inexplicable (Halévy 1905: 184), while others have offered completely different translations (for example, Dahood's translation of דמה as 'mighty castle', giving, 'praise to you in the mighty castle' [1968: 110]).

In reviewing the findings of this section the following may be said: the root נדר is often found in Priestly legislative texts which take as their audience 'anyone', 'any man', 'all native born Israelites' and 'all humanity'. The very inclusiveness of such terms suggests that they were directed to the widest possible section of Israelite society. The literati, then, either know of a votive system which correlates to such a state of affairs, or for various ideological reasons have fabricated one for the pages of the Old Testament.

Economic Standing

As we have just seen, the Old Testament authors seem to stress the fact that the votive system is inclusive. Any Israelite, they seem to suggest, may initiate a vow to Yahweh. In what remains of this chapter, I should like to re-examine some of the evidence discussed above. This time, however, I shall attenuate my analysis to focus on the biblical authors' reports regarding personal wealth and its relation to votive praxis. In so doing, I shall demonstrate that from an *economic* point of view this portrait of inclusion remains consistent throughout the Old Testament vow-texts; in the biblical authors' view anyone, regardless of their economic standing, may initiate a petition to Yahweh.

The Non-Privileged Strata

In Lev. 27.8 it is made clear that participation in the votive system was not solely restricted to wealthy Israelites. This verse relates the proper procedures to be observed when poor persons cannot pay back their vows. It reads: 'But if one cannot afford (הוא מם־מך ואם) the [fixed] equivalent he shall be presented before the priest and the priest shall assess him—according to what the vower can afford (the priest shall assess him)'. The word used here is מך, which B. Levine has traced back to the related roots מוך and מכך, meaning 'to be in straits'. He writes: 'the sense is that of "reduction" to poverty' (1989: 175).

This law concerns the regulations to be followed by the priest when encountering Israelites who may have vowed beyond their means, or perhaps, who were unaware exactly how much the '[fixed] equivalent' would actually cost them.[10] This cultic flexibility towards the poor can

---

10. As Levine notes: 'In situations where the denial of ritual expiation would render vowers and offenders seriously disabled, and adversely affect their standing as members of the Israelite community, accommodations became necessary' (1974: 109).

occasionally be witnessed in other instances where the worshipper simply cannot pay the fixed price. In Lev. 14.21, for example, the subject who 'is poor and his means are insufficient', also pays whatever he can afford. (The idiom used here, תשיג יד, is the same as that found in Lev. 27.8.)

In sum, the איש of Leviticus 27, when measured by economic criteria, could indeed be 'anyone'.[11] Whoever this person is, it is clear that he or she cannot afford what most other Israelites (mentioned in vv. 1-7) can. As such, v. 8 demonstrates that the literati either believed, or wanted it to be believed, that poor persons could make vows in ancient Israel.[12] Taken at face value this text also indicates that the priests had institutionalized a policy for handling economically disadvantaged votaries.

Another interesting portrait of the vowing 'rights' of the poor can be found in Numbers 15. Verses 14-15 read:

> And when a stranger [that] shall live with you or amongst you throughout the ages will present an offering by fire of pleasing odor to Yahweh as you do, so shall it be done, 15 [by the] congregation. There shall be one law for you and for the stranger, an eternal law throughout the ages, you and the stranger shall be alike before the Lord.

This text, which concerns itself with the type of offerings to be given for a vow or a freewill offering (v. 3), offers a revealing glimpse into the

11. Alison Grant has engaged in a statistical survey of the form איש in the Old Testament. Out of 2174 attestations it refers to 'anyone or everyone belonging to a particular group (sex or nation or other defined group)' 1427 times (1977: 2). In other instances, however, the word איש by itself, carries a socially-specific definition. Kutler has identified a variety of specialized meanings for the term, such as 'retainer, soldier, husband or resident' (1980: 56). Elsewhere, איש connotes a male with some type of special status or profession, such as an 'elite soldier' (Kutler 1982: 69). Yet a meaning that signifies a person with specialized skills or social status certainly does not seem to be suggested in the passage examined above. Rather, it would seem that the term here is aimed at the broadest possible demographic constituency.

12. Nevertheless, this passage may not serve as an accurate representation of the economic identity of pre-exilic votaries. For in the opinion of most scholars, this Priestly text stems from an age far removed from this period (Eissfeldt 1965: 189; Driver 1897: 59; De Vaux 1965: 466; Benzinger 1927: 377; Kennedy n.d.: 177). G. von Rad has noted the 'rationalising substitution of a monetary payment for sacrifice' inherent in this account (1962: 262), while Noth, who viewed this chapter as a late supplement, speaks of the 'considerably advanced "secularization" of the cultic apparatus' (1968: 204). C. Meyers, however, in a brilliant analysis of the socio-economic and gender dynamics of this text, has argued for a much earlier dating of the passage (1988: 170-72; see also Meyers 1983).

literati's conception of the economic accessibility of the vow. For, as I noted above, this legislative section does not confine itself to addressing simply the citizen (אזרח), but the stranger (גר) as well.

That one law concerning the offering of vows is applicable to both the stranger and the citizen is quite revealing given the economic position occupied by the former in Israelite society. William Robertson Smith's discussion of this term yielded the opinion that the גר was 'personally free but had no political rights' (1972: 75; see also Weber 1967: 35-36). In a detailed discussion of this issue, J. Milgrom notes: 'Although some *gerim* did manage to amass wealth (Lev. 25.37), most were poor and were bracketed with the poor as recipients of welfare (cf. Lev. 19.10; 23.22; 25.6)' (1990: 398). B. Levine has observed that legislative terms directed at the גרים were often also used on those 'who suffered from lack of legal redress, such as the poor, the widow and the orphan, along with the foreigner' (1989: 134).

Another dimension of the socio-economic position of the גר was underscored in Mayer Sulzberger's seminal, yet overlooked, study of labor in ancient Israel. In Sulzberger's estimation the גר is not 'merely an alien outsider(s) visiting the country or temporarily sojourning in it', but '*the* great labor force of the Hebrew commonwealth' (1923: 25,31).

In Numbers 15, then, the literati give us two explicit details indicating that even the poorest elements of Israelite society could participate in the votive system.[13] First, as noted above, the interplay of the terms גר and כל אזרח would seem to include the entire population of ancient Israel in the votive system. Secondly, this text assumes that the גרים a politically and legally powerless strata of economically non-privileged laborers, make vows.[14]

In Jonah 1 there is another depiction of non-privileged persons participating in the votive system. What makes this text so interesting, is the fact that the supplicants here are actually the מלחים or 'sailors' mentioned in v. 5. It must be stressed that the vowers in this case are anonymous, ordinary individuals, who do not possess great wealth.[15]

---

13. Thus, it should come as no surprise that there is Punic as well as Palmyrene evidence which indicates that slaves also made vows. See *KAI* 79 and *PNO* 14:5.

14. It should be mentioned that this is another late priestly text (Gray 1906: 168; Heinsich 1936: 63; McNeile 1911: 79; Budd 1984: 166; Noth 1968: 114; Eissfeldt 1965: 189). Nearly all the evidence suggesting that the non-privileged strata made vows emanates from the post-exilic period.

15. See Chapter 4 for a discussion of this vow.

Interestingly, a similar state of affairs can be identified in a late Punic votive stelae. A certain Cleon, a worker or perhaps an overseer in a salt mine (אש בממלהת), vows a copper altar to the deity.[16]

Conclusion: Non-Privileged Economic Strata

In this chapter it has been shown that as far as the Old Testament literati were concerned, 'anyone' could make a vow in ancient Israel. This point was demonstrated through an examination of various laws regarding the procedures for votive payment. The laws examined employ highly inclusive terminology when discussing this practice. These texts yield the impression that no particular demographic category was obstructed from initiating a petition to Yahweh.

Once this theme of inclusion was identified I proceeded to concentrate solely on the relationship between the vow and the non-privileged classes of ancient Israel. Did the literati, in their sporadic explicit statements on the subject, also depict indigent supplicants as being permitted to make vows? My results suggest that they did. The clearest instance is furnished by Lev. 27.8, where the authors of the Old Testament acknowledge that the priest may conceivably encounter a supplicant who cannot afford the 'fixed equivalent'.

A similar conclusion could be deduced from Num. 15.14. Here, it is intimated that the גר—a social element that the literati usually categorize with the poor—could also engage in this religious act. Elsewhere, ordinary sailors make a vow to Yahweh. In the literati's view then, great wealth was not a prerequisite for the making of a vow to the God of Israel.

My review of the explicit data regarding the economic identity of votaries is now complete. This information now needs to be analysed in light of the tacitly-assumed mechanisms discovered in Part I. I shall begin with the observation that both our implicit and explicit evidence seem to lead to the identical conclusion: poor Israelites could and did make vows in ancient Israel.

In Chapter 4 I called attention to the mechanism of 'autonomous regulation of content'. The supplicant had the right to decide what he or she would request from and promise to the deity. The existence of this mechanism makes the case for the economic accessibility of the vow increasingly plausible. Since votaries may offer the deity what they want,

16. *KAI* 66 = *CIS* 143 = *NE* 427b = *KI* 59 = *NSI* 40.

or, to put it more concretely, what they can afford, their economic standing does not in and of itself constitute an obstacle to the initiation of a vow.

A poor person who desperately wants a child, for example, may offer Yahweh an incentive commensurate with his or her current fiscal capabilities. Of course, had there existed external criteria (namely, ones imposed by the religious authorities) as to what *must* be offered to Yahweh, such a supplicant might have had great difficulty participating in this particular religious act. This ability to self-regulate what exactly it is that Yahweh is to receive suggests that the making of vows was not restricted solely to those who could afford a potentially restrictive 'standard fee'.

It has also been noted that supplicants autonomously decide *when* the deity is to receive his or her just compensation. There appears to be no 'time limit' for the payment of a vow (that is, 'autonomous regulation of compensation'). Since immediate payment is not—or cannot be—demanded by the religious authorities it would seem that this practice would be quite alluring to economically non-privileged Israelites. The period which elapsed during the weaning of a child (as in the case of Hannah) or for bemoaning one's impending death and virginity (Jephthah's daughter), might have been used by less celebrated Israelites to accumulate the capital required for the payment of the vow.

It is possible to imagine the case of a hypothetical supplicant not possessing great wealth, nor great status within his community. A situation of need arises and he feels sufficiently motivated to petition Yahweh for a rather expensive request. He is fully aware at the moment of the vow's initiation that should the request actually be granted, he will be permitted to spend as much time as necessary in gathering the resources required for the payment of his costly promise. This renders the vow economically accessible, since the worshipper knows that there is no sanction or stigma attached to the individual who requires an extended period of time to pay back vows.

If the situation were such that the cultic apparatus insisted that vows be paid back *one day* after they are granted by Yahweh, one could easily argue for the economic restrictiveness of this practice. For the supplicant would be forced to vow solely within his or her *present* fiscal means, which might indeed be meager. Yet as has been seen, payment to Yahweh can be made when the supplicant's economic situation permits him or her to do so, as opposed to when the cult demands payment.

I should also like to mention that the votive process permits the individual to espouse a sort of 'easy come, easy go' attitude—one that makes the vow appear to be *subjectively* accessible. Should a vow not be fulfilled by Yahweh, the supplicant fully understands that absolutely nothing has been lost. For the initiation of a petition does not require any form of 'up-front' material commitment (see also Cartledge 1992: 136). Accordingly, the votary is in a 'no lose' situation; should the deity be impervious to his or her pleas the supplicant has incurred no material loss. This particular mechanism of the Israelite vow, leads me to speculate that poor Israelites may have *frequently* turned to the vow.

In Chapter 3 I looked at two examples of east Semitic vows. While in no way representative of all vows in this milieu, a comparison with this system opens up the possibility of less accessible alternatives to the northwest Semitic votive system. These texts reveal a mechanism in which votive initiation was written as opposed to oral. Given the high rates of illiteracy in this period, it may be surmised that trained scribes composed the petitions of east Semitic votaries. Thus, it is plausible to assume that some sort of compensation would be owed to the scribes or temple personnel who assisted in the initiation of the vow.

Yet in the oral northwest Semitic system, the votary need not advance any material resources for the potentially costly services of scribes, temple advisors, writing materials and so on. For, as has already been noted, this spoken petition can be made in complete solitude. Moreover, the making of a vow demands no fiscal commitment from the supplicant, and again this would seem to facilitate the widespread participation of indigent Israelites.

To this point then, I have yet to identify any aspect of the votive process which might be potentially restrictive to members of non-privileged economic strata. Non-privileged economic standing does not seem to be an obstacle to taking part in the Israelite votive system. Insofar as *both* the implicit and explicit data point to participation in the votive system by the poor, it is difficult to imagine that the making of vows was the unique prerogative of privileged economic strata. Instead, it seems likely that 'anyone' who needed something from the deity, regardless of their economic status, could petition Yahweh for assistance.

Chapter 6

SOCIAL ACCESSIBILITY

In contrast to the purely economically determined 'class situation' we
wish to designate as 'status situation' every typical component of the life
fate of men that is determined by a specific, positive or negative, social
estimation of *honor* (M. Weber, 'Class, Status, Party' [1958]).

Heterodox Elements

It has been shown that the authors of the Old Testament write of a
votive system that invites the participation of even the most indigent
Israelites. As far as the literati were concerned, a person's economic
standing did not preclude him or her from making a vow. This explicit
evidence corroborated my earlier findings based on implicit evidence:
both led me to conclude that economically non-privileged strata actively
participated in the votive procedure.

Since I have already discussed in detail the economic identities of the
biblical supplicants, I shall now widen the parameters of my inquiry to
include an examination of their social identities. In particular, I am interested in examining this issue with reference to the relative 'Yahwist
standing' of the votaries. Those seen engaging in this practice often
receive a positive or negative estimation of honor from the Old Testament authors. What do the sources explicitly relate about the votive
behavior of heterodoxies, those who are not in good 'Yahwist standing'?

My analysis will employ the same format used in the previous chapter.
First, I shall examine the (rather scant) explicit evidence in which vows
are made by heterodox persons. This evidence will then be analysed in
light of the tacitly-assumed mechanisms discovered in Part I. In so doing,
I shall be able to generate a hypothesis regarding the participation of
heterodox elements in the Israelite votive system.

Good and Bad Yahwists

In the epic vows exemplary devotees of Yahweh are often portrayed as making petitions to their God. An example is pious Hannah, whose steadfast devotion to her deity is beyond question. There is also the patriarch Jacob, as well as Jephthah, brave defender of the Yahwistic faith. The somewhat less celebrated—but equally pious—Elkanah, husband of Hannah, is also depicted as making a vow. His observance of a yearly ritual brings him and his family to Shiloh.[1] In this passage (1 Sam. 1.21) the authors of the Old Testament offer their audience a model of a good Yahwist, responsibly fulfilling his votive duties:

ויעל האיש אלקנה וכל־ביתו

לזבח ליהוה את־זבח הימים ואת־נדרו

So this man, Elkanah, and his entire household went up to
sacrifice to Yahweh the annual slain offering[2] as well as his vow[3]

Yet, the literati do not hesitate to offer examples of non-exemplary Yahwists engaging in exactly the same practice as honorable Elkanah, pious Hannah and others. Individuals who are not devout and who have been accorded a 'negative social estimation of honor' (Weber 1958:187) by the authors of the Old Testament, are also depicted as participating in the votive procedure.

In Prov. 7.14 there appears a woman apparently in the process of accosting a young man. After having kissed the boy she says:

זבחי שלמים עלי

היום שלמתי נדרי

'Slain offerings of *šelāmîm* I owe,[4] today I fulfilled my vows'[5]

1.   Contrary to the opinion of some commentators, Elkanah's sojourn has nothing to do with the repayment of Hannah's original vow (Hertzberg 1964: 28; contra H.P. Smith 1899: 12; Stoebe 1973: 99-100). There are no biblical vows where the person who makes the vow dispatches someone else to pay it. Clearly, Hannah is intent on compensating the deity in person, a task which is accomplished in v. 24.

2.   For an excellent discussion of the term זבח הימים see Levine 1974: 132-35.

3.   On the discrepancies between the LXX and MT versions see McCarter 1980: 55. ואת־נדרו is a Masoretic addition, yet as Eslinger has noted, variants of the LXX leave us just as puzzled as to what exactly Elkanah is doing (1985: 85). For a comparison of the Greek and Hebrew texts of 1 Sam. 1 see Walters 1988.

4.   On the translation 'slain' see G.B. Gray 1971: 6; see also van der Weiden 1970: 69. To be rejected is Scott's translation, 'I have sacrificial meat on hand' (1965: 64) which seems completely incongruous with any of the words in this verse. As Stuart has pointed out, the term עלי, when used in this sense, refers to a 'duty' or

Over the last fifty years exegetes have attempted to determine the social identity of the woman featured in this cryptic verse. Some have suggested that the person in question is a prostitute (Thompson 1963: 105 n. 5; Levine 1974: 42). G. Boström advanced the ambitious theory that the solicitous woman was a foreigner and a member of an aphroditic cult. Consequently, her behavior is an expression of a ritualistic act of cultic prostitution (Boström 1935).

Boström's theory has been upheld by some commentators (for example, McKane 1970: 331-40; H. Ringgren and Zimmerli 1962: 35-36), while others have contested his reading of this difficult passage. L.A. Snijders, in examining the term אשה זרה, has concluded that the woman is not a foreign devotee of an exotic cult, but a native Israelite who is actually viewed as a social deviant: 'In our opinion "*zara*" indicates the aspect of the "deviating", the unfaithfulness with respect to her "house", community and Jhwh' (1954: 104).

Recently, Karel van der Toorn has argued that while this woman is indeed prostituting herself, this is not her normal status. As will be seen in the next chapter, it is van der Toorn's hypothesis that this woman is an ordinary Israelite supplicant who engages in this practice only as a last resort. Other scholars have refrained from portraying the woman as

an 'obligation' (1852: 210). This interpretation is demanded by the context if the assumption is made that the biblical writer is àware of the legislation of Lev. 7.16 which requires that the sacrifice be eaten on the day that it is offered. For similar usages see Num. 30.7, 9, 15. Most scholars have accepted this view (Toy 1904: 150; Greenstone 1950: 72; Levine 1974: 42; Ringgren and Zimmerli 1962: 34). Oesterley translates 'sacrifices of peace offerings are with me' (1929: 52). Levine makes the suggestion that the זבחי שלמים may have served as an accompaniment to another gift being offered by the votary (1974: 43).

5.   In order to support his theory of a foreign cultic prostitute about to entice a young man to engage in a ritualistic act, Boström maintained that שלמתי could be translated modally ('I must fulfill', 'heute löse ich meine Gelübde ein...' 1935: 105). Van der Toorn has recently defended this translation: 'This modal use of the afformative is sparingly but sufficiently attested in Hebrew' (1989: 198). While he also accepts this translation in order to further his theory that a poor Israelite is resorting to prostitution in order to pay her vows, the evidence for such a practice is still slim (see Chapter 7). It seems more likely that the woman in question has already paid her vows and is using the lure of the sacrificial meal as a device for appealing to the religious sensibilities of the young man (but see McKane 1970: 337, for a review of this argument). Thus, when the woman says 'slain offerings of *šelāmîm* I owe', she may be referring to the fact that she is obliged to consume the meal on this day (cf. Lev. 7.16).

a professional or temporary prostitute. Instead, they maintain that she is an Israelite adulteress (Oesterley 1929: 50; Toy 1904: 149; Barucq 1964: 83; Delitzsch 1890: 163).

In the last few years, some commentators have abandoned any attempt at pinpointing the social identity of this individual. Instead, they wish to concentrate on the larger symbolic role she plays within Proverbs and the world-view of the Old Testament literati. Philip Nel, for example, has taken the זרה of chapter 7 as 'symbolized evil' (1982: 120). Thus, this woman does not represent a practitioner of an ignoble profession, so much as the power of evil in its dialectical relation to wisdom.

Claudia Camp has perhaps made the most significant contribution to the argument by pointing out that the true social identity of the woman may simply be beyond our grasp. Like Nel, Camp opts for a more metaphorical interpretation of this figure:

> This variation and ambiguity, combined both with the apparently typical laissez-faire attitude in Israel toward prostitutes and with the failure of any other biblical authors to stereotype *real* women negatively (even harlots), recommends the conclusion that this poetic figure in Proverbs is a stereotype, a crystallized picture of the attractions and dangers of any and every sexually liminal woman; it does not portray a particular real person or class of persons (1985: 116).

In a later article Camp adds:

> We must be clear, however, that neither Proverbs 2 nor 7 is attempting to describe the actions of a particular given woman. The language of deviant sexual behavior *is* being used symbolically, but not as a mere cipher for deviant worship. Rather, it is a symbol of the forces deemed destructive of patriarchal control of family, property, and society. Because control of women's sexuality is a sine qua non of the patriarchal family, it is no accident that the forces of 'chaos' are embodied in a woman who takes control of her own sexuality (1991: 27).

Following Camp and Nel, I prefer to underscore the more generalized *symbolic significance* of the woman portrayed in Proverbs 7. Whether she is a prostitute, devotee of a foreign cult, temporary prostitute or an adulteress, there seems little doubt that the writers of this text deplore this person. She is singled out as an object of derision because she does not conform to the precepts of a correct Yahwistic life.

Yet even though this character is held in such utter contempt and even though she personifies those qualities which the literati clearly abhor, *she is nevertheless depicted as making a vow*. Accordingly, her

status as a non-exemplary Yahwist does not prohibit her from participating in the votive system. A similar state of affairs can be identified in
Jer. 44.25. Here, the backsliding ex-Judaeans are mockingly encouraged
to fulfill their vows. As has already been seen, these expatriate Judaean
women are making vows to the Queen of Heaven, not Yahweh.[6]

Thus, the authors of the Old Testament explicitly relate that heterodox
elements make vows. Apparently, there is no correlation between the
leading of a correct and pious Yahwistic life and the right to engage in
this practice. Petitioning Yahweh is not the unique prerogative of exemplary Yahwists, nor is it a privilege earned through steadfast devotion to
the deity. Instead, the literati believe—or want us to believe—that any
one, regardless of their fidelity to this deity, may initiate a vow.

Conclusion: Heterodoxies

Unfortunately, the Old Testament does not offer very much explicit
evidence regarding vows made by heterodox individuals or groups.
Jeremiah's mocking denunciation permits access to the Old Testament
authors' view that ex-Yahwists had the right to make vows. The vow of
the Israelite woman examined above also suggests that the literati believed
that impious persons may engage in this religious practice. Aside from
these two examples, there is very little explicit evidence regarding heterodox vows. If forced to rely solely on this data, it would be difficult to say
much about the participation of heterodoxies in this religious practice.

Bearing this in mind, I shall nevertheless advance the following hypothesis: heterodox Israelites could, and did, make vows to Yahweh and
other deities. The initial impetus for making this statement is provided by
the two explicit examples cited above. This evidence points to the
possibility that members of heterodoxies could participate in this religious act. As a means of substantiating this claim, however, I shall need to
engage in an examination of mechanisms and accessibility. In so doing, I
shall be able to offer an explanation as to *why* the votive system may
have been accessible to these Israelites.

The fact that a vow may be first, made individually, secondly, made
privately (that is, not in the presence of the cultic apparatus) and thirdly,
spoken directly to the deity, would theoretically permit heterodox
Israelites to take an active part in the votive process. As noted in
Chapters 1 and 2, a vow may be initiated in complete solitude—away

6. See Chapter 3.

from the supervisory glances of the religious authorities. The indirect route to divine ears—via the priest or any other intermediary—is unknown to the authors of the Old Testament vow-texts. In Chapter 3, it was observed that a simple act of speech is all that it takes for anyone to petition the gods. The votary's right to use his or her own mouth when vowing to Yahweh again underscores the radical autonomy that the unique structure of the votive system permits its patrons. For neither the mouth of the priest nor the hand of the scribe is needed to initiate a vow.

The heterodox votary in a Yahwist society certainly benefited from the right to avoid any contact with priests or other members of the community. It may be easily imagined how a clandestine worshipper of Baal, living in a community where a Yahwistic 'official religion' is in place, need not fear that he or she will be discovered making a vow to the 'wrong' god. As such, heterodox individuals are the beneficiaries of the anonymity granted by the votive system. Even if the existence of a community comprised mostly of pious Yahwists were postulated, it can be imagined that heterodox individuals could make their vows to the goddess Asherah with impunity.

The mechanisms described above permit not only the participation of heterodox individuals, but heterodox impulses, made by otherwise pious persons, to be expressed. A preposterous demand—such as an elderly, childless woman vowing for a son—need not be subjected to the scrutiny, and consequently the strictures, of other members of the community. The unorthodox desire remains the 'little secret' of the supplicant and her deity. It is only upon the unlikely fulfillment of the far-fetched request that the supplicant will feel obliged to divulge the contents of her vow.

Accordingly, the three mechanisms discussed above taken together proffer all types of incentives to members of heterodoxies. For there is no *social* price to pay for making a vow. Words spoken in solitude are comparatively unproblematic. Nobody is around to monitor them, to tax them, or to devote them to memory. This includes priests, scribes (as in the written east-Semitic system discussed in Chapter 3), intrusive neighbors, pernickety moralists and others who by virtue of their presence would somehow alter the contents of a person's vow. Votive initiation, quite simply, is the supplicant's affair; if he or she so chooses, no other member of society needs to know that a vow has even been made.

Before closing this chapter, I should like to discuss how one other type of heterodox element may have had a special affinity for the vow.

Here, I am speaking about persons who, by the standards of their day, were morally unscrupulous. In this study it has been repeatedly demonstrated that if the supplicant is so inclined, he or she may abuse the Israelite votive system. All these abuses are facilitated by the aforementioned administrative anonymity of this practice. That is, if one were to perceive that his or her vow had been fulfilled, there is nothing—other than honor—which prevents that person from paying the deity less than promised, or even nothing at all. As noted in Chapter 4, the practice under consideration allowed the supplicant as much time as he or she desires in paying back the vow. It may be assumed, then, that some would exploit this loophole by postponing the payment of their vow indefinitely. Since a vow can be made privately, away from the supervision of the cultic apparatus, it may also be imagined that some were less than generous when it came to making a promise to the deity. Such individuals, it could be speculated, would not hesitate in promising Yahweh an item worth a 'whore's fee'.

The private nature of votive initiation as well as the fact that it costs nothing could engender one final abuse: a person could petition Yahweh endlessly, every day, every hour on the hour.[7] It goes without saying that the content of such vows did not have to concern itself with offspring or victory in battle, but a variety of superfluous amenities whose nature and form may only begin to be imagined.

If such a scheme seems far-fetched to the reader, it must be stressed that it certainly did not to the biblical authors. The fact that such liberties were taken is more than adequately attested in the various sapiential exhortations to be examined in Chapter 8. The Old Testament's considerable concern with transgressions such as these suggests that some, at least, took advantage of the considerable autonomy offered by the votive system. Needless to say, I do not assume that every supplicant sought to defraud the cultic apparatus. Here, I have only tried to demonstrate that the very constitution of this procedure provided the morally marginal to take almost unparalleled liberties with Yahweh and his earthly representatives.

---

7. Cartledge opines: 'People did not make vows to request minor favors or to avoid effort when they had other options...vows were employed when divine intervention was perceived as essential' (1992: 27). While such a state of affairs is suggested by the explicit evidence, the implicit evidence leads to speculation in different directions.

The authors of the Old Testament explicitly tell us that both good *and* bad Yahwists make vows. An analysis of the implicit evidence reveals how and why this may have been so. It seems that the Israelite votive system is quite well tailored to any individual who, for whatever reasons, wished to avoid contact with representatives of the 'official religion'. By allowing the supplicant to avert any encounter with the religious authorities, this practice must have been highly accessible to those harboring sympathies for deities other than Yahweh or those who worshipped him in an unorthodox manner. Accordingly, one's level of devotion to Yahweh does not appear to have any bearing upon a person's right to initiate a vow.

Chapter 7

WOMEN AND THE VOW:
ANOTHER CRITIQUE OF EXPLICIT EVIDENCE

> Of possible greater significance for an understanding of women's religious participation and the total religious life of the community is the hidden realm of women's rituals and devotions that take place entirely within the domestic sphere and/or in the company of other women (P. Bird, 'The Place of Women in the Israelite Cultus').

Women and the Vow: A Re-evaluation

Biblical scholars have often made the observation that women actively participated in the Israelite votive system. C. Brekelmans speaks of the tendency of women 'to take vows quite frequently' (1963: 2553). Wendel writes: 'Women, in particular, seem to have been quite quick to make vows' (1931a: 25). Löhr opines: 'As regards the vow...women seem to have possessed a remarkable freedom' (1908: 38). And Karel van der Toorn remarks:

> In the margins of the official cult, Israelite women often engaged intensively in religious activities of various kinds. Vows ranked especially high in their devotional life (1989: 204).[1]

All these exegetes have reached this conclusion, in large part, by focusing on biblical passages that explicitly refer to women making vows. Since the vow-texts which they have examined feature female supplicants, they have maintained that *women in general* actively took part in this practice.

I should like to devote this chapter to re-appraising not so much this conclusion, but the means by which it was reached. I shall argue that the *quantity* of explicit evidence which unequivocally supports the claim that

---

1. Other researchers have also examined various Old Testament vow-texts with an eye towards demonstrating that women frequently engaged in this religious practice (Peritz 1898: 127-29; Otwell 1977: 170; Gruber 1987: 38).

women made vows in ancient Israel is actually quite small. Too small, in fact, to warrant drawing this connection between the vow and women. Furthermore, when looked at as a whole, the vow-texts that we possess are often contradictory or ambiguous regarding women's votive behavior.

This chapter, then, serves to underscore some of the advantages of the methodology forwarded in this research. As will been seen, a study based on explicit details alone would not necessarily prove that women frequently made vows in ancient Israel. It is only when the explicit approach is supplemented by an analysis of the implicit evidence that this conclusion gains in plausibility.

Hannah's Vow

Since there is no Ugaritic evidence which testifies to vows made by women I shall begin my analysis by turning to the Old Testament. In 1 Samuel 1 the literati furnish us with a portrait of a woman making her vow independently of both her husband and the Yahwistic priesthood.[2] C.J. Vos remarks: 'There seems to be no hesitancy on her [Hannah's] part to approach Yahweh directly and independently' (1968: 152). Hannah does not ask her husband Elkanah's permission to make the vow, nor to pay it back to Yahweh. This behavior does not seem consonant with the late legislation of Numbers 30 where it is stated that a husband has the right to annul his wife's vows should he 'hear' about them. As Löhr has noted :

> In no way will the possibility be raised in the text that Elkanah could object to the vow. On the contrary, if one reads the entire narrative with unbiased judgment one must agree with the two cited verses that the husband remains fully in the background. Hannah, it appears, possesses a thoroughly unrestricted freedom to make a vow (1908: 38; also see Emmerson 1989: 381).[3]

2.   See Chapter 2.

3.   This discrepancy with the legislation of Num. 30 has led some scholars to conclude that the P source evinces a new tendency to limit a woman's right to engage in cultic practices (Peritz 1898: 114; Löhr 1908: 38-40). This viewpoint has been contested by Gruber, who has cogently argued that P permits women greater participation in cultic activity than had originally been thought (1987), though it would seem that our data are presently too limited to yield any conclusions as to a trans-historical decrease or increase in the rights of the female votary.

How can Elkanah's silence in this episode be explained? Either this text was authored prior to the legislation of Numbers 30 and its author does not know of such regulations, or Elkanah had heard the vow, but did not object to it. Or perhaps Hannah had never told her husband about the vow and thus he could not raise any objection. While, I would incline towards the first of these explanations, it is safe to say that there is simply not enough evidence to draw any firm conclusions.

The Evidence from Deuteronomy

Apart from Hannah's vow, there are no other epic vows which feature women supplicants. Most of our remaining evidence consists of legalistic passages concerning various aspects of votive praxis. In Deuteronomy 12 it is reported that votive contributions must be consumed 'before Yahweh your God...in the place that Yahweh your God will choose' (Deut. 12.18). This entire section (vv. 12-18) utilizes second-person singular masculine forms, as well as masculine pronominal suffixes in addressing the hypothetical subject. In vv. 11-13 the passage is essentially reiterated, and here the listener is addressed with second-person plural masculine forms. Once again, masculine pronominal suffixes are employed.

The argument could conceivably be made that only men are being addressed by these laws, and therefore by the time of D women are not assumed to be participants in the votive system. Some commentators, however, have suggested that the wives of the men are also being addressed in this passage, albeit tacitly (Knobel 1861: 259; G.A. Smith 1950: 167). While I would agree with this assessment, it must be stressed that nothing in this passage *explicitly* states that women were allowed to make vows.

P's Partiality

It becomes increasingly apparent when reading P that explicit testimony regarding women's vows is quite limited. In fact, after examining P's votive legislation one could conceivably come to the conclusion that women rarely ever made vows.

The vow-texts of Lev. 27.2; 22.21, and Num. 30.3 are all prefaced by the idiomatic expression כי איש, 'when a man'. This term has often been translated as 'when anyone' or 'when a person'.[4] In Num. 30.4, for the

---

4.   In Chapter 5 I argued that such terms were inclusive and most likely referred to women as well. In this chapter, however, I am attempting to prove a point about the

first and only time in the Old Testament, the expression כי אישה, 'when a woman', is encountered. Accordingly, it does not seem perfectly accurate to conclude that the term א יש כי is gender-neutral. Given that the legislation of Lev. 27.2 and 22.21 uses the term אש כי, but not כי אישה, while Num. 30.3-4 uses both, it could be argued that only the latter verse actually addresses women votaries.

Lev. 7.16 also persistently utilizes the masculine possessive pronominal suffix when discussing the nature of sacrifice performed in fulfillment of a vow. By the same token, Num. 15.3-16; 29.39 and Lev. 23.38 all make use of masculine verbs, and in particular, masculine pronominal suffixes when referring to this practice.

It is probable that the failure to mention women in these passages is due to the sociologically imprecise nature of legal terminology. It would not be unreasonable to suggest that these texts, while grammatically addressed to men, actually intend to address women as well. In this chapter, however, I am attempting to demonstrate the inherent limitations of the explicit approach. For these reasons, I again emphasize that with the exception of Numbers 30, not a single law from P can be said to demonstrate clearly the participation of women in the votive system.

The majority of scholars who argue that the vow was commonly practiced by women have yet to confront this claim. Instead, many have pointed to Num. 6.2, where it is stated that women may initiate Nazirite vows. This evidence is often forwarded as a means of showing that women could make vows with the same frequency and aplomb as their male co-religionists. Ismar Peritz, in his groundbreaking article 'Woman in the Ancient Hebrew Cult', suggested that since female votaries could take Nazirite vows, it stands to reason that the use of masculine forms in the passages cited above should not be read literally:

> In view of this clear evidence of woman's participation in the Nazirite vow, we have reason to suppose that woman is included in the legislation of the ordinary vow (Nu. 15.1-3), although we find it in a general way addressed to man without specific mention of woman (1898: 128-29).

It must be stressed, however, that a Nazirite vow is quite different in its formal mechanics from an 'ordinary', positive vow.[5] The former is a

drawbacks of the explicit method. Namely, that the explicit evidence will make little sense unless supplemented by implicit evidence. For these reasons, I am engaging in an unyieldingly explicit reading of the data. My goal is to show how infrequent unequivocal attestations of women's participation in the votive system actually are.

5.   See Appendix 1 for a discussion of this issue.

negative vow of personal consecration made to Yahweh; it makes no particular demands, and is essentially a symbol of one's devotion to the deity. The positive vow, on the other hand, is a somewhat selfish, promise made by a worshipper who *needs some tangible item or outcome*. In its structure and content it is quite different from the vow of a Nazirite.

It should also be mentioned that none of the male-oriented legislation discussed above seems to be interested in legislating Nazirite vows. Rather, these laws are only concerned with regulating various sacrificial aspects of the positive vow. In light of these observations, it must be concluded that female participation in the Nazirite vow does not necessarily prove female participation in the positive vow.

The question then remains: where in P do we find irrefutable evidence of women making vows? The answer has been sought, quite justifiably, in Numbers 30. Here, a detailed passage articulates the fact that the father or husband of a woman may annul her vows on the day on which he 'hears' about them (Num. 30.4-7).[6] Conversely, if a man hears about the vow of his wife or daughter and offers no objection, then her vows shall stand (Num. 30.7-9).

Some exegetes reason that this chapter demonstrates a state of gender inequality. Milgrom notes: 'This law reflects the sociological reality that women in biblical days were subservient to their fathers or husbands' (1990: 250).[7] Another explanation for this law can be sought in the fact that males wished to wield some degree of social control over women in their immediate environment. Two facts dovetail nicely to support this explanation. First, as P. Hiebert has perceptively observed, the widow (אלמנה) of Num. 30:10 'has no male authority figure to pass judgment on the validity of her vow' (1989: 130; see also E. MacDonald 1931: 59, 65; Peritz 1898: 129; Vos 1968: 93). In the same verse it is also noted that a divorcee does not require any sort of affirmation from a male in order to carry out her vows. Accordingly, the legislation does not seek to restrict women in general, but only those women who reside under the 'jurisdiction' of a male.

The text in question seems to give two distinct messages concerning

---

6.   For a discussion on the effects of redaction on the basic original motifs of this text see Wendel 1931a: 25.

7.   A more severe assessment is rendered by Clamer:

'The Jewish woman, in fact, almost always found herself in a state of dependence vis-à-vis a man, be it her husband when she was not married, be it her husband when she was' (1946: 433).

the vowing rights of ancient Israelite women. One the one hand, it clearly demonstrates that in some capacity the rights of the male are greater than those of the female. No male, as far as we can tell, can have his vow annulled by his father, mother or wife (Gruber 1987: 38; Boström 1935: 113; also see Ruether 1982: 56).

It seems clear that the votive rights of men and women are characterized by a fundamental asymmetry. Yet, it should also be recalled that while the vowing rights depicted in Numbers 30 are not indicative of a state of equality, the fact that women can make vows is of some significance. They are, after all, permitted to initiate the dialogue with Yahweh in privacy and without the prior approval of a male. This would suggest that women had the freedom to make a variety of economic decisions in the form of the necessary inducements and enticements which are offered to the deity.[8]

Additionally, as Löhr has noted, the power of the male to annul the vow is certainly not all-encompassing; there exist definite restrictions which are placed on *his* right to reject a woman's petition (1908: 38). First, he must annul the vow on the day he finds out about it. Should he wait any longer than this period his objection will no longer be binding (v. 15). Secondly, at no place in this text is it stated that a woman is required to tell a man about her vow; one might speculate that many vows could have been concealed in this manner by the female supplicant.

The Evidence From Proverbs
Two other instances of vows made by biblical women are found in the book of Proverbs. In Proverbs 31, a text whose resemblances to Egyptian wisdom literature have been noted (McKane 1970: 407), there appear the instructions of a mother to her royal son. In verse two she begins his lesson with the following words:

2   מה־ברי ומה־בר־בטני ומה בר־נדרי[9]

2   No, my son[10], No, son of my wombs, No, son of my vows[11]

---

8.   See Chapter 4.

9.   She calls him בר נדרי. The construct state is formed with the Aramaism בר (Barucq 1964: 228; Oesterley 1929: 281; contra Stuart 1852: 422), and the plural נדרי, literally 'son of my vows'.

10.   The proper translation of the particle מה has caused all sorts of difficulties. Scott offers the rather bulky 'How now my son' (1965: 183). Dahood, when looking at attestations of this word in the Keret Epic, translates 'What ails my son' (1963: 60). While others have opted for the typical Hebrew usage 'what my son' (Stuart

The Book of Proverbs features one more vow-text in which a woman is seen participating in the votive system (Prov. 7.14). In this passage there is a characterization of an adulteress (?) who is alleged to have made a vow. More will be said about this passage later.[12]

This brings me to the Phoenician and Punic sources. Many of these texts clearly demonstrate the participation of women in the votive system.[13] *KAI* 109 suffices as a typical expression of this phenomenon:

1	לאדן לבעל חמן מלך
2	אמר נדר אש נדר א
3	[ ] כברת בת

1	To the Lord, to Baal Hamon, a sacrifice of a
2	lamb (?)[14] A vow which AKBRT
3	daughter of [ ] vowed.

Such vows made by women, while not comprising nearly one half of all Phoenician and Punic votive texts, nevertheless occur frequently enough to indicate that women in these cultures did actively participate in the votive system.

The Illicit Female Vow
To this point it has been observed that there is very little explicit biblical evidence regarding women as votaries. Further, nearly all the legislation regarding the vow is couched in language which, on the surface at least, is intended solely for males. In this last section I should like to delineate another reason why the explicit evidence should be treated with suspicion.

When looked at as a whole the portraits of women votaries evince a sort of representational polarity. In the account of Hannah's vow there appears a pious matriarch, one who obviously possesses the approval of the biblical literati. There seems little doubt that this devout Yahwist, who approaches the deity with the utmost respect and who gives birth

1852: 421; Toy 1904: 539; Greenstone 1950: 330). I prefer the translation 'No my son' since it fits nicely with the beginning of v. 3, which is also a negative command (see Barucq 1964: 228).

11. Most commentators have compared this vow to that of Hannah's (Scott 1965: 184; Oesterely 1929: 281; Stuart 1852: 422; Toy 1904: 540; Greenstone 1950: 330).

12. See the preceding chapter for textual exegesis.

13. See *KAI* 40, 87, 88, 155, 164 and *CIS* 378 and 515 for examples.

14. The reading of this word is somewhat controversial, though it does not change the fact that a woman is making a vow. The reader is conveniently referred to *EH* 55 and *KAI* 109 for extended discussions of the exegetical history of this phrase.

to one of Israel's most celebrated personas, receives a glowing literary depiction. Yet the hagiographic reception accorded to this woman is rather exceptional. In two other vow-texts, the reader is confronted with images of women who are anything but devout Yahwists.

In Jeremiah 44 the prophet's excoriation of a clan of Judaeans living in Egypt reveals that a group of women routinely made vows to the Queen of Heaven. In v. 25 the prophet exclaims:

25b

אתם ונשיכם
ותדברנה בפיכם ובידיכם מלאתם
לאמר עשה נעשה את־נדרינו אשר נדרנו
לקטר למלכת השמים
ולהסך לה נסכים
הקים תקימנה[15] את־נדריכם
ועשה תעשינה את־נדריכם

25b   'You and your wives have spoken with your mouths and
        executed [it] with your hands, saying: "we will certainly fulfill
        our vows to burn incense[16] to the Queen of Heaven, and to pour
        out libations to her." Fulfill your vows! Carry out your vows[17]!'

Jeremiah's reference to 'wives' in v. 25 is consonant with the opinion of this chapter, emphasized repeatedly, that women in particular are worshippers of this goddess. In v. 15 'all the men who knew that *their wives* made offerings to other gods respond to Jeremiah's gloomy augury. In vv. 17 and 20 women are mentioned as taking part in 'the insolent response' (Delcor 1982: 103) to the prophet, while v. 19 seems to suggest that, in accordance with the law of Num. 30.4-17, the men

15. On the peculiarity of this feminine form see Keil 1872: 428.

16. Carroll has suggested that קטר retains the meaning of 'to burn', as in sacrifice (1986: 740).

17. The usage here of the verbs קמה and עשה provides an interesting insight into votive terminology. The latter is attested in Deut. 23.24 in relation to vows. As such, it may more or less confidently be concluded that עשה in the context of a vow-text refers to the fulfillment of a vow. As for קמה, it also appears in a vow-text (Num. 30.5, 6, 8, 12, 15). There, however, it refers to the fact that the woman's vow shall stand. As such the usage of the verb seen in Jer. 44.25 as 'fulfill' is entirely different. Working from analogies it seems certain that קמה can be used in relation to *the fulfillment* of an oath or covenant (Deut. 8.18; 1 Kgs 6 and 12; Gen. 26.3; Jer. 23.20). Hence, it is likely that here it also refers to the fulfillment of a vow. As Wendel notes, this latter connotation seems to be a peculiarity of the *hiphil* (1931a: 98).

had ratified their wives' vows.[18] In v. 24 it is again specifically noted that women constitute part of the group which Jeremiah is about to address angrily.

Which brings me back to v. 25, where the prophet prefaces his remarks with the words 'you and your wives'. In fact, LXX reads 'You women', and as such the address might have been pointedly directed at only one sex (Bright 1965: 262; Weiser 1955: 377; Dennefeld 1946: 372). Thus, in this passage the literati make a vigorous association between heterodoxy, women and the making of vows.[19] It should be added that their sympathies obviously lie with the exasperated prophet who repeatedly singles out these women in his scornful rebukes.

Similarly, in Prov. 7.14 there is a depiction of a female votary whom the literati clearly abhor. As has been seen in the preceding chapter, this passage features a woman who is apparently attempting to lure a young man into sexual activity. K. van der Toorn has maintained that this scene sheds light on various aspects of women's everyday religious life. He views this woman not as a prostitute, but as an average Israelite woman who engages in a form of temporary prostitution as a means of accruing the necessary revenue required to remit one of her vows (1989: 198-99). Against this interpretation, I should like to argue that the character depicted in this passage should not be construed as typical or representative of Israelite women.

Van der Toorn asserts that in ancient Israel 'women, often short of means to keep their solemn engagements toward the deity, were frequently led to prostitute themselves in order to fulfill their vows' (1989: 193).[20] The married woman in Prov. 7.14 is seen as engaging in this behavior not because she is a member of a sexual cult, and not because

18. The women seem to be insinuating that they are only partly guilty (Peake n.d.a: 206).

19. S. Ackerman has suggested that the worship of this goddess constituted a significant component of women's religion (1989: 110; see also Ackerman 1992: 11; Bright 1965: 265; Bennett 1895: 201). For an examination of the private character of this cult see Weinfeld 1972a: 153.

20. Crucial to his theory is the assumption that in Prov. 7.14 the woman is speaking to the young man in the present tense. Following Boström's exegetical lead, it is suggested that the adulteress is not saying 'I have fulfilled my vows' but 'I must fulfill' or 'I am going to fulfill' (van der Toorn 1989: 198). For the original statement of this position see Boström 1935: 106-10. See Chapter 6 for a philological examination of this verse.

she is an adulteress and therefore wants to, but because she has to. Van der Toorn writes:

> In my opinion, her vows were ordinary vows. She is confronted with a problem. How is she going to fulfill her vows? Apparently, *the term of her engagement has expired* and the promised offerings are *due* today. What can she do? Her husband, she explains, has gone on a long journey; he took the bag of money with him, and will not be home until full moon (vv. 19-20)... The only way out that she can think of, or so she suggests, is prostitution. Of course, she is no common whore! (1989: 198 [emphasis mine]; see also Garrett 1990)

Van der Toorn goes on to argue that such a scenario must have occurred frequently in the lives of Israelite women. As corroborating evidence he points to Numbers 30 where it is stipulated that a woman's vow had to be approved by her husband or father:

> Ordinarily, vows were paid in movable goods, and there is no reason to assume that this was different in the case of women. In her case, though, it was her father or husband who had to furnish the promised goods. Without means of her own, the woman was forced to rely on her father or husband for the fulfillment of her vow. Since the latter had a stake in the matter, he was entitled to a say as to the validity of the vow. A woman could have her reasons, however, for hiding her vow from her husband. *When the time of payment had come*, she found herself in an awkward position. Unless she resorted to prostitution as a way to acquire the necessary means, she had to retract her promise, which was considered a very serious offense (Deut. 23:22[21]; Eccl 5:3) (1989: 200 [emphasis mine])

Van der Toorn has yet to explain why Numbers 30 can be adduced as support for his prostitution theory. In this chapter it is revealed that the father or husband annuls the conditions of the vow—what is requested and what is offered. He does not, however, concern himself with *the means* by which the vow should be paid.

I should also like to suggest that van der Toorn's argument underestimates the capacity of women to earn income through non-sexual activity. Even if the premise is accepted that a woman could find herself in a situation where she does not have the necessary means to fulfill her vow, the question as to why her only recourse would be to sell her body must be posed. A myriad of other revenue-enhancing activities could be expected to have been practised by such an individual.[21]

---

21. Van der Toorn also points to Deut. 23.18-19, where the subject is warned not to bring a 'whore's fee' into the temple in fulfillment of a vow. Yet, as argued earlier,

Also problematic are van der Toorn's repeated references to deadlines or time limits for the payment of the vow. In the passage quoted above, van der Toorn refers to the 'terms of her engagement' expiring. But where in the Old Testament is there a set time limit regarding votive compensation? As has already been shown, the supplicant is allowed to self-regulate the moment of votive remittance. It seems unlikely that the woman could have been running out of time, and was forced to go to the kind of drastic eleventh-hour lengths to fulfill her vow, as van der Toorn suggests.

Lastly, I should like to state that van der Toorn has not taken into consideration the very real possibility that the literati are offering a distorted and biased portrait of a type of woman which they do not like. It seems clear that the reader is being here confronted with an instance of the 'negative female imagery' discussed in the preceding chapter (Camp 1985: 115-16). In a recent refutation of van der Toorn's theory Camp observes:

> Against van der Toorn, I think it is unlikely that we should imagine a social situation in which married women regularly engaged in acts of harlotry... what information we have about the postexilic period suggests to me that in Proverbs 7 we are confronting not a social reality of wanton wives but rather a sociopsychological reality of men threatened by a multiply stressed social situation, including internal religio-political power struggles, economically oppressive foreign rule, and the pressures of cultural assimilation (1991: 28-29).

I agree with Camp's assessment. This figure stands as a sort of 'ideal type' image of the dangerous woman. In Proverbs 5 involvement with such a person is portrayed as spawning the most awful of destinies. There is absolutely no reason to believe that the authors of Proverbs 7 would be immune from offering a similarly figurative and polemical presentation of a sexually active woman.

With these considerations in mind, it should be stressed that the literati have offered neither a rounded nor a dependable portrait of women's votive behavior. As the Hannah episode, Jer. 44.25 and Prov. 7.14 indicate, when it comes to woman as supplicant, we are more likely to receive hyperbole than accurate data. A sort of 'virgin/whore' complex

the biblical term 'whore's fee' does not refer to a tangible cash transaction. Instead, it stands as a metaphor for the practice of bringing inadequate items to the temple as payment for the vow. See Chapter 5 for evidence, as well as a refutation of the widespread belief that this verse concerns itself with prostitution.

has surfaced, whose parameters are demarcated by opposites: pious matriarch is against the whore or backslider. As such, I find it difficult to accept that the explicit information related in these texts offers much insight into the dynamics of normative women's piety in ancient Israel.

Conclusion: Women

Many scholars who have used the explicit approach have concluded that women frequently made vows in ancient Israel. My own re-evaluation of this data has served to qualify and problematize this conclusion.

While the Old Testament furnishes a generous supply of vow-texts only a few of these directly refer to women. With the exception of Numbers 30, none of the legal passages makes specific reference to female votaries. Texts such as Lev. 27.2 and 22.21 seem specifically to *exclude* women from this practice—a state of affairs which stands in contrast to testimony received in Proverbs and 1 Samuel.

Aside from its contradictory nature, this same evidence is susceptible to the charge of offering distorted portraits of female supplicants. Those women who are depicted as making vows are either models of piety or exemplars of Yahwistic infidelity. Taken at face value these stereotypical depictions do not permit the drawing of any precise inferences regarding the types of Israelite women who engaged in this practice. They also arouse the suspicion that the misogynist assumptions of the (male) literati saturate their accounts of votive activity.

If forced to rely solely on the sparse and equivocal data discussed in this chapter, I would draw the following conclusion: women did indeed make vows in ancient Israel, though it is impossible to make any judgment as to the *extent* to which they participated in this practice. This claim is substantially different from that reached by those scholars cited above. The latter spoke of Israelite women who 'frequently' and enthusiastically engaged in this particular practice.

Both the preceding conclusions are predicated solely on explicit evidence. And here again one of the primary drawbacks of the explicit approach is encountered: its complete lack of explanatory power. This method fails to elucidate, in any way, *why* women may have been attracted to this particular religious act. It is only when the explicit evidence is combined with an analysis of the implicit data that a convincing case for women's intense participation in the votive system may be put forward. By coupling these species of evidence I shall attempt to suggest two interrelated hypotheses which may explain this circumstance.

In her article 'The Place of Women in the Israelite Cultus' Phyllis Bird makes reference to 'the hidden realm of women's rituals and devotions that take place entirely within the domestic sphere and/or in the company of other women' (1987: 409). The notion of the domestic or private sphere offers a useful analytical tool for the study of Israelite women and the vow. A few brief orientating remarks on research into the public/private distinction will thus be necessary.

Anthropologist Rayna Reiter's observation in her study of a village in the Southern French Alps serves as a good example of the type of gender stratification often witnessed in the public and private domains:

> Private and public forms of sociability were clues to the very different lives of women and men. Women spend their time working and living within a realm that is defined as their own, which has many informal prerogatives attached to it, the realm of their households. It is a domain quite distinct from the more public, highly differentiated spheres where men predominate in activities within the economy, politics, or the church. (1975: 253; see also Rosaldo 1974; Lamphere 1974; Rogers 1975: 733, 735, 745; Nicholson 1982)

In an important article on this issue, M.Z. Rosaldo calls attention to an often encountered sexual asymmetry in which 'the vast majority of opportunities for public influence and prestige, the ability to forge relationships, determine enmities, speak up in public, use or forswear the use of force are all recognized as men's privilege and right' (1980: 394; see also Bird 1991: 105).

Among biblical scholars, Phyllis Bird has perhaps gone further than any other in applying this dualistic model to the study of Israelite religion. Bird writes:

> In all of the primary institutions of the public sphere, which is the male sphere, women have limited or marginal roles, if any. Thus leadership roles in the official cultus are rarely women's roles or occupied by women. Conversely, however, women's religious activities—and needs—tend to center in the domestic realm and relate to women's sexually determined work. As a consequence, those institutions and activities which appear from public records or male perspective as central may be viewed quite differently by women, who may see them as inaccessible, restricting, irrelevant, or censuring (1987: 400).

In the comment which heads this chapter Bird raises the possibility that much, though not all, of the religious life of Israelite women may have been concentrated in this 'private sphere'.

The quotations above present the reader with only a cursory introduction to research on the relation of women to the public and private
spheres. It must be stressed that an intense debate has raged among
feminist scholars concerning the efficacy, proper application and basic
assumptions of this paradigm. Some researchers have challenged notions
regarding the alleged powerlessness of women within this sphere (for
example, Rogers 1975; Rosaldo 1980: 394; Tilly 1978: 172). In a study
of peasant societies Susan Carol Rogers has called attention to the ways
in which women exert power *throughout* their communities by using
the domestic sphere as a sort of base of operations (1975: 733, 735; see
also Meyers, 1988: 173-181; Jobling 1991: 244).

Carol Meyers notes a tendency for the 'private/public' distinction to
become so analytically rigid as to blind us to the considerable interactions which occur between these two spheres (Meyers 1988: 32; see
also Dubois *et al.* 1985: 113).[22] Others have expressed concerns about
the political dangers inherent in employing such a model. As Ellen Carol
Dubois and her colleagues opine: 'By using this public/private distinction
are we reenforcing the oppression we are trying to remedy?' (1985: 113).
Finally, Sylvia Junko Yanagisako speaks of 'an emerging consensus that
this dichotomy is analytically unproductive and empirically unfounded'
(1979: 191; contra Nicholson 1982: 734; also see Rapp 1979).

With all of these valid qualifiers and objections kept in mind, it is still
possible to make a claim which is more or less unproblematic. It does
not seem implausible to assume that in ancient Israel, as in many other
societies, women were typically relegated to the domestic or private
sphere (Meyers 1988: 43, 174) and constrained to lead lives which were
qualitatively less public than those of their male co-religionists. This state
of affairs goes a long way towards explaining why women may have
been inclined to participate in the votive system.

According to the Old Testament authors, the making of vows is as a
legitimate act of Yahwistic devotion. This conclusion may be inferred
from the numerous legislative passages in which proper forms of votive
payment are discussed by these theocratic historians. What makes the
vow somewhat distinct, however, is that while it is 'officially sanctioned'
it has no compulsory public character. As my analysis of the implicit and
explicit data in Chapter 2 revealed, votive activity could take place within
private settings (that is, outside 'officially-sanctioned' sacred precincts).

22. A similar critique was made of the 'official/popular religion' dichotomy in my
Introduction.

Insofar as it seems likely that women were constrained to lead lives in the domestic sphere or at least less public lives than Israelite men, the vow would stand as one of the few 'official' practices which conformed to their particular social circumstances. A correspondence is thus observed between the social space in which many women's (religious) activities were concentrated and the mechanisms of the Israelite vow, since the latter offers its patrons the option of initiating their petitions in precisely this domain.

My second hypothesis as to why the vow was popular among women is not entirely unrelated to the first. In Chapter 2 of this study it was shown that a petition need not be initiated in the public setting of a sanctuary or temple. Accordingly, a woman knew that her vow did not need to be regulated, overseen or validated by any male authority figure. This observation harmonizes nicely with the literati's explicit statement in Numbers 30 that husbands and fathers can only be expected to learn of a woman's vows *after* they have been made.[23]

Being a private affair, the Israelite vow provided female supplicants with a sort of impenetrable personal religious space, which could not be infiltrated by husbands, brothers, fathers, male members of the Yahwistic cult, or any one else for that matter. Once situated within the impenetrable space provided by the votive system—and precisely because of its impenetrability—Israelite women could engage in a variety of acts which were usually forbidden to them in other spheres of social and religious life.

In Chapter 3 I noted that the northwest Semitic vow allowed the supplicant to speak directly to the deity. Needless to say, this is a luxury which was denied to Israelite women in 'official', public settings. As Gayle Rubin once noted in her famous article 'The Traffic in Women: Notes on the "Political Economy" of Sex', modern capitalism is only a recent heir to a long tradition 'in which women do not talk to god' (1975: 164). A reading of the books of Leviticus, Numbers and Deuteronomy should sufficiently demonstrate that there exist very few public, communal religious practices which permit women to communicate directly with Yahweh. The northwest Semitic vow, however, is a

---

23. Note that this passage does not stipulate that women *must* tell their husbands or fathers about their vows. Accordingly, it seems likely that a woman did not have to reveal that she made a vow. As noted earlier, this might have been the case in the Hannah episode. Bird raises the possibility that women might intentionally make vows that were extremely costly (1987: 410).

practice which affords any given supplicant the right to speak to the gods *without the mediation* of another person. We may speculate then, that Israelite women were attracted to a practice which permitted them direct access to the ear of the deity.

Another mechanism of the Israelite vow consists of the supplicant's right to self-regulate the expense of the item offered to the deity (that is, autonomous regulation of content) as well as the moment of votive fulfillment (namely, autonomous regulation of compensation). Here again, the vow would seem to provide women with a type of power which they were normally not granted in other departments of life. A sort of 'economic empowerment' can be envisioned, whereby women could, uncharacteristically, set 'the terms of the deal'.[24] It is essential to recall that in doing so, they did not need to solicit the fiscal counseling of any man.

The explicit evidence relinquished by the Old Testament literati hints at a votive system in which women frequently made vows. A study of mechanisms, however, permits us not only to speculate that women often made vows, but to offer an explanation as to *why* this may have been so. As has been shown, a vow may be initiated in the private sphere of social life. It seems plausible to assume that it was precisely to such a sphere that many Israelite women were relegated. The vow, then, would appear to be a convenient medium through which women could pursue their religious needs.[25] Furthermore, I have argued that this practice afforded Israelite women types of religious options and liberties which they were typically denied in a highly patriarchal society. It is for these reasons that I submit that this practice was accessible to Israelite women.

---

24. This entails the right to decide how much and when the deity will be compensated.

25. Bird has suggested that the Israelite vow, amongst a series of other religious practices, was 'better suited to women's spiritual and emotional needs and the patterns of their lives than the rituals of the central sanctuary, the great pilgrimages and assemblies, and the liturgical calendar of the agricultural year' (1987: 401).

Part III

THE VOW AND THE 'OFFICIAL RELIGION'

Chapter 8

THE BALANCE OF POWER

> To this day, no decision of church councils, differentiating the 'worship' of God from the 'adoration' of the icons of saints, and defining the icons as merely a devotional means, has succeeded in deterring a south European peasant from spitting in front of the statue of a saint when he holds it responsible for withholding a favor even though the customary procedures were performed (M. Weber, *Economy and Society: An Outline of Interpretive Sociology*).

Counter-Power

In the preceding chapters I have drawn attention to various unwritten rules ('mechanisms') of the Israelite votive system. Once extracted from the text I have tried to envision how these votive norms may have impacted upon members of 'popular religious groups' who wished to make vows.

To this point, this study is devoted almost exclusively to examining the behavior of Israelite votaries. Yet as I noted in my Introduction, a 'popular religious group' must be understood as existing in relation to an 'official religion'. In this chapter, I shall examine how the norms of the votive process affected those persons whose job it was to maintain the cult of Yahweh. (For purposes of analysis I shall assume that the regulations found in the Old Testament represent the votive policies of an 'official religion'.) How did members of this organization, be they priests, cultic functionaries or law writers, figure in the votive system as reconstructed in my analysis? How did they react to the considerable autonomy which the vow permitted its patrons? What conclusions may we draw regarding the interactions that took place between Israelite supplicants and the 'official religion'?

As a means of engaging these questions, I shall concentrate my discussion on the concept of 'power'. This sociological construct offers an

analytical tool by which to understand a somewhat unusual phenomenon: the 'official religion' was *powerless* to regulate, prescribe or
control the votive activity of the populace.

Power

Since there are many distinct and sociologically sophisticated approaches
to the question of power, it will be necessary to articulate clearly the
definition which will be employed in the following discussion.[1] According
to Max Weber: '"Power" (*Macht*) is the probability that one actor
within a social relationship will be in a position to carry out his own will
despite resistance, regardless of the basis on which this probability rests'
(1964: 152; see also Weber 1958: 180). Jürgen Habermas observes that
Weber 'has defined power as the possibility of forcing one's own will,
whatever it may be, on the conduct of others' (1990: 173).

It is important to recall that power in this sense cannot be seen as a
quality that one person possesses. As Dennis Wrong remarks: 'the sociological concept of power must not imply that it is an attribute of an actor
rather than a relation between actors, whether individuals or groups'
(1988: 2; see also Elias 1978: 116 and Bendix 1977: 290). An elabora-
tion of this point can be found in Raymond Aron's observation that
'[t]he actors may be the United States and France, collective actors in
social interaction, or a professor and his students' (1989: 279).

The specific power relation I wish to scrutinize occurs between
votaries who are members of 'popular religious groups' and those persons affiliated with the management of the 'official' cult of Yahweh. The
question of interest to me concerns the nature of the interaction between
these two groups. In particular, who was more capable of 'carrying out
their own will' within the context of the votive relationship?

Historically, the power relation between 'popular religious groups'
and 'official religions' has been a somewhat one-sided affair. As I noted
in my Introduction, it could be safely said that an 'official religion' is
more likely to carry out its will than any other religious group within a
society. Yet within the context of the votive relationship—and solely
within this context—an entirely different situation is observed. My interpretation of the evidence indicates that in this particular arena the religious
authorities were incapable of forcing members of 'popular religious
groups', and votaries in general, to obey their commands. In the

---

1. For an important oversight of some of the major issues and theorists involved
in the study of power, see Wrong 1988 and Wartenberg 1992.

following discussion, I shall lend textual support to this claim. Then, I shall suggest an explanation for this state of affairs.

'Late' Regulations

I shall begin by searching for literary instances in which 'official' Yahwism attempted to carry out its will—to exert power over would-be votaries. Perhaps the most appropriate place for such a search is in those sections of the Old Testament which directly issue commands, laws or instructions to those who will be making vows.

In the legislative sections of the Old Testament there occasionally appear laws that attempt to regulate the behavior of hypothetical supplicants. As I mentioned in Chapter 2, all these laws share one basic characteristic: they are exclusively preoccupied with the payment stage of the vow. The authors of the Hebrew Bible devote a significant degree of explicit details to the issue of *where* a vow should be paid. Not a word, however is said about where vows should be made.

The literati also discuss, in considerable detail, those procedures to be observed upon the fulfillment of a vow. Lev. 22.17-25, which by dint of its placement in H is probably our oldest votive legislation, will serve as the starting point for this inquiry.[2] This passage states that the supplicant must sacrifice a perfect, non-blemished animal as payment for a vow (22.19-22).[3] Accordingly, this law which attempts to control private (Noth 1965: 162) and individual (Levine 1989: 151) votive praxis, makes no attempt to regulate how, where, and with what demands a vow should be initiated. Instead, it is solely concerned with how a vow should be paid.

---

2. The relative antiquity of this passage can also be proven by the fact that it subsumes only the נדר and the נדבה under the general categories of burnt offerings and שלמים offerings, whereas in later priestly legislation, as will become clear, the נדר, נדבה and תודה are all classified together. As B. Levine has noted:

> Thus, Leviticus 22:21, following, speaks of the *šelāmîm* only in connection with the *neder* and *nedābāh*, whereas the *tôdāh* is treated under a separate heading (verse 29 f.) That Leviticus, chapter 7, is subsequent to chapter 22 is evident from the relative dating of the Holiness code...which encompasses Leviticus, chapters 17-26, *vis à vis* the other priestly writings of the Pentateuch...(1974: 43).

For related treatments of this issue see Dussaud 1921: 102; Heinsich 1935: 100; de Vaux 1965: 417 and Thompson 1963: 220 n. 2.

3. In contrast to the נדבה offering which can consist of a defective animal (v. 23). As such, it would appear that the rules regarding the נדר were much more stringent than those regarding the latter (Levine 1989: 152).

In Numbers 15 there appears another law which only refers to the types of votive behavior practised upon fulfillment of the vow.[4] In Lev. 7.16-17 it is related that the flesh of a נדר or a נדבה offering may be eaten even on the third day after sacrifice.[5] Here, as in Lev. 23.37-38 and Num. 29.39, references to the *making* of the vow are entirely absent. A similar circumstance prevails in Deuteronomy 12 and Leviticus 27 where the various 'equivalents' (that is, cash commutations) for items vowed are named.[6]

A basic pattern emerges in these passages: P's votive regulation does not endeavor to regulate the behavior of the votary as he or she makes a vow. Accordingly, it leaves such decisions as the content of the vow (namely, what is requested and promised), the moment of initiation, the liturgical formulation of the petition, where it is to be made, and so on, completely to the discretion of the supplicant.

It is certainly curious that the same authors who have articulated such detailed rules concerning the payment stage of the vow have absolutely nothing to say about its initiation. Why do the religious authorities attempt to exert their will solely in the arena of votive fulfillment? Why do they refrain from regulating the inchoate stages of the procedure?

Mechanisms and the Cultic Apparatus

An examination of the basic mechanisms of votive initiation provides us with the most plausible responses to these questions.

I began this study by observing that nearly all biblical vows were made by individuals. In Chapter 2 it was demonstrated that the votive petition need not be made within the confines of the temple. A close reading of the Hannah episode (1 Samuel 1) also suggested that even when a vow is made in the presence of a priest, the latter has little knowledge of the contents of the petition. This ability to circumvent cultic functionaries may have something to do with a (northwest Semitic) votive system which permits supplicants to vocalize their petitions directly to the deity, without any form of human mediation. The fact that the initiation of a vow could be made individually and did not

---

4. Here again, the נדר and נדבה are grouped together without reference to the תודה (Milgrom 1990:118). This law, which stipulates that an additional meal offering be sacrificed with the animal in fulfillment of an עולה or זבח (vv. 3-13), is once again aimed at individual and frequently employed religious practices.

5. Unlike the passages examined above, this chapter classifies the תודה (Lev. 7.12) with the נדר and נדבה.

6. For a discussion of this text see Chapter 5.

necessitate any *interpersonal contact* would seem to provide the most logical explanation for the absence of regulation concerning votive initiation. For how can the priests effectively regulate a practice which they cannot see?[7] How can they prescribe a behavior which does not require their services? For these reasons, short of altering the entire constitution of this very ancient practice, there was little that the priests could do to monitor the initiation stage of the vow.[8]

As noted above, the authors of the Hebrew Bible request that vows be paid in a temple. If we extrapolate from the account of Hannah's vow, it would seem that the priest's presence is required for the process of votive remission. This moment may have provided the perfect, albeit *the only*, opportunity for the cultic authorities to participate in the votive procedure. My suggestion is that this accounts for the abundance of Old Testament laws concerned with votive payment. Realizing the impossibility of effectively legislating the components of the vow that occur in the initial stages of the procedure, the literary wing of the Yahwist party concentrated all of its energy on making sure that proper cultic protocol would be enforced upon remission.

Votive Abuses

However, this inability to monitor the initiation phase of a vow left the representatives of the Yahweh cult—or any Israelite 'official religion'—vulnerable to innumerable abuses. Since votive initiation is individual and private, the priest is essentially unaware of the contents of the contract that the worshipper has entered into with the deity. Thus, when a subject visits the sacred precincts to pay a vow, the priest has no means of gauging whether the supplicant is adhering to the original promise which he or she made. There always exists the danger that Yahweh is being

---

7.   Of all the students of the Israelite vow, it was Brekelmans who came closest to this conclusion. He writes:

> there is no law prescribing such votive offerings; only the place which they are to be offered is prescribed... By their very nature [they]... cannot be prescribed (1963: 2552).

8.   Given the tremendous antiquity of this practice (Peake 1902: 872; Brekelmans 1963: 2552; McFadyen 1928: 654; Phillott 1873: 3449; Brekelmans and Goldstain 1987: 1342), it might not be unreasonable to assume that the religious authorities conceded that it would be impossible to alter this system fundamentally. There is great truth in the observation by Phillott that 'The law therefore did not introduce, but regulated the practice of vows' (1873: 3449; see also Fohrer 1972: 210 and Gehman 1970: 985).

lied to, that a 'cheater' (in Malachi's terms [1.14]), has somehow deceived both the deity and his earthly representatives.[9] This type of duplicity is of tremendous concern to the religious authorities in the following bipartite respect. First, there could be a considerable loss of income from supplicants who offered valueless items—items worth a 'whore's fee'— to the temple.[10] Secondly—and even more of a threat to the cultic apparatus—it provided the supplicant with a parallel channel of approach to the deity. It was Weber's view that 'the priests sought to monopolize the regular management of Yahweh worship and all related activities' (1967: 168). It is certainly easy to imagine how the private, unmediated contact with Yahweh afforded by the Israelite vow would serve to undermine cultic efforts aimed at exclusively controlling Yahweh worship. As Cartledge notes: 'an individual could appeal directly to God through a vow and thus effectively bypass the "normal channel" of access through the priest' (1992: 31).

The fact that the initial dialogue with Yahweh is private allows supplicants to usurp momentarily the role of the priest. Votaries may address the deity in their own idiosyncratic manner. They may supersede the intricate system of symbolic acts and rituals that the cultic apparatus insists are necessary for contacting Yahweh. Worshippers approach the deity using their own symbolic language, at a moment which they alone feel is sacred, and in a place which they feel is appropriate.

It might not be an exaggeration to claim that for a short period of time, the votary functions as his or her own priest, behaving in accordance with his or her own personal understanding of the deity's character (how he is to be summoned, what may be requested of him, what types of enticements he prefers, and so on.). In offering a parallel channel of access to Yahweh, the votive system would hypothetically permit the worshipper to modify and if necessary ignore, various practices which the cultic apparatus maintains are inviolable.

Needless to say, this radical autonomy does not harmonize well with the priestly enterprise of monopolization. In fact, it relegates members of the cultic apparatus to a secondary status; they are only left to collect the physical residue of a votary's personal transaction with Yahweh.

9. Or, a scenario could be imagined in which a supplicant pays two shekels to the religious authorities, but promised four in the original vow.

10. By the same token, the votary who conveniently 'forgets' to pay back the vow altogether, is also depriving the Yahwistic cult of a potential source of revenue. For a discussion of the term 'whore's fee', see Chapter 4.

Powerlessness: 'God Will Get You For That'
It is in light of these considerations that the antecedents of some of our
more polemical vow-texts may be understood. In these passages it is
insinuated that Israelites are prone to behave unscrupulously when it
comes to making vows; that remittance is delayed or completely ignored;
that promises are altered; that Yahweh himself is being cheated.

The literati's fear of being the object of such deception can be
detected in various passages from the wisdom literature. I will begin by
juxtaposing two wisdom texts which convey nearly identical messages to
supplicants:[11]

Deut. 23.22	כי־תדר נדר ליהוה אלהיך לא תאחר לשלמו כי־דרש ידרשנו יהוה אלהיך מעמך והיה בך חטא
Eccl. 5.3	כאשר תדר נדר לאלהים אל־תאחר לשלמו כי אין חפץ בכסילים את אשר־תדר שלם
Deut. 23.23	וכי תחדל לנדר לא־יהיה בך חטא
Eccl. 5.4	טוב אשר לא־תדר משתדור ולא תשלם
Deut. 23.24	מוצא שפתיך תשמר ועשית כאשר נדרת ליהוה אלהיך נדבה אשר דברת בפיך
Eccl. 5.5	אל־תתן את־פיך לחטיא את־בשרך ואל־תאמר לפני המלאך כי שגגה היא למה יקצף האלהים על־קולך וחבל את־מעשה ידיך

Deut. 23.22	When you make a vow to Yahweh your God, do not delay in fulfilling it. For Yahweh your God will certainly require it from you and you will have incurred guilt.[12]

11. G. von Rad was the first to arrive at the now accepted conclusion that the
Deuteronomic passage in question retains more stylistic and thematic similarities to
the wisdom literature than to a typical Deuteronomic law (1966: 148; see also
Merendino 1969: 290; Weinfeld 1972b: 270).

12. Many commentators have translated the phrase חטא בך as 'sin in thee'
(G.A. Smith 1950: 275; Reider 1937: 219; H. Robinson 1907: 176; Craigie 1976:

Eccl. 5.3	When you make a vow to God, do not delay in fulfilling it, for there is no pleasure[13] in fools; that which you vow, fulfill.[14]
Deut. 23.23	However, if you refrain from making a vow you will not incur guilt.
Eccl. 5.4	It is better that you do not make a vow than if you were to vow and not fulfill.
Deut. 23.24	You will perform the utterance of your lips and you will do that which you voluntarily vowed to Yahweh your God; [that] which you spoke with your mouth.[15]
Eccl. 5.5	But do not let your mouth cause you[16] to sin.[17] Do not say in front of the messenger that it was a mistake. Why should God become angry at your voice and destroy your possessions?

Both texts seek to apprise the reader of the dangers of votive delinquency. If someone transgresses, he or she will incur guilt (Deut. 23.22), encounter the wrath of God (Eccl. 5.5) or risk damage to his or her property at the hands of Yahweh (Eccl. 5.5). What he or she will not encounter—and this is crucial—is any form of this-worldly punishment for this votive impropriety. For neither of these texts articulates what *the cultic apparatus* will do to the unscrupulous supplicant. Instead, *Yahweh*

303; Driver 1903: 268; von Rad 1966: 145 and Carmichael 1974: 194). Though not necessarily incorrect, a more natural translation would seem to be *JPS*'s 'you will have incurred guilt' or 'et pour toi il y aurait péché' (Buis and Leclercq 1963: 158; see also Clamer 1946: 661).

13. The translation 'there is no delight [or pleasure] in fools' (Wright 1883: 360; Delitzsch 1877: 287; Barton 1909: 124; Lauha 1978:96) is certainly more justified than the often seen 'He has no pleasure in fools' (Lattes 1964: 66; A. Williams 1922: 59; Scott 1965: 226; Levy 1912: 94; Crenshaw 1987: 114). Since חפץ is a substantive (as in 1 Sam. 15.22) and there is no personal pronoun present the latter translation must be rejected.

14. As Lauha notes, some witnesses preserve the pronoun את, thus his translation 'du aber-was du gelobst, das erfülle!' (1978:99).

15. For a discussion of this verse see Chapter 3.

16. The term בשרך connotes the body or the whole person (Crenshaw 1987:117; Barton 1909:124).

17. Here amending לחטיא, an obvious error, to a more acceptable *hiphil* causative להחטיא (Gordis 1951: 238; Ginsburg 1970: 339). There is no reason to suppose that the reference here is to negative vows as some have suggested (Ginsburg 1970: 339; Weiss 1858: 195).

alone is identified as the agent responsible for the delegation of punitive sanctions.[18]

The curious absence of tangible penalties to be meted out to votive delinquents can be seen once again in Num. 30.3:

איש כי־ידר נדר ליהוה

או־השבע שבעה לאסר אסר על־נפשו

לא יחל דברו

ככל־היצא מפיו יעשה

> If a man makes a vow to Yahweh or swears an oath of abstention[19]
> upon himself he will not break his word[20] he will do everything he
> has said[21]

Again, this legislation does not make reference to this-worldly forms of legal penalty to be dispensed by an earthly institution. The absence of any specific punitive measures is somewhat conspicuous in a text which generally does not hesitate to impose (often draconian) penalties upon transgressive actions (for example, Lev. 7.21, 25; 17.4; 19.8; 20.10; Num. 15.30; 18.6; 19.11).

I believe this state of affairs can also be understood in terms of the mechanisms of votive initiation. The authors of these passages under-

---

18. Notice that in Mal. 1.14 a 'curse' is placed on the 'cheater' though no specific, this-worldly penalty is noted by the angry prophet. See also the somewhat cryptic passage in Prov. 20.25.

19. Many commentators have been quick to note that this text, in the words of Noth, 'permanently differentiated' the positive vow, נדר, from the negative vow, אסר (1968: 224). In our earliest sources no such distinction is drawn; נדר apparently represents both positive and negative vows (Noth 1968: 224; Snaith 1967: 321; see also Clamer 1946: 432; Baentsch 1903: 648; G.B. Gray 1906: 414; Holzinger 1903: 146; Mcneile 1911: 161). The verb אסר here carries the connotation of 'prohibition' as in biblical Aramaic examples such as Dan. 6.8, 13 (see also G.B. Gray 1906: 414 for examples from Syriac and mishnaic Hebrew). This has led some scholars to suggest that the form here is in fact an Aramaism (Baentsch 1903: 648).

20. יחל appears here in the *hiphil*, the root being חלל, thus literally 'he shall not profane his word'.

21. Thus, in the case of a female, revealingly, patriarchal figures (that is, father, husband)—as opposed to cultic institutions—possess the necessary power to annul a vow. In these examples the reins of social control are compliantly passed to the spheres of domestic patriarchal authority. The wholly limited role played by the priests in these scenarios is striking; the religious authorities themselves do not threaten the unscrupulous male supplicant, nor do they take it upon themselves to regulate directly the votive praxis of women.

stand quite well that they cannot know either when a vow is made or what actually was promised to Yahweh. This leaves them no recourse other than frightening votaries into compliance by reminding them of the prospect of divine retribution. In so doing, the literati attempt to dissuade would-be delinquents with the threat that 'god will get you for that'. Thus, it is divine punishment, but not cultic retribution, that the unscrupulous votary will suffer.[22]

The Ethos of Honesty

The above discussion has demonstrated that the unique constitution of the votive system would permit immoral Israelites to realize their ethical shortcomings. I should like to qualify this statement somewhat by suggesting that it is highly probable that most supplicants *did* faithfully fulfill their vows to Yahweh. That votive delinquency was known to the literati seems very likely given the contents of the wisdom passages discussed above. Nevertheless, after witnessing the deity's astonishing ability to grant requests, it would seem improbable that most individuals would doubt the deity's equally developed capacity to punish an unscrupulous supplicant.

The dangers inherent in not remitting a vow are alluded to in a variety of ancient Near Eastern texts. Oppenheim relates the story of the 'bad conscience' of a Hittite king who has failed to make proper payment (1956: 193). In the Akkadian literature, Garelli has observed similar responses amongst the ranks of unprincipled supplicants:

> ...two young employees fell sick and were in danger of dying. The two managers quickly found themselves some interpreters of dreams (*šaʾilātum*), and the consulted deity responded that they should not keep vowed goods (*ikribū*). Thus, the sickness was a divine punishment (1962: 192).[23]

The wrath of a defrauded deity is also articulated in one of the older northwest Semitic vow-texts. In the Ugaritic Keret epic Lady Hurriya gives birth to the very children that the king had apparently requested in

22. Parenthetically, this observation suggests an interesting direction for future research. Is there a difference between practices punished by Yahweh and those punished by his earthly representatives? Is the threat of divine retribution indicative of a certain powerlessness to deploy terrestrial coercive power?

23. See Garelli 1963: 255-56, who discusses the potentially disastrous consequences of withholding payment (see also the Hittite evidence reported in Cartledge 1992: 103).

a vow. The passage in question seems to suggest that Keret was negligent in compensating the deity.[24]

20 *w tqrb.wl*d* bn l*h*	And she approached [the time] to bear him a son[25]
21 *w tqrb. wl*d*.b*nm*[26] l*h*	and she approached [the time] to bear him sons
22 *mk.b šbᶜ.šn*t**	Indeed, in the seventh year
23 *bn.krt.kmhm.tdr*	the sons of Keret were as had been vowed[27]

24. Here following the reading of *KTU* 1.15 III.

25. *w tqrb wld*. The exact translation is still not clear. I shall begin with *qrb*. This G stem carries the basic definition of 'to approach' or 'to draw near'. Some have maintained that 'she' (Lady Hurriya), the wife of Keret, is literally approaching (Virolleaud 1942–1943: 154; Amir 1987: 87; Sauren and Kestemont 1971: 206). Another view assumes that the time of birth is approaching (Gibson 1978:92; J. Gray 1964: 19). De Moor and Spronk have translated *qrb* as 'soon afterwards' based on Arabic *'aqraba*, 'to make things happen in very short intervals' (1982: 176). In a similar vein, but based on Akkadian evidence, the usage of *qrb* 'im Falle des Beginns einer Aktion' has been noted (Dietrich, Loretz and Sanmartín 1976a: 436), while others have taken *tqrb* as a synonym for 'she conceives' (Ginsberg 1946: 23; Caquot, Sznycer and Herdner 1974: 541; Xella 1982: 169 and Jirku 1962: 98). A completely different translation has been suggested by Tsumura, based on Akkadian *karābu*, who suggests 'and she will bless [him]' (1979: 782).

wld presents even more difficulties. Some take this form as an inf. abs. (G or D, de Moor and Spronk 1982: 176; Tsumura 1979: 782). In an analysis which reviews the merits and demerits of other approaches Dietrich, Loretz and Sanmartín observe: 'It should therefore be better to understand *qrb* as a verb, which adds a temporal determination to the *infinitivus absolutus* which announces the immediately approaching birth: "and she approaches to give birth = she will shortly give birth"' (1976a: 435). This differs slightly from Tsumura's conclusion that the primae waw verb *wld* can be rendered 'to give birth (to many)' (1982: 176).

26. *KTU* reads *bnm* here, as do Gordon (1965: 195) and Gibson (1978: 92). I favor this reading against that of Ginsberg, who reads *bnt* (1946: 23). Gordon (1949: 75) translates 'her two sons' though this seems unlikely (see also Margalit 1976: 190; Caquot, Sznycer and Herdner 1974: 541).

27. *bn krt kmhm tdr* Ginsberg provided the key to the understanding of this verse by associating *kmhm* with Arabic *mahmā*, 'whatever'. Hence the interpretation, 'The sons of Keret were even as *had been stipulated in the vows*' (1946: 23, 41). De Moor and Spronk, however, have persuasively argued for *k* + *mh* + enclitic *m*, akin to Heb. כמה (1982:177). They have also rejected Ginsberg's passive translation of *ndr*. They write:

24 *ap bnt.ḫry* (25) *kmhm.*	even the daughters of Hurriya, as had been vowed
25 *w tḫss*.a*ṯ*r*t**	But Asherah remembers
26 *ndrh.*	his vow[28]
26 *w ilt.* [...][29]	Indeed, the Goddess...
27 *w tšu.gh.w**[tṣḫ]	and she raises her voice and [screams]
28 *ph mʿ. ap.k*[rt]	'look here does Keret...
29 *u ṯn.ndr**[ ]	and two vows[30]
30 *apr....*	I will break...'[31]

Because an N-stem or a passive D-stem are not possible, *tdr* should be an otherwise unattested passive G-stem of *NDR* if we would defend a passive translation of the phrase. It would seem less strenuous to suppose that the deities who pronounced the blessing (lines 17-19) are the subject of *tdr* G (1982: 177).

If a passive translation of *tdr* is accepted, it is possible that the vow was made by Keret (see Ginsberg 1946: 23; Caquot, Sznycer and Herdner 1974: 541; Aistleitner 1964: 97). If de Moor and Spronk are followed, however, it must be assumed that the vow in question was made by the god(s). And this, in fact, is a very popular translation (Virolleaud 1942–1943: 155; Gordon 1949: 155; de Moor 1987: 207; Amir [hesitantly] 1987: 87; Sauren and Kestemont 1971: 207). In response to this opinion, and in particular to the views of de Moor and Spronk, I would make the following observations. The handful of attestations of *ndr* known from the Ugaritic sources do not permit the conclusion that a passive G-stem did not exist in the Ugaritic language. Admittedly, there has yet to surface one passive rendering of this verb in the entire northwest Semitic register. On the other hand, the same corpus of texts has yet to produce a single instance of a deity making a vow. What could the *gods* be vowing for here in the Keret epic? Furthermore, de Moor's translation 'the sons of Kirtu were just as (the gods) had promised' is unlikely (1987: 207) since the root *ndr* cannot be translated 'to promise'. For the time being, and with the accurate observations of de Moor and Spronk regarding the impossibility of a passive translation of *ndr* kept in mind, I would assume that the vows mentioned here were actually made by Keret. Lastly, it should be noted that there is no previous reference to the vows mentioned in this passage. Ginsberg speculates that the vow was made in the missing lines of col. 2 (1946: 22; contra Gibson 1978: 92 n. 4).

28. Following Ginsberg, *ḫss* is to be taken as cognate with Akkadian *ḫasāsu* which *CAD* renders as 'to remember' (6 'H' 123).

29. The original reading of a lone *p* here has given rise to many theoretical conjectures. This reading, however, is not accepted by *KTU* (see also de Moor and Spronk 1982: 177).

30. Most early commentators read *uṯn* here, 'to change' (Ginsberg 1946: 24; Caquot, Sznycer and Herdner 1974: 542; J. Gray 1964: 20; Xella 1982: 169; Jirku 1962: 99; Amir 1987: 87). As early as 1964, however, Aistleitner read *u ṯn*, thus 'seine beiden Gelübde' (1964: 97). His reading is confirmed by *KTU*. Hence a reading like de Moor and Spronk's 'Woe ! two vows you have broken' (1982: 177) is more likely.

31. I assume that the root here is *PRR* 'to break,' a verb usually associated with

Although the reading and translation of this text are not certain, it seems likely that Keret's ensuing illness is a direct result of his failure to compensate Asherah (Jirku 1962: 98; Parker 1979: 695; Parker 1989: 85; Cartledge 1992: 111-12). Verse 25 informs the reader that Asherah 'remembers' the vows of Keret and in verse 27 'she raises her voice and screams'. From this point on, Keret's fortunes change rapidly. Whereas in vv. 20-24 the monarch finally procures the offspring he has so desperately desired, the succeeding narrative chronicles his sudden illness and the rise of his usurper son, Yassib. Accordingly, it would seem that such improvident behavior is an invitation to severe displays of divine anger.

In the Israelite milieu, a similar ethos seems to prevail. As the Jephthah incident shows (Judg. 11.30-40), votive fulfillment at any cost is favored by the literati. As Trible has observed, Jephthah's decision to offer his daughter to Yahweh as a burnt offering testifies to the 'inviolability of the vow spoken to the deity' (1989: 103; see also Wendel 1931a: 151-52).[32] I have argued in this chapter, however, that this sense of inviolability did not arise as a consequence of the fear of cultic retribution. Rather, it may be attributed to the existence of an ancient and rather intuitive belief in the massive retributive capacities of an irascible deity.

Whereas King Keret—an abstract literary figure whose actions conform to the exigencies of epic narrative—has wantonly defied the gods, it is my assumption that most supplicants would not. Even though the private nature of the vow precludes the possibility of any priestly role in administering punishment for lack of payment, only the boldest of supplicants could ignore the possibility of divine retribution.

Conclusion

In the preceding discussion I concluded that the Yahwistic cult was incapable of carrying out its own will (that is, exerting power) within the context of the votive relationship. The priesthood's uncharacteristic powerlessness was viewed as a consequence of the mechanical structure of the northwest Semitic votive system. Since a vow may be initiated individually and privately, it is nearly impossible for members of the 'official religion' to monitor effectively any aspect of this practice. While

the breaking of treaties (de Moor and Spronk 1982: 177). Yet the children have already been delivered—what exactly is the goddess going to annul?

    32. See also Chapter 3.

none of this suggests that all or even most Israelites were delinquent in their votive behavior, it does mean that there was little to stop non-exemplary Yahwists, disaffected elements and other 'deviants' from carrying out their will if they so desired.[33]

The wisdom passages examined above suggest that the issue of votive delinquency was of considerable concern to the biblical authors. I speculated that this may be attributed to the fact that it not only deprived the cultic apparatus of wealth, but also subverted their efforts to control completely all aspects of Yahweh worship. Be that as it may, the literati never articulate any concrete punitive measures to be meted out to unethical supplicants. This task was left solely to the deity. This, I argued, was not an oversight on the part of the biblical authors. Rather, it suggests a conscious recognition that coercive measures are futile in the arena of votive initiation.

Of course, the votive relationship is only one aspect—admittedly a very small aspect—of religious life in ancient Israel. It should not necessarily be taken as an instance of social behavior whose implications were revolutionary, 'counter-hegemonic' or even politically efficacious. It can, however, offer a model for how 'popular religious groups' may exercise what I call 'counter-power' against the 'official religion' whose commands they are expected to obey.

In his absorbing study, *Weapons of the Weak: Everyday Forms of Peasant Resistance*, anthropologist James Scott discusses the manner in which the poor peasants of a Malaysian village attempt to resist the onslaught of a more powerful capitalist class. Scott's central argument, I believe, may be of use to students of 'popular religious groups':

> For these reasons it seemed to me more important to understand what we might call *everyday* forms of peasant resistance—the prosaic but constant struggle between the peasantry and those who seek to extract labor, food, taxes, rents, and interest from them. Most forms of this struggle stop well short of outright collective defiance. Here I have in mind the ordinary weapons of relatively powerless groups: foot dragging, dissimulation, desertion, false compliance, pilfering, feigned ignorance, slander, arson, sabotage, and so on. These Brechtian—or Schweikian—forms of class struggle have certain features in common. They require little or no coordi-

---

33. See Chapter 6 for a further discussion of this issue. I should also note that those who defrauded the cultic apparatus may have done so not out of disrespect for the deity but out of disdain for the religious authorities. It is not unusual for critics of a particular religious establishment to claim that they love the god in question, but despise his alleged earthly representatives and institutions (see below).

nation or planning; they make use of implicit understandings and informal networks; they often represent a form of individual self-help; they typically avoid any direct, symbolic confrontation with authority. (1985: xvi)

In the current literature on 'popular religion' a growing interest in the various ways in which powerless groups wield such weapons of the weak against 'official religions' can be identified. One interesting, small-scale manifestation of such counter-power can be seen in the promulgation of anti-clerical attitudes and behavior. The recent collection of anthropological essays, *Religious Orthodoxy and Popular Faith in European Society*, has dealt extensively with this theme. Ellen Badone has examined the considerable animosity which the peasants of Brittany harbor toward Catholic priests. As an example of how such resentment expresses itself, Badone offers this analysis of a remark recorded during her fieldwork:

'he doesn't even need one and yet he has ten' quips the *rogue* bartender in a Monts d'Arée café. As this comment suggests, priests are viewed as being potentially oversexed, despite their theoretical chastity. If heightened sexual power can be taken as a metaphor for social power, the bartender's comment is additionally revealing. It conveys the anomalous position of the priest who presumably lacks the sexual prowess of ordinary men but wields considerable social power over them (1990b: 148; see also Brettell 1990; Behar 1990; Taylor 1990; Dubisch 1990: 117).

In applying these insights to the domain of Israelite 'popular religious groups' an attempt could be made to identify instances of such small-scale, low-risk, indirect, non-symbolic confrontation with the powers that be. It does not seem at all implausible to speculate that the Israelite votive system would be a handy 'weapon of the weak' for individual members of oppressed or socially disaffected groups to wield against an 'official religion'. Those votaries who, for whatever reasons, wished to defraud the cultic apparatus could do so with relative impunity.

In a more broadly theoretical sense these considerations remind us that no 'official religion' is an omnipotent institution, capable of carrying out its will at all times and under all circumstances. Conversely, 'popular religious groups' should not be construed as totally powerless. Instead, they attempt to exert their will—counter-power—whenever and wherever the opportunity presents itself. A task for future research lies in identifying the innumerable ways in which 'popular religious groups' subvert the considerable power of the reigning orthodoxy. What are the necessary sociological preconditions for the emergence of counter-power?

At what point (and how) does this counter-power seriously threaten the existing power of a dominant group? How do 'official religions' typically react to these threats to their hegemony?

CONCLUSION

'The sociologist,' according to Anthony Giddens, 'is someone who states the obvious, but with an air of discovery' (1987: 2).

In this study I have concluded that the Israelite vow was accessible to women, heterodox elements and non-privileged economic strata. I was not able to identify any mechanism of the votive procedure which would restrict members of these 'popular religious groups' from participating in this act. It was argued that the mechanisms of individual initiation, privacy, spoken invocation, autonomous regulation of content and autonomous regulation of compensation all served to render the vow highly accessible to these particular groups of Israelites.

As I noted at the beginning of this inquiry, this conclusion is not entirely novel. A handful of biblical scholars—after only cursory deliberation—were capable of identifying a connection between 'popular religion' and the Israelite vow. The authors of the Old Testament themselves report that women, the poor and heterodox elements can and do engage in this particular religious practice.

If any discovery was made in this contribution it consisted of the development and deployment of a variety of sociological and text-critical methods for the study of Israelite religion. Throughout this work I have stressed that these were of an experimental nature. As such, it is presumed (and hoped) that they will be interrogated, modified and eventually superseded by students of biblical 'popular religion'. As a means of expediting this process this final chapter will consider not only the advantages of these initiatives, but also some of their drawbacks.

'Popular Religious Groups' and 'Official Religion'

'Popular Religious Groups' Reassessed

I began this study by advancing local definitions of the terms 'popular religious groups' and 'official religion'. A dialectical approach was employed whereby the former was defined in opposition to the latter.

Assuming that the Hebrew Bible represented the views of an 'official Yahwism' (and at some point, perhaps, an 'official religion') then those denounced in this text as heretics, apostates, backsliders, and so forth, stand as potential 'popular religious groups'. It was noted that 'official religion' is often associated with an economically dominant class. Accordingly, non-privileged strata could plausibly be categorized under the 'popular' heading. Lastly, since all available data indicated that the Yahwist cult was governed in its principal functions by males, and privileged men's religious activity, I targeted Israelite women as another group for investigation.

Admittedly, there is a tremendous lack of analytical precision in the groups I have selected. A term such as 'the non-privileged strata' tends to consolidate far too many distinct groups (such as peasants, plebeians, resident aliens, and so on) under one generic heading. To speak of 'women' as a category for sociological analysis is to ignore the fact that they *never* constitute a homogenous group. While all women in a society may share common experiences (such as subjection to a patriarchal order or relegation to the 'private' sphere) this does not mean that, sociologically speaking, they are identical. Some women are the wives, sisters, and mothers of the most prominent members of the 'official religion', if not important players within this group.[1] Yet others are residents of the most peripheral, economically disadvantaged and politically powerless village in the kingdom.

Specificity, then, is a virtue when it comes to defining a 'popular religious group'. The more precision one can achieve in describing the sociological constituency under consideration, the more valid one's results are likely to be. Given the paucity of available vow-texts it was difficult to achieve any degree of specificity in this study. The northwest Semitic data simply does not provide enough examples of Israelite votaries to permit the drawing of narrow analytical categories. Accordingly, I was obliged to select my 'popular religious groups' in terms of very broad and sociologically imprecise criteria.

Researchers should also aim for specificity when demarcating the temporal parameters within which their 'popular religious groups' are to be found. Susan Ackerman's recent monograph *Under Every Green Tree: Popular Religion in Sixth-Century Judah* stands as a good example. While I have substantive disagreements with her definition of,

---

1. Just as members of non-privileged classes may be perfectly pious devotees of an 'official religion' (see Berlinerblau 1995).

and her method for extracting information about, 'popular religion', these will not be engaged here. As indicated by the title of this study, Ackerman has concentrated her research within a relatively compact sociological time and space. This stands in opposition to the temporally peripatetic analysis offered in the present monograph. In this study—for the reasons mentioned above—a composite image of both the Israelite vow and 'popular religious groups' was sketched on the basis of data spanning the entire pre-exilic and early post-exilic periods.

Students of 'popular religious groups' should also take into consideration what I shall refer to as 'subjective solidarity'. Extrapolating somewhat from Marx's discussions of class solidarity and class consciousness, I would note that there must be clarity about whether the members of the group being targeted were subjectively aware that they were in fact a group.[2] If this were indeed the case then it could be assumed that their social action was, in part, predicated upon this very awareness. For example: Baalists living within a Yahwist society most probably retained a healthy cognizance of being an 'us' in contradistinction to a Yahwist 'them'. Accordingly, many of their actions were motivated by the realization that they belonged to a 'negatively-esteemed' status group.

But can we draw the same inference regarding women and the non-privileged classes of Antiquity? I believe that such subjective solidarity was lacking among these 'popular religious groups' when *taken as aggregates*. However, this does not preclude the possibility that clusters of Israelite women (for example, residents of a small village or adherents of a particular god[dess]) or non-privileged persons (such as slaves under one master or peasants of one over-taxed region) might have retained the type of 'in-group' feeling discussed above.

Thus, it may be expedient to draw a distinction between 'organic' and 'inorganic' 'popular religious groups'. By the former I mean those groups whose members maintained some consciousness of possessing similar material or ideal interests. By the latter, I mean groups whose existence has been postulated by academicians for purposes of scholarly analysis. It is unlikely that the 'members' of such groups evinced any awareness of constituting a 'we' insofar as their members have been artificially bonded, so to speak, by a modern researcher.

Turning to the 'official religion' construct, I recommend that future

---

2.   See for example Marx and Engels' discussion of the difference between an atomized and a unified proletariat in 'The Communist Manifesto' (1983: 89).

researchers adopt a more consistent stance than that taken in this study. In the present contribution I conveniently alternated between two conceptions of 'official religion' and its relation to the Hebrew Bible. In some places I have assumed that Old Testament verses revealed something about the votive policies of an 'official Yahwism' which was in fact an 'official religion'. Elsewhere, particularly in my introduction, I called into question the widespread assumption that the Hebrew Bible offers accurate information about the latter.

One of the most pressing challenges which confronts students of Israelite religion lies in establishing a more consistent approach to this issue. It may no longer be assumed that the views of the 'official religion' of ancient Israel, at all points of its history, can be effortlessly gleaned from the pages of the Old Testament. The truly crucial questions may be posed as follows: at which historical period(s) did the Yahwism discussed on the pages of the Hebrew Bible actually function as the real 'official religion' of ancient Israel? Which major social groups comprised its ruling apparatus and its constituents? Through what particular combination of coercion and consent did it exercise power? Who exactly were the Yahwist literati? What was their relation to other factions of the Yahwist party? What position did these Yahwist intellectuals occupy within the Israelite social order during those times in which their views did not constitute an 'official religion'? When a non-Yahwist 'official religion' was in place, what types of social groups comprised its ruling apparatus and constituency? What were the central tenets of this non-Yahwist 'orthodoxy?' Did their exist periods in Israelite history in which no 'official religion' could be identified?

The Method of Tacit Assumption

The Old Testament's capacity to furnish accurate information about the votive behavior of 'popular religious groups' stood as the second major issue addressed in my introduction. The reasons which motivated me to cast doubts upon the historical integrity of this document are certainly not new. William Dever reiterates the concerns of an entire generation of biblical scholars when he observes that 'the historical reconstruction enshrined in the Hebrew Bible in its present form (especially in Dtr) is late; highly selective in what it includes; elitist in perspective; and, in its final redaction, propagandistic in nature throughout' (1991:196).

Similarly, in this study it was argued that the majority of the vow-texts stem from the hands of passionate and partial 'theocratic historians'.

As such, an attitude of exegetical skepticism was recommended as the proper intellectual orientation for the student of Israelite 'popular religious groups'. My own skeptical impulses led me to develop a series of exegetical strategies which were declared to be 'cognizant of the snares of theocratic history'. A variety of text-critical methods with neologistic designations such as 'tacit assumption', 'explicit' and 'implicit evidence', 'accessibility' and 'restrictiveness' were advanced as a means of gaining insight into the basic skeletal structure of the Israelite votive system. It is to an evaluation of these initiatives which I shall now turn.

Explicit and Implicit Evidence
In my introduction I posed the following question: how can we study the religious life of social groups and strata which Old Testament historiographers have either maligned, misunderstood or relegated to obscurity?

One response may be stated as follows: the researcher will patiently wait for biblical archaeologists to unearth fresh evidence—peasant autobiographies, the remains of a women's cult installation, well-preserved scrolls featuring anti-Yahwistic diatribes, and so on. Such texts would provide new evidence for analysis; evidence in which 'popular religious groups' are not misrepresented; evidence rendered in the actual words and artifacts of those who have been ignored, disparaged and misrepresented by the biblical literati.

My own response to this question was predicated on the belief that archaeological harvests of this nature will not be immediately, nor abundantly, forthcoming. Simply put, if any advances in the study of Israelite 'popular religious groups' are to be made, they will not come by awaiting the discovery of new data. Progress will be achieved through the cultivation of new approaches to the evidence currently possessed; evidence furnished by impassioned theocratic historians. Without in any way casting aspersions upon the archaeological enterprise, I would stress that it is the quality of the instruments of analysis, not the quantity of the data, which will facilitate the making of significant and lasting contributions to the study of the social world of Antiquity; archaeologists, exegetes, sociologists, gender theorists, anthropologists are among those who stand to play an important role in this undertaking.

The method of tacit assumption was formulated as a corrective to the tendency of Old Testament scholars to read explicit biblical statements as veridical assessments of Israelite religious life, be it 'official' or 'popular'. It was proposed that threads of 'implicit evidence' be teased out from the well-crafted tapestry which is the Hebrew Bible. The strands of information extracted in this manner shared two qualities which led me to believe that they retained a certain degree of autonomy from the partisan statements of theocratic historians.

First, such details were indifferent to the ideological agenda of the Yahwist party; they bore no discernible connection to the political and theological imperatives of the biblical literati. Secondly, the latter seem uninterested in drawing attention to these details. In some cases the mechanisms I identified were literally submerged within the text. Elsewhere, they were repeated over and over again in a formulaic manner. As far as the Old Testament writers were concerned, these details were neither important nor controversial and merited no particular literary ornamentation or intellectual consideration.

The method of tacit assumption is useful in that it permits the generation of an autonomous body of evidence which may be contrasted with the tale of the explicit evidence. It was through an examination of this implicit evidence that I constructed a hypothetical portrait of the laws of motion of the votive process. In so doing, an explanation was offered as to *why* it was that 'popular religious groups' made vows in ancient Israel. As noted in the Introduction, it was this explanatory dimension which was lacking in all previous studies of this religious practice.

The method of tacit assumption was also helpful in clarifying the meaning of various cryptic vow-texts. Reference to the 'whore's fee', I argued, may be best understood in light of the mechanism of autonomous regulation of content (Chapter 4). The literati's repeated warnings regarding delinquent votive behavior would seem to be attributable to the clergy's inability to monitor the private and individual process of initiation (Chapters 1, 2 and 8). Malachi's rebuke of 'the cheater' seems motivated by a similar concern (Chapter 4), and so on. It may be said, then, that implicit details serve to illuminate the meanings and antecedents of ambiguous explicit details.

A final advantage of this approach arises from its capacity to circumvent distortions of accuracy attributable to 'intentional misrepresentation'. In the Introduction I maintained that many of the details which appear on the pages of the Old Testament cannot be read as facts, but as deliberate attempts to malign those who failed to adhere to the literati's 'party line'. The mechanisms discovered in this research, however, cannot be easily correlated with the ideological impulses of the biblical authors. With the exception of the mechanism of 'spoken initiation', these banal assertions were buried within the Old Testament. They could not be noticed unless one set out to look for them—and then to look for them again in other vow-texts. It is highly improbable that the literati would traverse such a circuitous route in order to report 'facts' which their readers, in Collingwood's phrase, 'ought to know'.[3]

While the method of tacit assumption may enable us to avoid the hazards of 'intentional misrepresentation', it does not proffer the same advantages with respect to 'unintentional misrepresentation'. The latter is to be distinguished from the former in that there is no deliberate attempt on the part of the literati to defame other groups. Instead, the inaccurate information received may be attributable to the biblical authors' misunderstanding or lack of awareness regarding the activities of 'popular religious groups'.

The difficulties this creates for the researcher may be best illustrated by the following example. Let us imagine that heterodox Israelites always made *group vows*, covertly, to their deities. Following the theory of 'unintentional misrepresentation' it might be presumed that the authors of the Old Testament were completely unfamiliar with this practice of group initiation. Accordingly, when they wrote (disparagingly) about heretical votaries they tacitly and erroneously assumed that the latter initiated vows in a manner reminiscent of Yahwists (that is, individually).

This highlights an unavoidable drawback of the method of tacitly-assumed mechanisms: just because the literati tacitly assume a mechanism does not mean that it is a reliable account of votive behavior among groups which the literati did not know or understand. If the extraction of mechanisms permits us, to some restricted degree, to transcend ideological partiality, it does not ensure that *non-ideologically motivated historical inaccuracies* will also be transcended.

Accessibility Reviewed

When studying accessibility I was looking for lines of correspondence between the aforementioned mechanisms of the Israelite vow and the normative behavioral patterns of a 'popular religious group'. A fit occurs when a group's pattern of social behavior interlocks with a specific mechanism. A practice which is restricted is one where a rule of

---

3.   I should stress that although the explicit and implicit evidence were in relative agreement as regards the vow, this will not necessarily always be the case. When other acts of Israelite worship are subjected to the method of tacit assumption it is likely that a fundamental asymmetry will arise between the claims which may be inferred from the two sources of data.

the votive procedure is radically incompatible with one or more of these normative dispositions.

My assumptions regarding the relevant behavioral patterns of the groups targeted in this study may be briefly summarized as follows. Members of economically non-privileged strata share the characteristic of having comparatively little material wealth. It may be surmised that they would avoid religious practices which demanded significant expenditures of their already limited resources, while seeking out those practices which might increase them. Heterodoxies could be said to live in a state of high tension with leaders and devotees of any given 'official religion'. The desire to avoid confrontation with the more powerful institutions of the reigning orthodoxy may be seen as a paramount consideration for members of this group. Women, as I noted in Chapter 7, were relegated to a secondary status within the male-dominated cult of Yahweh. Additionally, their religious activities may have been confined to, and concentrated within, the private or domestic sphere of the Israelite social world. It could be assumed that Israelite women actively sought out those practices which not only could be undertaken within the private sphere, but also granted them types of autonomy which they were usually denied within a highly gender-stratified society.

When measuring the accessibility of the vow I was searching for an inherent congeniality between the mechanisms I discovered and the behavioral patterns of the groups I wished to scrutinize. This approach is problematic, however, in that it is quite difficult at present to make *any* accurate statements about the normative dispositions of these particular populations. Israelite peasants, it seems, never speak in their own voices. One thinks of Max Weber's observation in *Ancient Judaism*: 'the free peasants of ancient Israel stand in the deep shadow of mute sources which give us almost nothing beyond the fact of their existence and original power position' (1967: 23). In Weber's estimation, the religious life of such a group can only be 'indirectly determined' (1967: 24). When discussing Israelite women, Bird reaches a similar position:

> The question about the place of women in the Israelite cultus exposes a defect in traditional historiography—beginning already in Israelite times. It is a question about a forgotten or neglected element in traditional conceptions and presentations of Israelite religion, which typically focus on the activities and offices of males (1987: 398)
>
> Since women rarely emerge in the text from behind the facade of generic male terminology, it is impossible to determine with certainty the extent of their participation in prescribed or reported activities (1987: 408).

An analogous point is made by Morton Smith when he reminds us that 'psalms celebrating the tender mercies of Asherah' have not been included within the 'cult collection' of the Yahwist party (1987: 14).

These remarks underscore a major difficulty for the study of 'popular religious groups': insofar as there is almost no first-hand or reliable information regarding the lives these Israelites led, there are few means of ascertaining what their normative behavioral patterns might have been. It is entirely possible that in pre-exilic Israel, for reasons only known to the ancients, the non-economically privileged classes made very expensive material sacrifices to their deities. Instead of seeking a religious practice which did not demand costly expenditures of personal or family wealth, these strata gravitated towards exorbitant displays of piety. While such a scenario may be unlikely, it must be acknowledged that there is currently very little data available to the historian who wishes to refute such a hypothesis. These considerations remind us that, at present, the study of 'popular religious groups' in Antiquity is a highly speculative enterprise.

The methods and theories employed in this study are by no means immune from criticism. Be that as it may, I believe that in scrutinizing the issues of the dialectical relation between 'official religion' and 'popular religious groups' and 'the explicit approach', I have been able to delineate some of the integral questions which confront students of Israelite 'popular religion'. Through the further innovation of text-critical strategies and the sober and responsible use of theories and methods culled from the social-sciences it is hoped that our understanding of the mute, anonymous and maligned groups of the biblical world will be broadened. Only in this manner will history's lost citizens be reinstated into modern consciousness.

Appendix 1

The Positive Vow

It is commonly held that the substantive and verbal forms of the root נדר can refer to two very distinct patterns of votive behavior (Wendel 1931a: 11). These are usually referred to as 'positive' and 'negative' vows.

This study has concentrated on what is typically understood to be the positive vow: a conditional vow where 'something or someone is vowed to Yahweh or to His sanctuary' (Brekelmans 1963: 2553; Snaith 1967: 321; Kennedy n.d.: 358; Greenstone 1939: 312). When making a positive vow the supplicant approaches the deity with a specific need, manifested in the form of a request. In return for the granting of this request, the votary offers the god(s) a tangible object or service as reimbursement. As just noted, such vows are conditional; only if the latter fulfills the request does the former have to fulfill the terms of his or her promise.

Biblical scholars have also traditionally maintained that the root נדר is employed as a means of referring to 'negative' or Nazirite vows. This species of vow is discussed in only one place in the Old Testament (Numbers 6).[1] Here, the agent apparently makes no demands of the deity. Rather, an 'Enthaltungsgelübde' (Baentsch 1903: 648) is made whereby the supplicant offers to abstain from intoxicants, shaving or trimming bodily hair or proximity with a corpse. When the terms of this (temporary) Nazirite vow have expired, specific offerings are to be made to Yahweh in a prescribed manner (Num. 6.13-20).

It appears that this process is initiated when a worshipper *voluntarily offers* the god some particular service or makes some particular pledge. Unlike positive vows, such vows seem to be *unconditional* acts of piety motivated by *unselfish* impulses. The supplicant places absolutely no conditions on his or her fulfillment of the vow; the votary offers to do something for Yahweh without placing any corresponding conditions on the deity.

In his article, 'Were Nazirite Vows Unconditional?', Tony Cartledge has boldly challenged this age-old distinction between positive and negative vows (1989; see also Cartledge 1992:18-26). Cartledge argues that Nazirite vows are as conditional as the so-called positive vows attested throughout the Old Testament and extra-biblical literature. He writes:

---

1.   In Ps. 132.3-5 David vows that he will not enter his house or sleep until he has found a temple for Yahweh. Cartledge has argued persuasively that this is not a vow but an oath (1992: 16). This leaves us with Num. 6 as our only example of the alleged negative vow.

> among those who became Nazirites as the result of a vow, the evidence indicates that these vows were most likely conditional promises of special service, held out on condition that a petition of the person making the vow should be granted by God (1989: 410).

By suggesting that some Nazirites offered their devotion to Yahweh in return for some (unspecified) payment by the deity, Cartledge has raised an interesting point. If this view could be substantiated then it would indicate that Nazirite vows were actually similar to the so-called positive vows and that the entire positive–negative distinction would be unnecessary.

While I do not find this argument implausible, I nevertheless have certain reservations about Cartledge's central thesis. To begin with, I must stress (as does Cartledge) that there is only one unequivocal example of a Nazirite vow in the Old Testament. As such, Cartledge must base the bulk of his reconstruction of the putative conditional Nazirite votive system on the mishnaic tractates *Nedarim* and *Nazir* and the writings of Josephus (1989: 421-22; Cartledge 1992: 22-23). The temporal distance of these sources from the Old Testament materials is large enough to make one hesitant to assume that similar processes are being discussed in the latter texts.

Secondly, the biblical data which addresses the issue of Nazirites (but not necessarily Nazirite vows) seems to suggest that one is *vowed into* this status *by another person*. The angel of the Lord performs this service in Judg. 13.4-7, Hannah does this in 1 Samuel 1, and according to Amos 2.11-12 such individuals were 'divinely appointed' (Cartledge 1989: 410). These passages indicate that one becomes a Nazirite as a consequence of someone else's act. If these are related to the Nazirite vows discussed in Numbers 6, then the mechanisms found here would be completely incongruous with any of those seen in the positive vow.

Thirdly, in Numbers 6 a variety of regulations are stipulated for those who take Nazirite vows. These rules are nothing like the rules pertaining to positive vows. In the latter, the initiation stage of the vow is entirely unregulated and there exist no laws about when, how, and under what circumstances a petition is to be made. Of course, payment of the vow is an entirely different matter. The verses of Numbers 6, however, describe a type of vow where cultic supervision is at a maximum throughout all stages of the votive procedure.

Finally, in v. 21 a reference seems to be made to another type of vow that theoretically the Nazirite may make. Why did the literati distinguish this type of vow from Nazirite vows if they did not believe that there was something distinct about the latter?

Unlike Cartledge, I believe that the positive and negative categories are still valid distinctions insofar as they suggest that there is something very different about the type of vow discussed in Numbers 6 and nearly all the others found in the Old Testament. While Cartledge's thesis should not be ruled out, suffice it to say that more evidence of Nazirite vows stemming from the pre-exilic and early post-exilic periods will be needed before it can be accepted as true.

פלא נדר

One of the great unanswered—and perhaps unanswerable—questions regarding the Israelite vow concerns the proper meaning of the occasionally-encountered phrase נדר פלא (Lev. 22.21, 27.2; Num. 15.3, 8, 6.2). The correct translation and interpretation of the verb פלא, which appears in both the *piel* and the *hiphil* (Wendel 1931a: 96; Milgrom 1990: 44), has beguiled over a century of exegetes. While many theories have been proposed, it is safe to say that none of them can be accepted as definitive. I shall begin this discussion with a review of the basic approaches which scholars have taken when attempting to translate this difficult phrase.

One very popular interpretation of the phrase פלא נדר renders it as 'to fulfill a vow' or 'to accomplish a vow' (Noth 1968: 112; Budd 1984: 165; G.B. Gray 1906: 173; McNeile 1911: 80; Snaith 1967: 148, 249; Heinsich 1935: 101; Heinsich 1936: 61; Elliger 1966: 295). Unfortunately, not one proponent of this translation has offered any reason for favoring this reading. This interpretation is obviously derived from context, and in this capacity it is not at all implausible.

A second school of thought, usually associated with Jewish commentators who are students of medieval rabbinic exegesis, maintains that the phrase refers to a vow specifically uttered. Milgrom notes: 'The versions render "express, make explicit", implying that the vow cannot be silent but must be articulated' (1990: 44, 118; Greenstone 1939: 153; Hoffman 1906: 111). Yet there does not seem to be any evidence which suggests that the root פלא may bear this connotation. Further, why does the vow have to be 'explicitly uttered' insofar as nearly all vows are assumed by the biblical literati to be 'expressed' or 'spoken' to Yahweh (see Chapter 3)?

The third major school views the term as referring to something special or set apart. Thus Levine observes: 'The point is that the verb *hipli'*, with a final *alef*, is a variant of the verb *palah*, with a final *heh*, a verb whose meaning is clearly known: "to set apart"' (1989: 193). This classification is in line with Gesenius's observation that for this root 'the *aleph* has no consonantal value, and is only retained orthographically' (1985: 77).

This general notion of setting apart or separateness, or of being special, can be detected in the following translations: 'a separate vow' (Knobel 1857: 526; see also Strack 1894: 409), 'when anyone [makes] a solemn vow' (Bertholet 1901: 97, 76), 'do a special thing' (Cartledge 1989: 413; see also *idem* 1992: 21, 141-42). Similarly, Ehrlich writes: 'Here the expression indicates something special which stands outside of the ordinary. פלא נדר is a special sacrifice for the payment of the vow' (1909: 81; see also McNeile 1911: 80; Noth 1968: 202; *BDB*: 810).

Gold seems to synthesize all of these views in the remark 'a separate vow, or rather vowing a special vow, פלא (a vow) clearly pronounced' (1926: 21).

Another translation is proffered by Miller, who, on the basis of a Ugaritic parallel, has offered the unlikely theory that פלא is a confusion with מלא (1988: 147; and see Chapter 1). Yet this verb never governs the substantive נדר in any other vow-text at our disposal.

All these translations have their merits. Those that choose to emphasize the distinctiveness of the vow, or the fact that it is set apart, stand on the firmest philological ground. These particular definitions of the forms פלא and פלה are well attested in the Old Testament (*BDB*: 810). As such, any translation that undertakes to emphasize the connotation of something being extraordinary, special or distinct, would seem to be the most sound. Certain considerations, however, lead me to question the contextual appropriateness of this translation. For *why* are these vows considered to be so special? What it is about them which serves to set them apart?

It is difficult to find answers to such questions. In Lev. 27.2 and Num. 6.2 the consecration of a person to the temple can indeed be thought of as 'special'. But in Num. 15.3, 8 and Lev. 22.21, where the phrase also appears, animal sacrifices are mentioned and these certainly do not seem very extraordinary at all. In fact, the particular sacrifices mentioned in these two latter passages can be found in many other vow-texts which make no mention of the term פלא נדר (for example, Judg. 11.31; Lev. 7.11; contra Cartledge 1992: 141).

Neither does the notion of being 'set apart' seem to retain any significance across all these vow-texts. If one were to suggest that this term refers to a type of vow only set apart for special people at particular times, it would be refuted by the fact that a very wide cross-section of the populace appears in vow-texts which make use of the term (for example, Num 6.1: men and women, Lev. 27.8: poor persons, Lev. 22.17: any Israelite, Num. 15.13: every citizen and stranger; see Chapter 5). Thus, the fact that 'anyone' may engage in the practice forces questions about what may have been so distinct and special about this type of vow. Accordingly, a sociological reading of this phrase and its surrounding vow-texts clarifies little given that the supplicants in these passages are as varied as those found in others.

I would repeat, however, that the term does appear in two vow-texts in which the 'item offered' has unique social value. In Leviticus 27 the term is used in conjunction with a vow for the '[fixed] equivalent of a human being'. In Num 6.2 a similar usage is witnessed in the case of a Nazirite's vow. It is only in these particular instances that the notions of 'distinctiveness' or of something being extraordinary seem to be clearly articulated.

APPENDIX 3

שׁלם: *'To Fulfill a Vow'*

The verb שׁלם appears in Old Testament vow-texts a total of 16 times: 15 times in *piel* and once in the *pual* form.[1] Based on an examination of these texts it would seem better to translate the term as 'fulfill a vow' rather than 'pay a vow'. Insofar as the latter remotely suggests a 'money' transaction, it should be excluded from translations of the relevant vow-texts, for in none of these passages can it be inferred that money, shekels, and so on are being paid to Yahweh.

There exists only one vow-text which employs שׁלם and which articulates what exactly it is that is being offered to the deity. In 2 Sam. 15.7, Absalom states: ואשלם את־נדרי אשר־נדרתי ליהוה בחברון. In this instance he has allegedly offered his devotion to Yahweh. But in Leviticus 27, where payment of vows according to a tendered scale is clearly demonstrated, it is significant that the form שׁלם does not appear. Accordingly, this term has yet to be used in reference to 'money' transactions as regards vows.

In fact, the form seems generally reserved for passages which stress the more general nature of faithfully compensating Yahweh (for example, in the Psalms). In instances where the offer of a specific tangible item (such as animal sacrifice) is mentioned, the term does not appear. For now then, it may be more accurate to translate this verb as 'to fulfill' as opposed to 'to pay'.[2]

---

1.   But see Keller who counts 20 (1976: 40). The vow-texts that employ שׁלם are: 2 Sam. 15.7; Jon. 2.10; Isa. 19.21; Eccl. 5.3, 4; Pss. 76.12; 22.26; 61.9; 116.14; 116.18; 66.13; 50.14; Prov. 7.14; Job 22.27; Nah. 2.1 and Ps. 65.2 (*pual*).

2.   See also Cathcart 1973: 69 for a similar translation.

APPENDIX 4

The Etymological Status of נדר

To date, there have been three distinct schools of thought regarding the etymological lineage of the Hebrew root נדר. Two of these, it will be shown, are founded on assumptions which have been more or less discredited by the third. This last and most recent position has clearly superseded the first two and currently represents the most plausible reconstruction of the etymological standing of Hebrew נדר.

The Arabic Deviance School

The position I call the 'Arabic deviance hypothesis' is almost exclusively associated with the great German-speaking philologians of the late nineteenth and early twentieth century. These scholars, well trained in Arabic, naturally proceeded on the assumption—one seen less frequently among contemporary students of Hebrew philology—that Arabic could illuminate various complexities of the Hebrew language.

This school took as its methodological starting point the fact that Arabic retains only one root which is cognate to both Hebrew נדר and נזר. Accordingly, it was maintained that the presence of two roots in Hebrew was actually an aberration. Wellhausen writes: 'According to the rule נזר, not נדר, is the real Hebrew word for *naḍara*' (Wellhausen;[1] see also Robertson Smith 1972: 482-83; Pedersen 1914: 121).

The parameters of the argument were framed by the belief that the two roots found in Hebrew only occurred by accident, since Hebrew possessed two roots while the sister language only retained one to express both concepts. In 1898 Schwally offered the following explanation:

> I believe rather, that there existed in נ־ד־ר an inner-Hebraic consonantal shift, the fixed Terminus נזיר and its relative have not expanded since a very early period (1898: 137).

In a similar vein, Wendel observed that this state of affairs is attributable to a bifurcation of an original Hebrew root, which was most likely נזר:

> The original Hebrew root might have been נ־ד־ר or נ־ז־ר, having the sense of: to consecrate. In actuality, the probability leans more toward the form נ־ז־ר ... (1931a: 93).

The proponents of this theory took the standing of this root in Arabic as indicative of normative Semitic usage. The Hebrew root נדר was viewed as a secondary development, an offshoot of the root N-Z-R. For most scholars this suggested that a late split

---

1.   Cited in Wendel (1931a: 93). I believe, however, that the citation offered by Wendel may be incorrect.

had occurred whereby the Hebrew root נדר had become confused, for a variety of reasons, with the older root נזר.

The Consonantal Shift Theory

With the rise of a philological intelligentsia which specialized in Canaanite dialects, a new methodological starting point was adopted for the study of this problem. These exegetes founded their inquiry on the assumption that there once existed a proto-Semitic root N-D̲-R of which נדר and נזר are descendants. This discussion often led to some extraordinarily complicated theoretical schemes, most of them not straying too far from the version adumbrated by Albright.

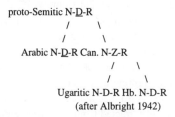

proto-Semitic N-D̲-R

Arabic N-D̲-R Can. N-Z-R

Ugaritic N-D-R Hb. N-D-R
(after Albright 1942)

Thus, Albright attempts to explain the usage of נזר instead of נדר in the Bar-Hadad inscription (see Chapter 1) as attributable to the fact that 'the Aramaeans employed Phoenician (Canaanite) spelling wherever possible, and consequently rendered their own *d*… with the character of *zayin*'[2] (1942: 26; see also Albright 1969: 161). In correspondence with the general view noted above, most scholars agreed that Aramaic נזר could be rendered as 'to vow' (Dunand 1942–1943: 43; Levi Della Vida 1943: 30; Keller 1976: 40; Gibson 1978: 4).

Complicating matters immensely, was H.L. Ginsberg's argument which claimed that נזר in the Bar-Hadad inscription should be translated as 'he prayed' not 'he vowed' (1945: 161 n. 8; see Chapter 1). In developing this theory, Ginsberg took the opportunity to suggest that the existence of these two forms in Hebrew 'is due to blending or contamination' (1945: 161, n. 8). Here, as with Albright and nearly all other commentators noted in this section, the root נדר is treated as a variant of Canaanite נזר, which itself traces its lineage to Proto-Semitic N-D̲-R.

The common denominator running through all these explanations is that the Hebrew root נדר is a derivative of an older proto-Canaanite form N-Z-R. As with the proponents of the Arabic Deviance hypothesis, it was held that נדר was a late offshoot of a completely different root.

Jesse Boyd and Proto-Semitic N-D-R

Pointedly ending a nearly forty-year silence on the subject, philologian Jesse Boyd offered a radically new interpretation of the etymological lineage of this word. Drawing on all Semitic languages, as well as a corpus of evidence which was not available to scholars of earlier generations, Boyd has offered a hypothesis which

---

2.   Albright originally wrote '*daleth*' here, but this was an error which he later corrected (see Levi Della Vida 1943: 30 n. 1).

essentially invalidates the conclusions of the aforementioned schools. While the abundance of data culled from all of the Semitic languages makes it impossible to summarize Boyd's argument, I should nevertheless like to outline its basic tenets.

Most importantly, Boyd has adduced convincing evidence to support the hypothesis that no etymological basis exists for the belief that the Semitic root N-D-R is a derivative of proto-Semitic N-D̲-R. As Boyd has demonstrated, *all* of the northwest Semitic languages preserve the roots N-D-R, N-D̲-R and N-Z-R, yet only N-D-R is found in each as meaning 'to vow' (1986: 66). Further, Tigre and Hebrew both preserve N-D-R and N-Z-R forms with distinct meanings (Boyd 1986: 72). As such, this would strongly argue for the distinction of these two roots in the hypothetical proto-Semitic language. Boyd goes on to conclude that Hebrew נדר does not stem from proto-Semitic N-D̲-R, *but from its own distinct proto-Semitic root*. As such, Boyd's hypothesis would directly discredit the fundamental assumptions upon which both the Arabic Deviance Hypothesis and the Consonantal Shift Theory were predicated. That is to say, neither anticipated the existence of a proto-Semitic root N-D-R. Rather, they maintained that the form entered Hebrew at a much later date, due to blending, consonantal shifts, the role of the newly-formed alphabet, and so on.

If any broader significance can be extracted from the aforementioned philological discussion it may be stated as follows: the distinction between נדר and נזר is not due to an aberrational deviation from one basic proto-Semitic root. Further, they are not identical sister concepts which became differentiated only in the Canaanite world. Instead, they could be looked at as two entirely different social processes whose distinct historical antecedents can be traced back to a philological distinction in a hypothetical proto-Semitic language.

A Nazirite's vow then, as I maintained above, could conceivably reflect a process which was quite distinct from, and perhaps not even related to, the institution of positive vow-making in ancient Israel. Earlier it was shown that Nazirite vows are different in their social function from positive vows. The philological material, insofar as it places a degree of etymological distance between these allegedly related roots, would seem to support a similar conclusion.

BIBLIOGRAPHY

Ackerman, S.
1989   '"And the Women Knead Dough": The Worship of the Queen of Heaven in Sixth-Century Judah', in Day 1989: 109-24.
1992   *Under Every Green Tree: Popular Religion in Sixth-Century Judah* (HSM, 46; Atlanta: Scholars Press).

Ackroyd, P.
1971   *The First Book of Samuel* (Cambridge Bible Commentary; Cambridge: Cambridge University Press).

Ahlström, G.W.
1979   '1 Samuel 1:15', *Bib* 60: 254.

Aistleitner, J.
1964   *Die mythologischen und kultischen Texte aus Ras Schamra* (Bibliotheca Orientalis Hungarica, 8; Budapest: Akadémiai Kiadó, 2nd edn).
1974   *Wörterbuch der ugaritischen Sprache* (Berlin: Akademie Verlag).

Albertz, R.
1978   *Persönliche Frömmigkeit und offizielle Religion: Religionsinterner Pluralismus in Israel und Babylon* (Calwer Theologische Monographien, 9; Stuttgart: Calwer Verlag).

Albright, W.F.
1942   'A Votive Stele Erected By Ben-Hadad I of Damascus to the God Melcarth', *BASOR* 87: 23-29.
1944   'A Vow to Asherah in the Keret Epic', *BASOR* 94: 30-31.
1969   'Samuel and the Beginnings of the Prophetic Movement', in *Interpreting the Prophetic Tradition: The Goldenson Lectures 1955-1966* (intro. H. Orlinsky; New York: Ktav): 151-176.

Almbladh, K.
1986   *Studies in the Book of Jonah* (Uppsala: Almqvist and Wiksell).

Alt, A.
1968   *Essays on Old Testament History and Religion* (trans. R.A. Wilson; Garden City, NY: Anchor Books).

Amir, D.
1987   *Gods and Heroes: Canaanite Epics From Ugarit (Including Some Epics Never Before Published in Hebrew)* (Hebrew) (Israel: Beth Ussishkin).

Andersen, F., and D. Forbes
1989   *The Vocabulary of the Old Testament* (Rome: Pontificio Instituto Biblico).

Anderson, A.A.
    1972   *The Book of Psalms* (NCB; 2 vols.; Greenwood, SC: The Attic Press).
    1989   *2 Samuel* (WBC, 11; Waco, TX: Word Books).
Anderson, G.
    1987   *Sacrifices and Offerings in Ancient Israel: Studies in Their Social and Political Importance* (HSM, 41; Atlanta: Scholars Press).
Anderson, P.
    1976   'The Antinomies of Antonio Gramsci', *New Left Review* 100: 5-78.
Ap Thomas, D.
    1956   'Notes on Some Terms Relating to Prayer', *VT* 6: 225-41.
Aron, R.
    1989   *Main Currents in Sociological Thought* 2: Durkheim–Pareto–Weber (trans. R. Howard and H. Weaver; Garden City, NY: Doubleday).
Asad, T.
    1983   'Anthropological Conceptions of Religion: Reflections on Geertz', *Man* 18: 237-59.
Badone, E.
    1990a   'Introduction', in Badone 1990: 3-23.
    1990b   'Breton Folklore of Anticlericalism', in Badone 1990: 140-62.
    1990 (ed.) *Religious Orthodoxy and Popular Faith in European Society* (Princeton, NJ: Princeton University Press).
Baentsch, B.
    1903   *Exodus–Leviticus–Numeri* (HKAT; Göttingen: Vandenhoeck und Ruprecht).
Barton, G.
    1909   *A Critical and Exegetical Commentary on the Book of Ecclesiastes* (ICC; New York: Charles Scribner's Sons).
Barucq, A.
    1964   *Le livre des Proverbes* (SB; Paris: Gabalda).
Bates, T.
    1975   'Gramsci and the Theory of Hegemony', *Journal of the History of Ideas* 36: 351-66.
Bax, M.
    1987   'Religious Regimes and State Formation: Towards a Research Perspective', *Anthropological Quarterly* 60: 1-11.
Behar, R.
    1990   'The Struggle for the Church: Popular Anticlericalism and Religiosity in Post-Franco Spain', in Badone 1990: 76-112.
Bendix, R.
    1977   *Max Weber: An Intellectual Portrait* (intro. G. Roth; Berkeley: University of California Press).
Bennett, W.H.
    1895   *The Book of Jeremiah: Chapters 21-52* (New York: Armstrong & Son).
    n.d.   *Genesis: Introduction; Revised Version With Notes, Giving an Analysis Showing From Which of the Original Documents Each Portion of the Text is Taken; Index and Map* (Edinburgh: T.C. and E.C. Jack).

Benz, F.
1972   *Personal Names in the Phoenician and Punic Inscriptions: A Catalog, Grammatical Study and Glossary of Elements* (Rome: Biblical Institute Press).

Benzinger, I.
1927   *Hebräische Archäologie* (Angelos-Lehrbücher, 1; Leipzig: Eduard Pfeiffer).

Berger, P.
1963   'Charisma and Religious Innovation: The Social Location of Israelite Prophecy', *American Sociological Review* 82: 940-50.

Berger, P., and T. Luckmann
1967   *The Social Construction of Reality: A Treatise in the Sociology of Knowledge* (Garden City, NY: Doubleday).

Berlinerblau, J.
1991   'The Israelite Vow: Distress or Daily Life?', *Bib* 72: 548-55.
1993   'The "Popular Religion" Paradigm in Old Testament Research: A Sociological Critique', *JSOT*: 60: 3-26.
1995   'Some Sociological Observations on Moshe Greenberg's *Biblical Prose Prayer as a Window to the Popular Religion of Ancient Israel*', JNSL: 21: 1-14.
1996   (forthcoming) 'Preliminary Remarks for the Sociological Study of Israelite "Official Religion"' in Baruch Levine Anniversary Volume (ed. L. Schiffman and W. Hallo; Winona Lake, IN: Eisenbrauns).

Berthier, A., and R. Charlier
1955   *Le sanctuaire punique d'El-Hofra à Constantine* (Paris: Arts et métiers graphiques).

Bertholet, A.
1899   *Deuteronomium* (KHAT; Tübingen: Mohr).
1901   *Leviticus* (KHAT; Tübingen: Mohr).

Bewer, J.
1952   *The Book of Jeremiah. II. Jeremiah Ch. 26-52 in the King James Version With Introduction and Critical Notes* (Harper's Annotated Bible 6; New York: Harper Brothers).

Beyerlin, W. (ed.).
1978   *Near Eastern Religious Texts Relating to the Old Testament* (trans. J. Bowden, OTL; Philadelphia: Westminster Press).

Bird, P.
1987   'The Place of Women in the Israelite Cultus', in Miller, Hanson and McBride 1987: 397-419.
1989   'Women's Religion in Ancient Israel', in *Women's Earliest Records From Ancient Egypt and Western Asia: Proceedings of the Conference on Women in the Ancient Near East* (ed. B. Lesko; BJS, 166; Atlanta: Scholars Press): 283-98.
1991   'Israelite Religion and the Faith of Israel's Daughters: Reflections on Gender and Religious Definition', in Jobling, Day and Sheppard 1991: 97-108.

Birnbaum, S.A.
1957   'Ostraca', in *The Objects From Samaria-Sebaste*, III (eds. J.W.

Crowfoot, G.M. Crowfoot and K. Kenyon; London: Palestine Exploration Fund).

Bossy, J.
1989   *Christianity in the West: 1400-1700* (Oxford: Oxford University Press).

Boström, G.
1935   *Proverbiastudien: Die Weisheit und das Fremde Weib in Spr. 1-9* (Lund: Gleerup).

Bouritius, G.J.F.
1979   'Popular and Official Religion in Christianity: Three Cases in Nineteenth-Century Europe', in Vrijhof and Waardenburg 1979: 117-65.

Boyd, J.
1986   'The Etymological Relationship Between *NDR* and *NZR* Reconsidered', *UF* 17: 61-75.

Brandes, S.
1990   'Conclusion: Reflections on the Study of Religious Orthodoxy and Popular Faith in Europe', in Badone 1990: 185-200.

Brekelmans, C.
1963   'Vow', in L. Hartman (ed.), *Encyclopedic Dictionary of the Bible* (New York: McGraw-Hill): 2552-54.

Brekelmans, C., and J. Goldstain
1987   'Voeu', in P-M. Bogaert *et al.* (eds.), *Dictionnaire encyclopedique de la Bible* (Belgium: Brepols): 1342-43.

Brett, M.G.
1987   'Literacy and Domination: G.A. Herion's Sociology of History Writing', *JSOT* 37: 15-40.

Brettell, C.
1990   'The Priest and His People: The Contractual Basis for Religious Practice in Rural Portugal', in Badone 1990: 55-75.

Brichto, H.
1963   *The Problem of 'Curse' in the Hebrew Bible* (*JBL* Monograph Series, 13; Philadelphia: Society of Biblical Literature and Exegesis).

Briggs, C., and Emilie B.
1907   *A Critical and Exegetical Commentary on the Book of Psalms*, II (ICC; Edinburgh: T. & T. Clark).

Bright, J.
1965   *Jeremiah: A New Translation with Introduction and Commentary* (AB, Garden City, NY: Doubleday).

Brown, P.
1982   *The Cult of the Saints: Its Rise and Function in Late Christianity* (Chicago: University of Chicago Press).

Brunet, G.
1985   'L'Hébreu Kèlèb', *VT* 35: 485-88.

Bruno, A.
1955   *Die Bücher Samuel: Eine rhythmische Untersuchung* (Stockholm: Almqvist and Wiksell).

1957	*Das Buch der Zwölf: Eine rhythmische und textkritische Untersuchung* (Stockholm: Almqvist and Wiksell).

Budd, P.
1984	*Numbers* (WBC, 5; Waco, TX: Word Books, Publisher).

Buis, P., and J. Leclercq.
1963	*Le Deutéronome* (SB; Paris: J. Gabalda).

Camp, C.
1985	*Wisdom and the Feminine in the Book of Proverbs* (Bible and Literature Series; Sheffield: Almond Press).
1991	'What's so Strange about the Strange Woman?', in Jobling, Day and Sheppard 1991: 17-31.

Candelaria, M.
1990	*Popular Religion and Liberation: The Dilemma of Liberation Theology* (Albany: State University of New York Press).

Caquot, A.
1960	'Les Rephaim ougaritiques', *Syria* 37: 75-93.

Caquot, A., M. Sznycer and A. Herdner
1974	*Textes ougaritiques. I. Mythes et légendes: introduction, traduction, commentaire* (Paris: Cerf).

Carmichael, C.
1974	*The Laws of Deuteronomy* (Ithaca, NY: Cornell University Press).

Carroll, M.
1992	*Madonnas that Maim: Popular Catholicism in Italy Since the Fifteenth Century* (Baltimore: The Johns Hopkins University Press).

Carroll, R.
1986	*Jeremiah: A Commentary* (OTL; Philadelphia: Westminster Press).

Cartledge, T.
1987	'Conditional Vows in the Psalms of Lament: A New Approach to an Old Problem', in K. Hoglund, E. Huwiler, J. Glass and R. Lee 1987: 77-94.
1988	'Vow', in *ISBE*, IV: 998-99.
1989	'Were Nazirite Vows Unconditional?', *CBQ* 51: 409-22.
1992	*Vows in the Hebrew Bible and the Ancient Near East* (JSOTSup, 147; Sheffield: JSOT Press).

Cathcart, K.
1973	*Nahum in the Light of Northwest Semitic* (BibOr, 26; Rome: Biblical Institute Press).

Cazelles, H.
1951	'La dîme israélite et les textes de Ras Shamra', *VT* 1: 131-34.

Chaney, M.
1986	'Systemic Study of the Israelite Monarchy', *Semeia* 37: 53-76.
1991	'Debt Easement in Israelite History and Tradition', in Jobling, Day and Sheppard 1991: 129-39.

Chapman, A.T., and A.W. Streane
1914	*The Book of Leviticus in the Revised Version, with Introduction and Notes* (Cambridge Bible For Schools and Colleges; Cambridge: Cambridge University Press).

Cipriani, R.

1976   'La religiosité populaire en Italie: deux recherches sur la magie et la politique dans le sud du pays', *Social Compass* 23: 221-31.

Clamer, A.

1946   *Tome 2 Lévitique-Nombres-Deutéronome* (La Sainte Bible; Paris: Letouzey et Ané, Éditeurs).

1953   *La Genèse: Traduite et commentée* (La Sainte Bible; Paris: Letouzey et Ané).

Clements, R.E. (ed.)

1989   *The World of Ancient Israel: Sociological, Anthropological and Political Perspectives: Essays by Members of the Society for Old Testament Study* (Cambridge: Cambridge University Press).

Coats, G.

1976   'Conquest Traditions in the Wilderness Theme', *JBL* 95: 177-90.

Collingwood, R.G.

1956   *The Idea of History* (London: Oxford University Press).

Cooke, G.A.

1903   *A Textbook of North-Semitic Inscriptions: Moabite, Hebrew, Phoenician, Aramaic, Nabataean, Palmyrene, Jewish* (Oxford: Clarendon Press).

Coppes, L.

1980   'Vow', *TWOT*, II: 557-58.

Coser, L.

1964   *The Functions of Social Conflict* (New York: The Free Press).

Cowley, A.

1923   *Aramaic Papyri of the 5th Century B.C.: Edited With Translation and Notes* (Oxford: Clarendon Press).

Craigie, P.

1976   *The Book of Deuteronomy* (ICC; Grand Rapids: Eerdmans).

1977   'Deuteronomy and Ugaritic Studies', *TynBul* 28: 155-69.

1983   *Ugarit and the Old Testament* (Grand Rapids: Eerdmans).

Crenshaw, J.L.

1970   'Popular Questioning of the Justice of God in Ancient Israel', *ZAW* 82: 380-95.

1987   *Ecclesiastes: A Commentary* (OTL; Philadelphia: Westminster Press).

Cross, F.

1972   'The Stele Dedicated to Melcarth by Ben-Hadad of Damascus', *BASOR* 205: 36-42.

1973   *Canaanite Myth and Hebrew Epic: Essays in the History of the Religion of Israel* (Cambridge, MA: Harvard University Press).

Dahood, M.

1963   'Hebrew-Ugaritic Lexicography I', *Bib* 44: 289-303.

1966   'Hebrew-Ugaritic Lexicography IV', *Bib* 47: 403-19.

1968   *Psalms 2: 51-100. Introduction, Translation, and Notes* (AB; Garden City, NY: Doubleday).

Davies, G.H.

1962   'Vows', *IDB*, IV: 792-93.

Day, P. (ed.)
1989   *Gender and Difference in Ancient Israel* (Minneapolis: Fortress Press).
Deissler, A., and M. Delcor.
1961   *Les petits prophètes* (La Sainte Bible, 8; Paris: Letouzey et Ané).
Delavault, B., and A. Lemaire.
1976   'Une stèle "Molk" de Palestine dédiée à Eshmoun? RES 367 reconsidéré', *RB* 83: 569-83.
Delcor, M.
1982   'Le culte de la "Reine du Ciel" selon Jer. 7,18; 44,17-19, 25 et ses survivances', in W.C. Delsman *et al.* (eds.), *Von Kanaan bis Kerala: Festschrift für Prof. Mag. Dr. Dr. J.P.M. van der Ploeg O.P.* (Neukirchen: Butzon und Bercker Kevelaer).
Delitzsch, F.
1877   *Commentary on the Song of Songs and Ecclesiastes* (trans. M.G. Easton; Edinburgh: T. & T. Clark).
1889   *A New Commentary on Genesis* (trans. S. Taylor; Edinburgh: T. & T. Clark).
1890   *Biblical Commentary on the Proverbs of Solomon* (trans. M.G. Easton; Clark's Foreign Theological Library; Edinburgh: T. & T. Clark).
Dennefeld, L.
1946   *Les grands prophètes* (La Sainte Bible, 7; Paris: Letouzey et Ané).
Dever, W.
1987   'The Contribution of Archaeology to the Study of Canaanite and Early Israelite Religion', in Miller, Hanson and McBride 1987: 209-47.
1990   *Recent Archaeological Discoveries and Biblical Research* (Seattle: University of Washington Press).
1991   'Unresolved Issues in the Early History of Israel: Toward a Synthesis of Archaeological and Textual Reconstructions', in Jobling, Day and Sheppard 1991: 195-208.
Dhorme, E.
1910   *Les livres de Samuel* (EBib; Paris: Gabalda).
1984   *A Commentary on the Book of Job* (trans H. Knight; New York: Thomas Nelson).
Diakonoff, I.M., *et al.*
1991   'Introduction', in *Early Antiquity* (ed. I.M. Diakonoff; trans. A. Kirjanov; Chicago: University of Chicago Press).
Dietrich, M., and O. Loretz.
1980   'Die Bannung von Schlangengift: (*KTU* 1.100 und *KTU* 1.107:7b-13a.19b-20)', *UF* 12: 153-70.
Dietrich, M., O. Loretz and J. Sanmartín
1976a   'Zu WLD "Gebären" und "Knabe" im Keret-Epos', *UF* 8: 435-36.
1976b   'Die ugaritischen Totengeister *RPU(M)* und die biblischen Rephaim', *UF* 8: 45-52.
Dijkstra, M.
1979   'Some Reflections on the Legend of Aqhat', *UF* 11: 199-210.
Dijkstra, M., and J. de Moor
1975   'Problematical Passages in the Legend of Aqhâtu', *UF* 7: 171-215.

Doeve, J.W.
1979　　'Official and Popular Religion in Judaism', in Vrijhof and Waardenburg 1979: 325-39.

Driver, S.R.
1897　　*An Introduction to the Literature of the Old Testament* (International Theological Library; New York: Charles Scribner's Sons, 6th edn).
1903　　*A Critical and Exegetical Commentary on Deuteronomy* (ICC; New York: Charles Scribner's Sons).
n.d.　　*The Minor Prophets: Nahum, Habakkuk, Zephaniah, Haggai, Zechariah, Malachi: Introductions, Revised Version with Notes, Index and Map* (The Century Bible; Edinburgh: T.C. & E.C. Jack).
1909　　*The Book of Genesis: With Introduction and Notes* (London: Methuen, 7th rev. edn).
1913　　*Notes on the Hebrew Text and the Topography of the Book of Samuel: with an Introduction on Hebrew Paleography and the Ancient Versions and Facsimiles of Inscriptions and Maps* (Oxford: Clarendon Press).
1965　　*A Critical and Exegetical Commentary on Deuteronomy* (ICC; Edinburgh: T. & T. Clark, 3rd. edn).
1984　　*Notes on the Hebrew Text and the Topography of the Book of Samuel: With an Introduction on Hebrew Paleography and the Ancient Versions and Facsimiles of Inscriptions and Maps* (2nd rev. edn; Indiana: Alpha Publications).

Driver, S., and G.B. Gray.
1921　　*A Critical and Exegetical Commentary on the Book of Job: Together with a New Translation*, II (ICC; New York: Charles Scribner's Sons).

Dubisch, J.
1990　　'Pilgrimage and Popular Religion at a Greek Holy Shrine', in Badone 1990: 113-39.

Dubois, E.C. *et al.*
1985　　*Feminist Scholarship: Kindling in the Groves of Académe* (Urbana, IL: University of Illinois Press).

Dunand, M.
1939　　'Stèle araméenne dédiée à Melqart', *Bulletin Musée de Beyrouth* 3:65-76.
1942–1943　'A propos de la stèle de Melqart de musée d'Alep', *Bulletin Musée de Beyrouth* 6:41-45.

Dupont-Sommer, A.
1958　　*Les inscriptions araméennes de Sfiré (Stèles 1 et 2)* (Extrait des mémoires présentés par divers savants à L'Académie des Inscriptions et Belles-Lettres, 15; Paris: Imprimerie Nationale).

Durkheim, E.
1965　　*The Elementary Forms of the Religious Life* (trans. J. Swain; New York: The Free Press).
1974　　*Sociology and Philosophy* (trans. D.F. Pocock; New York: The Free Press).

Dussaud, R.
1921　　*Les origines cananéennes du sacrifice Israélite* (Paris: Leroux).

Ehrlich, A.
1909   *Randglossen zur hebräischen Bibel: Textkritisches, Sprachliches und Sachliches.* II. *Leviticus, Numeri and Deuteronomium* (Leipzig: Hinrichs).

Eisenstadt, S.N.
1981   'The Format of Jewish History—Some Reflections on Weber's Ancient Judaism', *Modern Judaism* 1: 54-73.

Eissfeldt, O.
1965   *The Old Testament: An Introduction (including the Apocrypha and Pseudepigrapha, and also the Works of Similar Type From Qumran). The History of the Formation of the Old Testament* (trans. P. Ackroyd; New York: Harper & Row, Publishers).

Elias, N.
1978   *What is Sociology?* (trans. S. Mennell and G. Morrissey; New York: Columbia University Press).

Elliger, K.
1950   *Das Buch der zwölf kleinen Propheten.* II. *Die Propheten Nahum, Habakuk, Zephania, Haggai, Zacharia, Maleachi* (*Das Alte Testament Deutsch*, 25; Göttingen: Vandenhoeck & Ruprecht).
1966   *Leviticus* (*HAT*, 4; Tübingen: Mohr).

Ellis, E.E.
1962   'Vow', in *The New Bible Dictionary* (ed. J.D. Douglas; London: The Inter-Varsity Fellowship): 1313.

Emmerson, G.I.
1989   'Women in Ancient Israel' in Clements 1989: 371-94.

Engels, F.
1969   *The Peasant War in Germany* (trans. V. Schneierson; Moscow: Progress Publishers).
1974   *Ludwig Feuerbach and the Outcome of Classical German Philosophy* (New York: International).

Eslinger, L.
1985   *Kingship of God in Crisis: A Close Reading of 1 Samuel 1–12* (Bible and Literature Series; Decatur: Almond Press).

Fahey, T.
1982   'Max Weber's *Ancient Judaism*', *American Journal of Sociology* 88: 62-87.

Farrar, F.W.
n.d.   *The Minor Prophets* (New York: Anson D.F. Randolph & Co.).

Fisher, L.
1971   'Two Projects at Claremont', *UF* 3: 25-32.
1975 (ed.)   *Ras Shamra Parallels: The Texts from Ugarit and the Hebrew Bible*, II (AnOr, 50; Rome: Pontificium Institutum Biblicum).

Fitzmyer, J.
1967   *The Aramaic Inscriptions of Sefire* (BibOr, 19; Rome: Pontifical Biblical Institute).

Fohrer, G.
1972   *History of Israelite Religion* (trans. D. Green; Nashville: Abingdon Press).

Fokkelman, J.P.
    1981   *Narrative Art and Poetry in The Books of Samuel: A Full Interpretation Based on Stylistic and Structural Analyses*. I. *King David 2 Sam. 9–20 and 1 Kings 1–2* (Studia Semitica Neerlandica 30; Assen: Van Gorcum).

Fontana, B.
    1993   *Hegemony and Power: On the Relation Between Gramsci and Machiavelli* (Minneapolis: University of Minnesota Press).

Fulton, J.
    1987   'Religion and Politics in Gramsci: An Introduction', *Sociological Analysis* 48: 197-216.

Gammie, J., and L. Perdue (eds.).
    1990   *The Sage in Israel and the Ancient Near East* (Winona Lake, IN: Eisenbrauns).

Garbini, G.
    1988   *History and Ideology in Ancient Israel* (trans. J. Bowden; New York: Crossroad).

Garelli, P.
    1962   'La religion de l'Assyrie ancienne d'après un ouvrage récent', *RA* 56: 191-210.
    1963   *Les Assyriens en Cappadoce* (Bibliothèque archéologique et historique de l'institut Français d'archéologie d'Istanbule, 19; Paris: Librairie Adrien Maisonneuve).

Garrett, D.
    1990   'Votive Prostitution Again: A Comparison of Proverbs 7:13-14 and 21: 28-29', *JBL* 109: 681-82.

Garsiel, M.
    1985   *The First Book of Samuel: A Literary Study of Comparative Structures: Analogies and Parallels* (Israel: Revivim Publishing House).

Gehman, H.
    1970   'Vow', in H. Gehman (ed.), *The New Westminster Dictionary of the Bible* (Philadelphia: Westminster Press): 984-85.

Gesenius, W.
    1985   *Gesenius' Hebrew Grammar* (eds. E. Kautzsch and A.E. Cowley; Oxford: Clarendon Press).

Gianto, A.
    1987   'Some Notes on the Mulk inscription from Nebi Yunis (RES 367)', *Bib* 68: 397-401.

Gibson, J.C.L.
    1975   *Textbook of Syrian Semitic Inscriptions*. II. *Aramaic Inscriptions: Including Inscriptions in the Dialect of Zenjirli* (Oxford: Clarendon Press).
    1978   *Canaanite Myths and Legends* (Edinburgh: T. & T. Clark, rev. edn).

Giddens, A.
    1987   *Social Theory and Modern Sociology* (Stanford: Stanford University Press).
    1992   *Capitalism and Modern Social Theory: An Analysis of the Writings of Marx, Durkheim and Weber* (Cambridge: Cambridge University Press).

Ginsberg, H.L.
1945 'Psalms and Inscriptions of Petition and Acknowledgement', in *Louis Ginzberg Jubilee Volume: On the Occasion of his Seventieth Birthday* (New York: The American Academy for Jewish Research): 159-71.
1946 *The Legend of King Keret: A Canaanite Epic of the Bronze Age* (BASORSup, 2-3; New Haven: American Schools of Oriental Research).

Ginsburg, C.
1970 *The Song of Songs and Coheleth (Commonly Called the Book of Ecclesiastes): Translated From the Original Hebrew, With a Commentary, Historical and Critical* (The Library of Biblical Studies; New York: Ktav).

Ginzburg, C.
1979 'Cheese and Worms: The Cosmos of a Sixteenth-Century Miller', in *Religion and the People: 800–1700* (ed. J. Obelkevich; Chapel Hill: University of North Carolina Press): 87-167.
1982 *The Cheese and the Worms: The Cosmos of a Sixteenth-Century Miller* (trans. J. and A. Tedeschi; New York: Penguin Books).
1985 *The Night Battles: Witchcraft and Agrarian Cults in the Sixteenth and Seventeenth Centuries* (trans. J. and A. Tedeschi; New York: Penguin Books).
1991 'The Name and the Game: Unequal Exchange and the Historiographic Marketplace', in Muir and Ruggiero 1991:1-10.

Glazier-McDonald, B.
1987 *Malachi: The Divine Messenger* (SBLDS, 98; Atlanta: Scholars Press).

Goffman, E.
1961 *Asylums: Essays on the Social Situation of Mental Patients and Other Inmates* (Garden City, NY: Anchor Books).

Gold, I.
1926 *Das Gelübde nach Bibel und Talmud* (Berlin: Itzkowski).

Good, R.
1980 'Supplementary Remarks on the Ugaritic Funerary Text RS 34.126', *BASOR* 239: 41-42.

Gordis, R.
1951 *Koheleth: The Man and his World* (Text and Studies of the Jewish Theological Seminary of America, 19; New York: The Jewish Theological Seminary of America).

Gordon, C.
1949 *Ugaritic Literature: A Comprehensive Translation of the Poetic and Prose Texts* (Scripta Pontificii Instituti Biblici, 98; Rome: Pontificium Institutum Biblicum).
1955 *Ugaritic Manual. II. Texts in Translation* (AnOr, 35; Rome: Pontificium Institutum Biblicum).
1965 *Ugaritic Textbook: Grammar, Texts in Transliteration, Cuneiform Selections, Glossary, Indices* (AnOr, 38; Rome: Pontificium Institutum Biblicum).

Gottwald, N.
1964 '"Holy War" in Deuteronomy: Analysis and Critique', *RevExp* 61: 296-310.

1985   *The Tribes of Yahweh: A Sociology of the Religion of Liberated Israel,
1250-1050 B.C.E* (Maryknoll: Orbis Books).

Graesser, C.
1972   'Standing Stones in Ancient Palestine', *BA* 35: 34-63.

Gramsci, A.
1975   *Selections from the Prison Notebooks of Antonio Gramsci* (eds. and
trans. Q. Hoare and G. Nowell-Smith; New York: International
Publishers).
1991   *Antonio Gramsci: Selections from Cultural Writings* (eds. D. Forgacs
and G. Nowell-Smith; trans. W. Boelhower; Cambridge, MA: Harvard
University Press).

Grant, A.
1977   '*Adam and Iš: Man in the OT', *Australian Biblical Review* 25: 2-11.

Gray, G.B.
1906   *A Critical and Exegetical Commentary on Numbers* (ICC; New York:
Charles Scribner's Sons).
1971   *Sacrifice in The Old Testament: Its Theory and Practice* (The Library
of Biblical Studies; New York: Ktav).
1976   *A Critical and Exegetical Commentary on Numbers* (ICC; Edinburgh:
T. & T. Clark, 2nd edn).

Gray, J.
1964   *The KRT Text in the Literature of Ras Shamra: A Social Myth of
Ancient Canaan* (Leiden: Brill, 2nd edn).

Greenberg, M.
1983   *Biblical Prose Prayer as a Window to the Popular Religion of Ancient
Israel* (Berkeley: University of California Press).

Greenstone, J.
1939   *Numbers: With Commentary* (The Holy Scriptures; Philadelphia: The
Jewish Publication Society of America).
1950   *Proverbs: With Commentary* (The Holy Scriptures; Philadelphia: The
Jewish Publication Society of America).

Grelot, P.
1972   *Documents araméens d'Egypte: introduction, traduction, présentation*
(Paris: Cerf).

Gruber, M.
1986   'Hebrew $q^e d^e š\bar{a}h$ and Her Canaanite and Akkadian Cognates', *UF* 18:
133-48.
1987   'Women in the Cult According to the Priestly Code', in J. Neusner, B.
Levine, and E. Frerichs (eds.), *Judaic Perspectives on Ancient Israel*
(Philadelphia: Fortress Press): 35-48.

Gunkel, H.
1917   *Genesis: übersetzt und erklärt* (Göttinger Handkommentar zum Alten
Testament, 1; Göttingen: Vandenhoeck & Ruprecht).

Gurevich, A.
1990   *Medieval Popular Culture: Problems of Belief and Perception* (trans.
J. Bak and P. Hollingsworth; Cambridge Studies in Oral and Literate
Culture, 14; Cambridge: Cambridge University Press)

Habermas, J.
1990 'Hannah Arendt: On the Concept of Power', in *Philosophical–Political Profiles* (trans. F. Lawrence; Cambridge, MA: MIT Press): 173-89.

Halévy, J.
1905 *Recherches bibliques: notes pour l'interprétation des psaumes, les chants nuptiaux des cantiques, les livres d'Osée, d'Amos de Michée etc.* III (Paris: Leroux).

Hallo, W.
1968 'Individual Prayer in Sumerian: The Continuity of a Tradition', *JAOS* 88: 71-89.

Haran, M.
1969 '*Zebaḥ Hayyamîm*', *VT* 19: 11-22.
1978 *Temples and Temple-Service in Ancient Israel: An Inquiry into the Character of Cult Phenomena and the Historical Setting of the Priestly School* (Oxford: Clarendon Press).

Harris, R.
1960 'Old Babylonian Temple Loans', *JCS* 14: 126-37.

Harvey, D.
1990 *The Condition of Postmodernity: An Enquiry into the Origins of Cultural Change* (Oxford: Basil Blackwell).

Heiler, F.
1958 *Prayer: A Study in the History and Psychology of Religion* (trans. S. McComb; New York: Oxford University Press).

Heinsich, P.
1930 *Das Buch Genesis: Übersetzt und erklärt* (Die Heilige Schrift des Alten Testament; Bonn: Peter Hanstein).
1935 *Das Buch Leviticus: Übersetzt und erklärt* (Die Heilige Schrift des Alten Testament; Bonn: Peter Hanstein).
1936 *Das Buch Numeri: Übersetzt und erklärt* (Die Heilige Schrift des Alten Testament; Bonn: Peter Hanstein).

Herdner, A.
1946–1948 'Dédicace araméenne au dieu Melqart', *Syria* 25: 329-30.
1973 'Une prière à Baal des Ugaritains en danger', *in Académie des inscriptions et belles-lettres: comptes rendus des séances de l'année 1972* (Paris: Éditions Klincksieck): 693-703.

Hertzberg, H.
1964 *1 and 2 Samuel: A Commentary* (trans. J. Bowden; OTL; Philadelphia: Westminister Press).

Hiebert, P.
1989 '"Whence Shall Help Come to Me?" The Biblical Widow', in Day 1989: 125-41.

Hitzig, F.
1863 *Die zwölf kleinen Propheten* (Kurzgefasstes exegetische Handbuch zum Alten Testament; Leipzig: S. Hirzel).

Hobsbawm, E.J.
1988 'History From Below: Some Reflections', in F. Krantz (ed.), *History From Below: Studies in Popular Protest and Popular Ideology* (New York: Basil Blackwell): 13-27.

Hoffmann, D.
1905   *Das Buch Leviticus: Übersetzt und erklärt*. I. *Lev. I-XVII* (Berlin: M. Poppelauer).
1906   *Das Buch Leviticus: Übersetzt und erklärt*. II. *Lev. XVII-Ende* (Berlin: M. Poppelauer).
Hoglund K., E. Huwiler, J. Glass and R. Lee (eds.)
1987   *The Listening Heart: Essays in Wisdom and Psalms in Honor of Roland E. Murphy, O. Carm* (JSOTSup, 58; Sheffield: JSOT Press).
Holladay, J., Jr.
1987   'Religion in Israel and Judah Under the Monarchy: An Explicitly Archaeological Approach', in Miller, Hanson and McBride 1987: 249-99.
Holstein, J.
1975   'Max Weber and Biblical Scholarship', *HUCA* 46: 159-79.
Holub, R.
1992   *Antonio Gramsci: Beyond Marxism and Post-Modernism* (London: Routledge & Kegan Paul).
Holzinger, H.
1903   Numeri (Kurzer Hand-Commentar zum Alten Testament; Tübingen: Mohr).
Horton, R.F.,
n.d.   *The Minor Prophets: Hosea, Joel, Amos, Obadiah, Jonah and Micah. Introduction, Revised Version With Notes, Index and Map* (The Century Bible; Edinburgh: T.C. and E.C. Jack).
Horwitz, W.
1979   'The Significance of the Rephaim', JNSL 7: 37-43.
Hulst, A.R.
1958   '*Kol Baśar* in der priesterlichen Fluterzählung', Oudtestamentische Studiën 12: 28-68.
Hyatt, J, P.
1939   'The Deity Bethel and the Old Testament', *JAOS* 59: 81-98.
Isambert, F.A.
1975   'Autour du Catholicisme populaire: réflexions sociologiques sur un débat', *Social Compass* 22: 193-210.
1977   'Religion populaire, sociologie, histoire et folklore', *Archives de Sciences Sociales des Religions* 43: 161-84.
1982   *Le sens du sacré: fête et religion populaire* (Paris: Les Editions de minuit).
Isopescul, O.
1908   *Der Prophet Malachias: Einleitung, Übersetzung und Auslegung* (Wien: Czernowitz).
Jackson, K.
1983   *The Ammonite Language of the Iron Age* (HSM, 27; Chico, CA: Scholars Press).
Jespen, A.
1952–1953   'Zur Melqart-Stele Barhadads', *AfO* 16: 315-17.

Jirku, A.
1962   *Kanaanäische Mythen und Epen aus Ras Schamra-Ugarit* (Gütersloh: Gerd Mohn).

Jobling, D.
1991   'Feminism and "Mode of Production" in Ancient Israel: Search for a Method', in Jobling, Day and Sheppard 1991: 239-51.

Jobling, D., P. Day and G. Sheppard (eds.).
1991   *The Bible and the Politics of Exegesis: Essays in Honor of Norman K. Gottwald on His Sixty-Fifth Birthday* (Cleveland: The Pilgrim Press).

Kalberg, S.
1994   *Max Weber's Comparative-Historical Sociology* (Chicago: University of Chicago Press).

Kalisch, M.M.
1872   *Leviticus Part 2: A Historical and Critical Commentary on the Old Testament* (London: Longmans).

Kaufmann, Y.
1972   *The Religion of Israel: From its Beginnings to the Babylonian Exile* (trans. M. Greenberg; New York: Schocken Books).

Keil, C. F.
1868   *The Twelve Minor Prophets*, II (trans. J. Martin; Biblical Commentary on the Old Testament; Edinburgh: T. & T. Clark).
1872   *Den Propheten Jeremia und die Klagelieder* (*BKAT*; Leipzig: Dürffling und Franke).

Keil, C. F. and F. Delitzsch.
1880   *Biblical Commentary on the Books of Samuel*, IX (trans. J. Martin; Clark's Foreign Theological Library, Fourth Series; Edinburgh: T. & T. Clark).

Keller, C.A.
1976   'נדר *ndr* geloben', in E. Jenni (ed.), *Theologisches Handwörterbuch zum Alten Testament* (Stuttgart: Verlag W. Kohlhammer): 39-43.

Kellogg, S.H.
1891   *The Book of Leviticus* (The Expositors Bible; New York: Armstrong and Son).

Kennedy, A.R.S.
n.d.   *Leviticus and Numbers: Introduction, Revised Version with Notes, index and Map* (The Century Bible; Edinburgh: T.C. & E.C. Jack).

Kittel, R.
1922   'Das erste Buch Samuel: 1:1-11', in *Die heilige Schrift des Alten Testamentes*. I (ed. A. Bertholet; Tübingen: Mohr).

Klein, R.
1983   *1 Samuel* (WBC, 10; Waco, TX: Word Books).

Klinger, E.
1987   'Vows and Oaths', in M. Eliade (ed.), *The Encyclopedia of Religion*. XV (New York: Macmillan): 301-305.

Knight, D., and G. Tucker (eds.)
1985   *The Hebrew Bible and its Modern Interpreters* (Chico, CA: Scholars Press).

Knobel, A.
1852   *Die Genesis* (Kurzgefasstes exegetisches Handbuch zum Alten Testament; Leipzig: Weidmann).
1857   *Die Bücher Exodus and Leviticus* (Kurzgefasstes exegetisches Handbuch zum Alten Testament; Leipzig. S. Hirzel).
1861   *Die Bücher Numeri, Deuteronomium und Josua* (Kurzgefasstes exegetisches Handbuch zum Alten Testament; Leipzig: S. Hirzel).
König, E.
1925   *Die Genesis: Eingeleitet, übersetzt und erklärt* (Gütersloh: Bertelsmann).
Koschaker, P., and A. Ungnad
1923   *Hammurabi's Gesetz. VI. Übersetzte Urkunden mit Rechtserläuterungen* (Sumerische Rechtsurkunden; Leipzig: Eduard Pfeiffer).
Kraus, H.-J.
1960   *Psalmen*, I (*BKAT*, 15; Neukirchen–Vluyn: Neukirchener Verlag).
Kselman, T.
1986   'Ambivalence and Assumption in the Concept of Popular Religion', in Levine 1986: 24-41.
Kutler, L.
1980   *Social Terminology in Phoenician, Biblical Hebrew and Ugaritic* (PhD. diss., New York University).
1982   'A Structural Semantic Approach to Israelite Communal Terminology', *JANES* 14: 69-77.
Labuschagne, C.J.
1964–1965   'Amos' Conception of God and the Popular Theology of His Time', in Papers Read at 7th and 8th Meetings of Die O.T. Werkgemeenskap in Suid-Afrika: 122-33.
Lamphere, L.
1974   'Strategies, Cooperation, and Conflict Among Women in Domestic Groups', in Rosaldo and Lamphere 1974: 97-112.
Landes, G.
1982   'Linguistic Criteria and the Date of the Book of Jonah', *Eretz Israel* 16: 147-70.
Lang, B.
1983   *Monotheism and the Prophetic Minority: An Essay in Biblical History in Sociology* (The Social World of Biblical Antiquity, 1; Sheffield: The Almond Press).
Lanternari, V.
1982   'La religion populaire: prospective historique et anthropologique', *Archives de sciences sociales des Religions* 53: 121-43.
Lattes, D.
1964   *Il Qoheleth o l'Ecclesiaste: Traduzione e commento* (Rome: Unione Delle Comunita' Israelitiche Italiane).
Lauha, A.
1978   *Kohelet* (*BKAT*, 19; Neukirchen–Vluyn: Neukirchener Verlag).
Lehmann, M.
1969   'Biblical Oaths', *ZAW* 81: 74-92.
Lesètre, H.
1912   'Voeu', in F. Vigouroux (ed.), *Dictionnaire de la Bible*, V: 2443-45.

Levi Della Vida, G.
1943   'Some Notes on the Stele of Ben-Hadad', *BASOR* 90: 30-31.
Levine, B.
1963   'Ugaritic Descriptive Rituals', *JCS* 17: 105-111.
1971   'Prolegomenon', in Gray 1971.
1974   *In the Presence of the Lord: A Study of Cult and Some Cultic Terms in Ancient Israel* (SJLA, 5; Leiden: Brill).
1989   *Leviticus* ויקרא: *The Traditional Hebrew Text with the New JPS Translation* (The Jewish Publication Society Torah Commentary; Philadelphia: The Jewish Publication Society).
Levine. B., and J.-M. de Tarragon
1984   'Dead Kings and Rephaim: The Patrons of the Ugaritic Dynasty', *JAOS* 104: 649-59.
Levine, D.
1986   'Religion, the Poor, and Politics in Latin America Today', in Levine (ed.) 1986: 3-23.
1992   *Popular Voices in Latin American Catholicism* (Princeton: Princeton University Press).
Levine, D. (ed.)
1986   *Religion and Political Conflict in Latin America* (Chapel Hill: University of North Carolina Press).
Levine, E.
1984   'Jonah as a Philosophical Book', *ZAW* 96: 235-45.
Levy, L.
1912   *Das Buch Qoheleth: Ein Beitrag zur Geschichte des Sadduzäismus. Kritisch untersucht, übersetzt und erklärt* (Leipzig: Hinrichs).
Lewis, I.M.
1989   *Ecstatic Religion: A Study of Shamanism and Spirit Possession* (London: Routledge & Kegan Paul, 2nd edn).
Lieberman, S.
1942   *Greek in Jewish Palestine: Studies in the Life and Manners of Jewish Palestine in the 2–4 Centuries C.E.* (New York: Jewish Theological Seminary of America).
Loewenstamm, S.
1980   'The Address "Listen" in the Ugaritic Epic and the Bible', in *The Bible World: Essays in Honor of Cyrus H. Gordon* (eds. G. Rendsburg, R. Adler, M. Arfa and N. Winter; New York: Ktav): 123-31.
Löhr, M.
1908   *Die Stellung des Weibes zu Jahwe-Religion und -Kult* (Leipzig: Hinrichs).
Loretz, O.
1981   'Ugaritische und hebräische Lexikographie (2)', *UF* 13: 127-35.
Luckmann, T.
1972   *The Invisible Religion: The Problem of Religion in Modern Society* (New York: Macmillan).
MacDonald, E.M.
1931   *The Position of Women as Reflected in Semitic Codes of Law*

(University of Toronto Studies Oriental Series, 1; Toronto: University of Toronto Press).

Maduro, O.
1982   *Religion and Social Conflicts* (trans. R. Barr; Maryknoll: Orbis Books).

Marcus, D.
1986   *Jephthah and His Vow* (Texas: Texas Tech Press).

Margalit, B.
1976   'Studia Ugaritica II: "Studies in *Krt* and *Aqht*"', *UF* 8: 137-92.

Margalith, O.
1983   '*Keleb*: Homonym or Metaphor?', *VT* 33: 491-94.

Marx, K., and F. Engels
1983   *The Communist Manifesto* (with an introduction by A.J.P. Taylor; New York: Penguin Books).
1991   *The German Ideology: Part One* (ed. C.J. Arthur; New York: International Publishers).

Mauchline, J.
1971   *1 and 2 Samuel* (NCB; London: Oliphants).

Mayes, A.D.H.
1979   *Deuteronomy* (NCB; London: Oliphants).

McCarter, P.K., Jr
1980   *1 Samuel: A New Translation with Introduction, Notes and Commentary* (AB; Garden City, NY: Doubleday).
1987   'Aspects of the Religion of the Israelite Monarchy: Biblical and Epigraphic Data', in Miller, Hanson and McBride 1987: 137-55.

McFadyen, J.
1928   'Vows (Hebrew)', in J. Hastings (ed.), *Encyclopaedia of Religion and Ethics*, XI (New York: Charles Scribners Sons): 654-56.

McKane, W.
1970   *Proverbs: A New Approach* (OTL; Philadelphia: Westminster Press).

McNeile, A.H.
1911   *The Book of Numbers. In the Revised Version: With Introduction and Notes* (Cambridge: Cambridge University Press).

Mead, G.H.
1962   *Mind, Self, and Society: From the Standpoint of a Social Behaviorist* (ed. and intro. C. Morris; Chicago: University of Chicago Press).

Mendelsohn, I.
1956   'Samuel's Denunciation of Kingship in the Light of the Akkadian Documents from Ugarit', *BASOR* 143: 17-22.

Merendino, R.
1969   *Das deuteronomische Gesetz: Eine literarkritische, gattungs- und überlieferungsgeschichtliche Untersuchung zu Dt. 12-26* (BBB, 31; Bonn: Peter Hanstein).

Meyers, C.
1983   'Procreation, Production, and Protection: Male–Female Balance in Early Israel', *JAAR* 51: 569-93.
1988   *Discovering Eve: Ancient Israelite Women in Context* (New York: Oxford University Press).

1991 "'To Her Mother's House": Considering a Counterpart to the Israelite *Bêt 'āb'* in Jobling, Day and Sheppard 1991: 39-51.

Milgrom, J.
1990 *Numbers* במדבר: *The Traditional Hebrew Text With the New JPS Translation* (The Jewish Publication Society Torah Commentary; Philadelphia: The Jewish Publication Society).

Miller, J.M.
1985 'Israelite History', in Knight and Tucker 1985: 1-30.

Miller, P., Jr
1985 'Israelite Religion', in Knight and Tucker 1985: 201-37.
1987 'Aspects of the Religion of Ugarit', in Miller, Hanson and McBride 1987: 53-66.
1988 'Prayer and Sacrifice in Ugarit and Israel', in *Text and Context: Old Testament and Semitic Studies for F.C. Fensham* (ed. W. Classon, JSOTSup, 48; Sheffield: JSOT Press): 139-55.

Miller, P., Jr., P. Hanson and S. McBride (eds.).
1987 *Ancient Israelite Religion: Essays in Honor of Frank Moore Cross* (Philadelphia: Fortress Press).

Moor, J. de
1969 'Ugaritic *hm*-Never "Behold"', *UF* 1: 201-202.
1976a 'Ugarit', *IDBSup*: 928-31.
1976b 'Rāpi'ūma-Rephaim', *ZAW* 88: 323-45.
1987 *An Anthology of Religious Texts From Ugarit* (Leiden: Brill).

Moor, J. de, and K. Spronk
1982 'Problematical Passages in the Legend of Kirtu 2', *UF* 14: 173-90.

Moore, George.
1903 'Vows, Votive Offerings', in T.K. Cheyne (ed.), *Encyclopaedia Biblica*, IV (London: Macmillan): 5252-55.

Muir, E., and G. Ruggiero (eds.)
1991 *Microhistory and the Lost Peoples of Europe* (trans. E. Branch; Baltimore: The Johns Hopkins University Press).

Murphy, J.
1873 *A Critical and Exegetical Commentary on the Book of Genesis with a New Translation* (intro. A. Hovey; pref. J. Thompson; Boston: Estes and Lauriat).

Nel, P.J.
1982 *The Structure and Ethos of the Wisdom Admonitions in Proverbs* (*BZAW*, 158; Berlin: de Gruyter).

Nesti, A.
1975 'Gramsci et la religion populaire', *Social Compass* 22: 343-54.

Nicholson, L.
1982 'Comment on Rosaldo's "The Use and Abuse of Anthropology"', *Signs* 7: 732-35.

Noth, M.
1965 *Leviticus: A Commentary* (trans. J.E. Anderson; OTL; Philadelphia: Westminster Press).
1968 Numbers: A Commentary. (trans. J. Martin; OTL; Philadelphia: Westminster Press).

Nowack, W.
1894   *Lehrbuch der hebräischen Archäologie*, II (Sammlung Theologischer Lehrbücher; Freiburg: Mohr).
O'Brien, J.
1987   'Because God Heard My Voice: The Individual Thanksgiving Psalm and Vow-Fulfillment,' in Hoglund, Huwiler, Glass and Lee 1987: 281-98.
Oesterley, W.O.E.
1929   *The Book of Proverbs: With Introduction and Notes* (London: Methuen).
1953   *The Psalms: Translated With Text-Critical and Exegetical Notes* (London: SPCK).
Oesterley, W.O.E., and H.H. Rowley
1963   'Vows', in *Dictionary of the Bible* (eds. F.C. Grant and H.H. Rowley; Edinburgh: T. & T. Clark, 2nd edn): 1024-25.
Oettli, S.
1893   *Das Deuteronomium und die Bücher Josua und Richter (mit einer Karte Palästinas)* (Kurzgefasster Kommentar zu den heilgen Schriften Alten und Neuen Testamentes; Munich: Beck).
Oppenheim, A.L.
1956   'The Interpretation of Dreams in the Ancient Near East: With a Translation of an Assyrian Dream-Book', in *Transactions of the American Philosophical Society*, XLVI (Philadelphia: The American Philosophical Society).
1977   *Ancient Mesopotamia: Portrait of a Dead Civilization* (rev. and ed. E. Reiner; Chicago: University of Chicago Press).
Otto, E.
1976   'Jakob in Bethel: Ein Beitrag zur Geschichte der Jakobüberlieferung', *ZAW* 88: 165-90.
Otwell, J.
1977   *And Sarah Laughed: The Status of Woman in the Old Testament* (Philadelphia: Westminster Press).
Pace, E.
1979   'The Debate on Popular Religion in Italy', *Sociological Analysis* 40: 71-75.
Palmer, A.
1899   *Jacob at Bethel: The Vision, the Stone, the Anointing: An Essay in Comparative Religion* (Studies on Biblical Subjects, 11; London: David Nutt).
Pareto, V.
1991   *The Rise and Fall of Elites: An Application of Theoretical Sociology* (intro. H. Zetterberg; New Brunswick, NJ: Transaction Publishers).
Parker, S.
1977   'The Historical Composition of *KRT* and the Cult of EL', *ZAW* 89: 161-75.
1979   'The Vow in Ugaritic and Israelite Narrative Literature', *UF* 11: 693-700.
1989   *The Pre-Biblical Narrative Tradition: Essays on the Ugaritic Poems Keret and Aqhat* (SBLRBS, 24; Atlanta: Scholars Press).

Payne, D.
1979   'Jonah From the Perspective of its Audience', *JSOT* 13: 3-12.
Peake, A.S.
1902   'Vow', in *A Dictionary of the Bible: Dealing with its Language, Literature and Contents, Including the Biblical Theology*, IV (ed. J. Hastings; New York: Chales Scribner's Sons,): 872-73.
n.d.a   *Jeremiah and Lamentations. II. Jeremiah 25 to 52, Lamentations: Introduction, Revised Version With Notes, Map and Index* (The Century Bible; Edinburgh: T.C. and E.C. Jack).
n.d.b   *Job: Introduction, Revised Version with Notes and Index* (The Century Bible; Edinburgh: T.C. and E.C. Jack).
Pedersen, J.
1914   *Der Eid bei den Semiten: In seinem Verhältnis zu verwandten Erscheinungen sowie die Stellung des Eides im Islam* (Studien Zur Geschichte und Kultur des Islamischen Orients, 3; Strasbourg: Trübner).
1947   *Israel: Its Life and Culture*, I–II (London: Oxford University Press).
1963   *Israel: Its Life and Culture*, III–IV (London: Oxford University Press).
Peritz, I.
1898   'Woman in the Ancient Hebrew Cult', *JBL* 17: 111-48.
Petersen, D.
1979   'Max Weber and the Sociological Study of Ancient Israel', *Sociological Inquiry* 49: 117-49.
Phillott, H.
1873   'Vows', in *Dictionary of the Bible: Comprising its Antiquities, Biography, Geography and Natural History*, IV (ed. H.B. Hackett; Cambridge: Riverside Press): 3449-51.
Picard, C.
1991   'Les sacrifices Molk chez les puniques: Certitudes et hypothèses', *Semitica* 39: 77-88.
Pirot, L., and A. Clamer.
1955   *Josué-Juges, Ruth-Samuel-Rois* (La Sainte Bible, III; Paris: Letouzey et Ané Éditeurs).
Plumptre, E.H.
1898   *Ecclesiastes; Or, The Preacher, With Notes and Introduction* (The Cambridge Bible for Schools and Colleges; Cambridge: University Press).
Polzin, R.
1989   *Samuel and the Deuteronomist: A Literary Study of the Deuteronomic History*, II (San Francisco: Harper & Row).
Portelli, H.
1974   *Gramsci et la question religieuse* (Paris: Éditions anthropos).
Pury, A. de
1975   *Promesse divine et légende culturelle dans le cycle de Jacob: Genèse 28 et les traditions patriarcales*, II (Paris: Gabalda).
Rad, G. von
1962   *Old Testament Theology. I. The Theology of Israel's Historical Traditions* (trans. D. Stalker; New York: Harper & Row).

1966   *Deuteronomy: A Commentary* (trans. D. Barton; OTL; Philadelphia: Westminster Press).

1972   *Genesis: A Commentary* (rev. edn, trans. J. Marks; OTL; Philadelphia: Westminster Press).

Raphaël, F.

1973   'Max Weber and Ancient Judaism', *Yearbook Leo Baeck* 18: 41-62.

Rapp, R.

1979   'Review Essay: Anthropology', *Signs* 4: 497-513.

Reider, J.

1937   *Deuteronomy: With Commentary* (The Holy Scriptures; Philadelphia: Jewish Publication Society of America).

Reiter, R.

1975   'Men and Women in the South of France: Public and Private Domains', in Reiter 1975: 252-82.

Reiter, R. (ed.)

1975   *Toward an Anthropology of Women* (New York: Monthly Review Press).

Renker, A.

1979   *Die Tora bei Maleachi: Ein Beitrag zur Bedeutungsgeschichte von Tôrā im Alten Testament* (Freiburg: Herder).

Richter, W.

1967   'Das Gelübde als theologische Rahmung der Jakobsüberlieferungen', *BZ* 11: 21-52.

Riessler, P.

1911   *Die kleinen Propheten oder das Zwölfprophetenbuch nach dem Urtext übersetzt und erklärt* (Rottenburg: Wilhelm Bader).

Ringgren, H.

1980   *Israelite Religion* (trans. David Green; Philadelphia: Fortress Press).

Ringgren, H., and W. Zimmerli.

1962   *Sprüche/Prediger: Übersetzt und erklärt* (Das Alte Testament Deutsch, 16; Göttingen: Vandenhoeck & Ruprecht).

Robertson, R.

1987   'Church–State Relations in Comparative Perspective', in *Church–State Relations: Tensions and Transitions* (eds. T. Robbins and R. Robertson; New Brunswick, NJ: Transaction Books): 153-60.

Robinson, H.

1907   *Deuteronomy and Joshua: Introductions, Revised Version with Notes, Map and Index* (The Century Bible; Edinburgh: T.C. and E.C. Jack).

Rodriguez, J.

1994   *Our Lady of Guadalupe: Faith and Empowerment among Mexican-American Women* (Austin: University of Texas Press).

Rogers, S.C.

1975   'Female Forms of Power and the Myth of Male Dominance: A Model of Female/Male Interaction in Peasant Society', *American Ethnologist* 2: 727-56.

Rosaldo, M.Z.

1974   'Women, Culture, and Society: A Theoretical Overview', in Rosaldo and Lamphere 1974: 17-42.

1980 'The Use and Abuse of Anthropology: Reflections on Feminism and Cross-cultural Understanding', *Signs* 5: 389-417.

Rosaldo, M.Z. and L. Lamphere (eds.)
1974 *Woman, Culture and Society* (Stanford: Stanford University Press).

Rosenau, P.
1992 *Post-Modernism and the Social Sciences: Insights, Inroads, and Intrusions* (Princeton, NJ: Princeton University Press).

Ross, J.P.
1967 '*Jahweh ṣebā ʾōṭ* in Samuel and Psalms', *VT* 17: 76-92.

Rowley, H.H.
1967 *Worship in Ancient Israel: Its Forms and Meaning* (London: SPCK).
1978 *Job* (NCB; Greenwood, SC: Attic Press).

Rubin, G.
1975 *The Traffic in Women: Notes on the 'Political Economy' of Sex*, in Reiter 1975: 157-210.

Ruether, R.R.
1982 'Feminism and Patriarchal Religion: Principles of Ideological Critique of the Bible', *JSOT* 22: 54-66.

Ryle, H.
1921 *The Book of Genesis: In the Revised Version with Introduction and Notes* (Cambridge: Cambridge University Press).

Sadri, A.
1992 *Max Weber's Sociology of Intellectuals* (New York: Oxford University Press).

Saggs, H.W.F.
1978 *The Encounter with the Divine in Mesopotamia and Israel* (London: Athlone Press).

Said, E.
1979 *Orientalism* (New York: Vintage Books).

Sapin, J.
1983 'Quelques systemes socio-politiques en Syrie au 2 millenaire avant J-C et leur evolution historique d'après des documents religieux (légendes, rituels, sanctuaires)', *UF* 15: 157-90.

Sarna, N.
1988 'Israel in Egypt: The Egyptian Sojourn and the Exodus', in Shanks 1988: 31-52.
1989 Genesis בראשית: The Traditional Hebrew Text with the New JPS Translation. (The Jewish Publication Society Torah Commentary; Philadelphia: Jewish Publication Society).

Sauren, H., and G. Kestemont
1971 'Keret roi de Hubur', *UF* 3: 181-221.

Scheil, V.
1915 'La promesse dans la prière babylonienne', *RA* 12: 65-72.
1916 'Notules', *RA* 13: 125-42.

Schenker, A.
1989 'Gelübde im Alten Testament: Unbeachtete Aspekte', *VT* 29: 87-91.

Schiper, I.
1959   'Max Weber on the Sociological Basis of the Jewish Religion', *Journal of Jewish Sociology* 1: 250-60.

Schluchter, W.
1984   'The Paradox of Rationalization: On the Relation of Ethics and the World', in Roth, Guenther and Wolfgang Schluchter, *Max Weber's Vision of History: Ethics and Methods* (Berkeley: University of California Press).

1989   *Rationalism, Religion and Domination: A Weberian Perspective* (trans. N. Solomon; Berkeley: University of California Press).

Schmidt, H.
1934   *Die Psalmen* (HAT, 15; Tübingen: Mohr).

Schneider, J.
1990   *Spirits and the Spirit of Capitalism*, in Badone 1990: 24-54.

Schult, H.
1976   'שמע, šmᶜ, hören', in *Theologisches Handwörterbuch zum Alten Testament*, II (ed. E. Jenni; Munich: Chr. Kaiser Verlag): 974-82.

Schultz, F.
1859   *Das Deuteronomium* (Berlin: Gustav Schlawitz).

Schwally, F.
1898   'Lexikalische Studien', *ZDMG* 52: 132-48.

Scott, J.
1977   'Hegemony and the Peasantry', *Politics and Society* 7: 267-96.

1985   *Weapons of the Weak: Everyday Forms of Peasant Resistance* (New Haven: Yale University Press).

Scott, R.B.Y.
1965   *Proverbs–Ecclesiastes: Introduction, Translation and Notes* (AB; Garden City, NY: Doubleday).

Scribner, R.W.
1984   'Ritual and Popular Religion in Catholic Germany at the Time of the Reformation', *JEH* 35: 47-73.

Segal, J.B.
1976   'Popular Religion in Ancient Israel', *JJS* 27: 1-22.

Segert, S.
1984   *A Basic Grammar of the Ugaritic Language: With Selected Texts and Glossary* (Berkeley: University of California Press).

Shanks, H. (ed.)
1988   *Ancient Israel: A Short History From Abraham to the Roman Destruction of the Temple* (Englewood Cliffs, NJ: Prentice–Hall).

Shea, W.
1979   'The Kings of the Melqart Stele', *Maarav* 1: 159-76.

Simmel, G.
1971   *On Individuality and Social Forms* (ed. Donald Levine; Chicago: University of Chicago Press).

1990   *The Philosophy of Money* (ed. D. Frisby. trans. T. Bottomore and D. Frisby; London: Routledge & Kegan Paul, 2nd edn).

Smith, G.A.
1950   *The Book of Deuteronomy: In the Revised Version with Introduction*

and Notes (The Cambridge Bible for Schools and Colleges; Cambridge: Cambridge University Press).

Smith, H. P.
1899   *A Critical and Exegetical Commentary on the Books of Samuel* (ICC; New York: Charles Scribner's Sons).

Smith, J, W. Ward and J. Bewer
1974   *A Critical and Exegetical Commentary on Micah, Zephaniah, Nahum, Habakkuk, Obadiah, and Joel* (ICC; Edinburgh: T. & T. Clark).

Smith, M.
1987   *Palestinian Parties and Politics that Shaped the Old Testament* (London: SCM Press, 2nd edn).

Smith, R.
1984   *Micah–Malachi* (WBC, 32; Waco, TX: Word Books).

Smith, W. R.
1972   *Lectures on the Religion of the Semites* (repr.; New York: Schocken Books [1894]).

Snaith, N.H.
1945   *Notes on the Hebrew Text of Jonah* (London: Epworth Press).
1957   'Sacrifices in the Old Testament', *VT* 7: 308-17.

1967   *Leviticus and Numbers* (The Century Bible; London: Nelson).

Snijders, L.A.
1954   'The Meaning of זר in the Old Testament', *Oudtestamentische Studiën* 10: 1-154.

Soden, W. von
1965   *'ikribu(m)'*, in *Akkadisches Handwörterbuch* (ed. W. Von Soden; Wiesbaden: Harrasowitz): 369-70.

Speiser, E.A.
1938   'The Nuzi Tablets Solve a Puzzle in the Books of Samuel', *BASOR* 72: 15-17.
1960   'Leviticus and the Critics', in *Yehezkel Kaufmann Jubilee Volume: Studies in Bible and Jewish Religion Dedicated to Yehezkel Kaufmann on the Occasion of his Seventieth Birthday* (ed. M. Haran; Jerusalem: Magnes): 29-45.
1964   *Genesis: Introduction, Translation and Notes* (AB; Garden City, NY: Doubleday).

Sperling, D.
1986   'Israel's Religion in the Ancient Near East' in *Jewish Spirituality: From the Bible Through the Middle Ages* (World Spirituality: An Encyclopedic History of the Religious Quest, 13; ed. A. Green; New York: Crossroad): 5-31.

Spurrell, G.J.
1896.   *Notes on the Text of the Book of Genesis* (Oxford: Clarendon Press, 2nd edn).

Steuernagel, C.
1900   *Übersetzung und Erklärung der Bücher Deuteronomium und Josua und allgemeine Einleitung in den Hexateuch* (HKAT; Göttingen: Vandenhoeck & Ruprecht).

1901   *Die Einwanderung der israelitischen Stämme in Kanaan: Historisch-*
              kritische Untersuchungen (Berlin: Schwetschke).

Stoebe, H.
1972   'Anmerkungen zur Wurzel *plʾ* im Alten Testament', *TZ* 28: 13-23.
1973   *Das erste Buch Samuelis* (KAT, 8; Gütersloh: Gerd Mohn).

Strack, H.
1894   *Die Bücher Genesis, Exodus, Leviticus und Numeri* (Kurzgefasster
              Kommentar zu den heilgen Schriften Alten und Neuen Testamentes;
              Munich: Beck; Münich: C.H. Beck).
1905   *Die Genesis: Übersetzt und ausgelegt* (Kurzgefasster Kommentar zu
              den heilgen Schriften Alten und Neuen Testamentes; Munich: Beck;
              Münich: C.H. Beck).

Stuart, D.
1987   *Hosea–Jonah* (WBC, 31; Waco, TX: Word Books).

Stuart, M.
1852   *A Commentary on the Book of Proverbs* (London: Delf & Trübner).

Sukenik, E.L.
1933   'Inscribed Hebrew and Aramaic Potsherds From Samaria', *PEFQS* 65:
              152-56.

Sulzberger, M.
1923   *The Status of Labor in Ancient Israel* (Philadelphia: The Conat Press).

Sweet, R.
1990   'The Sage in Mesopotamian Palaces and Royal Courts', in Gammie
              and Perdue 1990: 99-107.

Talmon, S.
1983   'Biblical *REP̱ĀʾÎM* and Ugaritic *RPU/I(M)**', *HAR* 7: 235-49.
1987   'The Emergence of Jewish Sectarianism in the Early Second Temple
              Period', in Miller, Hanson and McBride 1987: 587-616.

Tarragon, J.-M. de
1980   *Le culte d'Ugarit: d'après les textes de la pratique en cunéiformes*
              alphabétiques (Cahiers de la revue biblique, 19; Paris: Gabalda).

Taylor, L.
1990   'Stories of Power, Powerful Stories: The Drunken Priest in Donegal',
              in Badone 1990: 163-84.

Thenius, O.
1842   *Die Bücher Samuels* (Leipzig: Weidmann).

Thomas, D.W.
1960   '*Kelebh* "Dog": Its Origin and Some Usages of it in the Old
              Testament', *VT* 10: 410-27.

Thompson, E.P.
1966   *The Making of the English Working Class* (New York: Vintage Books).

Thompson, R.J.
1963   *Penitence and Sacrifice in Early Israel outside of the Levitical Law:*
              An Examination of the Fellowship Theory of Early Israelite Sacrifice
              (Leiden: Brill).

Tilly, L.
1978   'The Social Sciences and the Study of Women: A Review Article',
              Comparative Studies in Society and History, 20: 163-73.

Toorn, K. van der
    1989   'Female Prostitution in Payment of Vows in Ancient Israel', *JBL* 108:
          193-205.
Towler, R.
    1974   *Homo Religiosus: Sociological Problems in the Study of Religion*
          (New York: St. Martin's Press).
Toy, C.
    1904   *A Critical and Exegetical Commentary on the Book of Proverbs* (ICC;
          New York: Charles Scribner's Sons).
Trible, P.
    1989   *Texts of Terror: Literary–Feminist Readings of Biblical Narratives*
          (Overtures to Biblical Theology, 13; Philadelphia: Fortress Press).

Tropper, J., and E. Verreet
    1988   'Ugaritisch *NDY, YDY, HDY, NDD* und *D(W)D*', *UF* 20: 339-50.
Tsevat, M.
    1965   'Studies in the Book of Samuel', *HUCA* 36: 49-58.
Tsumura, D.T.
    1979   '*The Verba Primae WAW*, WLD, in Ugaritic', *UF* 11: 779-82.
Vaux, R. de
    1965   *Ancient Israel. I. Religious Institutions* (New York: McGraw-Hill).
Virolleaud, Ch.
    1941   'Les Rephaïm: Fragments de poèmes de Ras Shamra', Syria 22: 1-30.
    1942–1943 'Le mariage du Roi Kéret (3k): poème de Ras-Shamra', *Syria* 23:
          137-72.
Vorländer, H.
    1986   'Aspects of Popular Religion in the Old Testament', in *Concilium:*
          Popular Religion (eds. N,. Greinacher and N. Mette; Edinburgh: T. &
          T. Clark): 63-70.
Vos, C.
    1968   *Woman in Old Testament Worship* (Delft: Judels and Brinkman).
Vriezen, T.
    1967   *The Religion of Ancient Israel* (trans. H. Hoskins; Philadelphia:
          Westminster Press).
Vrijhof, P.H.
    1979a.   'Official and Popular Religion in Twentieth-Century Western
          Christianity', in Vrijhof and Waardenburg 1979: 217-43.
    1979b   'Conclusion', in Vrijhof and Waardenburg 1979: 668-99.
Vrijhof, P., and J. Waardenburg (eds.)
    1979   *Official and Popular Religion: Analysis of a Theme for Religious*
          Studies (Religion and Society, 19; The Hague: Mouton).
Walters, S.
    1988   'Hannah and Anna: The Greek And Hebrew Texts of 1 Samuel 1',
          JBL 107: 385-412.
Walzer, M.
    1988   *The Company of Critics: Social Criticism and Political Commitment in*
          the Twentieth Century (New York: Basic Books).

Ward, W.A.
1962   'Some Egypto-Semitic Roots', *Or* 31: 397-412.
Wartenberg, T. (ed.).
1992   *Rethinking Power* (SUNY Series in Radical Social and Political
        Theory; Albany: State University of New York Press).
Weber, M.
1958   *From Max Weber: Essays in Sociology* (eds. and trans., H. Gerth and
        C. Mills; New York: Oxford University Press).
1964   *The Theory of Social and Economic Organization* (ed. and intro. T.
        Parsons; trans. A. Henderson and T. Parsons; New York: The Free
        Press).
1967   *Ancient Judaism* (eds. and trans., H. Gerth and D. Martindale; New
        York: The Free Press).
1976   *The Protestant Ethic and the Spirit of Capitalism* (trans. T. Parsons;
        New York: Charles Scribner's Sons).
1978   *Economy and Society: An Outline of Interpretive Sociology* (eds. G.
        Roth and C. Wittich; 2 vols. ; Berkeley: University of California Press).
Weiden, J. van der
1970   *Le livre des proverbes: Notes philologiques* (BibOr, 23; Rome: Biblical
        Institute Press).
Weinfeld, M.
1972a   'The Worship of Molech and of the Queen of Heaven and its
        Background', *UF* 4: 133-54.
1972b   *Deuteronomy and the Deuteronomic School* (Oxford: Clarendon Press).
Weiser, A.
1955   *Das Buch des Propheten Jeremia: Kapitel 25: 15-52:34 (Das Alte
        Testament Deutsch*, 21; Göttingen: Vandenhoeck & Ruprecht).
1959   *Das Buch der zwölf kleinen Propheten. I. Die Propheten Hosea, Joel,
        Amos, Obadja, Jona, Micha übersetzt und erklärt (Das Alte Testament
        Deutsch*, 24; Göttingen: Vandenhoeck & Ruprecht).
Weisman, Z.
1967   'The Biblical Nazirite: Its Types and Roots', *Tarbiz* 36: 207-20
        (Hebrew).
Weiss, B.
1858   *New Translation and Exposition of the Book of Ecclesiastes with
        Critical Notes on the Hebrew Text* (Edinburgh: William Oliphant and
        Co).
Wendel, A.
1927   *Das Opfer in der altisraelitischen Religion* (Leipzig: Eduard Pfeiffer).
1931a   *Das israelitisch-jüdische Gelübde* (Berlin: Philo Verlag GMBH).
1931b   *Das freie Laiengebet im vorexilischen Israel* (Leipzig: Eduard
        Pfeiffer).
1958   'Gelübde', in *Die Religion in Geschichte und Gegenwart: Hand-
        wörterbuch für Theologie und Religionswissenschaft*, II (ed. K. Galling;
        Tübingen: Mohr): 1322-23.
Wenham, G.J.
1978   'Leviticus 27:2-8 and the Price of Slaves', *ZAW* 90: 264-65.

Westermann, C.
1981   *Genesis 12–36: A Commentary* (trans. J. Scullion; Minneapolis: Augsburg).

Westphal, A.
1956   'Voeu', in *Dictionnaire encyclopédiques de la Bible: les choses, les hommes, les faits, les doctrines*, II (ed. A. Westphal; Valence-sur-Rhone: Imprimeries réunies): 835-36.

Whitaker, R.
1972   *A Concordance of the Ugaritic Literature* (Cambridge, MA: Harvard University Press).

Whitelam, K.
1986   'Recreating the History of Israel', *JSOT* 35: 45-70.
1989   'Israelite Kingship. The Royal Ideology and its Opponents', in Clements 1989: 119-39.

Whybray, R.N.
1990   'The Sage in the Israelite Royal Court', in Gammie and Perdue 1990: 133-39.

Wichers, A.J.
1979   'Some Reflections on the Position of the Christian Religion in a Situation of Affluence: The Welfare State', in Vrijhof and Waardenburg 1979: 200-16.

Williams, A.
1922   *Ecclesiastes: In the Revised Version with Introduction and Notes* (Cambridge: Cambridge University Press).

Williams, P.
1989   *Popular Religion in America: Symbolic Change and the Modernization Process in Historical Perspective* (Chicago: University of Illinois Press).

Willis, J.
1971   'An Anti-Elide Narrative Tradition From a Prophetic Circle at the Ramah Sanctuary', *JBL* 90: 288-308.

Wilson, R.
1984   *Sociological Approaches to the Old Testament* (Philadelphia: Fortress Press).

Wolff, H.W.
1977   *Dodekapropheton 3 Obadja und Jona* (BKAT, 14; Neukirchen–Vluyn: Neukirchener Verlag).
1981   *Anthropology of the Old Testament* (trans. M. Kohl; Philadelphia: Fortress Press).

Wright, C.
1883   *The Book of Koheleth, Commonly Called Ecclesiastes: Considered in Relation to Modern Criticism, and to the Doctrines of Modern Pessimism, with a Critical and Grammatical Commentary. and a Revised Translation* (London: Hodder & Stoughton).

Wrong, D.
1988   *Power: Its Forms, Bases and Uses* (Chicago: University of Chicago Press).

Wutz, F.
1925   *Die Psalmen: Textkritisch, untersucht* (Munich: Kösel).

Xella, P.
    1978   'Un testo ugaritico recente (*RS* 24.266, *Verso*, 9-19) e il "sacrificio dei primi nati"', *Revista di studi fenici* 6: 127-35.
    1982   *Gli antenati di Dio: Divinità e miti della tradizione di Canaan* (Italy: Essedue Edizioni).
Yanagisako, S.
    1979   'Family and Household: The Analysis of Domestic Groups', *Annual Review of Anthropology* 8: 161-205.
Zalevsky, S.
    1978   'The Vow of Hannah, (1 Samuel 1)', *Beth Mikra* 74: 304-26 (Hebrew).
Zipor, M.
    1987   'What Were the *Kᵉlābîm* in Fact?', *ZAW* 99: 423-28.
Zyl, A.H. van
    1984   '1 Sam. 1:2-2:11—A Life–World Lament of Affliction', *JNSL* 12: 151-61.

INDEXES

INDEX OF REFERENCES

OLD TESTAMENT

108	89	1.15 III		1.22 II 16-17	84
109	139	20-30	98	1.22 II 18-21	85
110	110	1.15 III		1.119	58
155	139	20-24	162	1.119	61
164	53, 139	1.15 III		1.119 26-31	59, 60
201 1-5	62	20-23	160	1.119 28	60, 61
		1.15 III		1.119 30-31	60
KTU		24-30	161		
1.14 I-IV 35	86	1.15 III 25	162	*PNO*	
1.14 IV		1.15 III 27	83, 162	14.5	121
36-44	49, 58	1.20-22	84		
1.14 IV		1.22 II 16-21	49, 58, 98	*V AB, D*	
36-43	73, 86, 98			47	85

INDEX OF AUTHORS

JOURNAL FOR THE STUDY OF THE OLD TESTAMENT
SUPPLEMENT SERIES